Comb. J.   19·11·80   £6·95

THE INTERRUPTED JOURNEY

THE INTERRUPTED JOURNEY:

Two Lost Hours Aboard a Flying Saucer

by John G. Fuller

Introduction
by Benjamin Simon, M. D.

SOUVENIR PRESS

Copyright © 1966 by John G. Fuller

Map of the constellation Pegasus
© 1965 by The New York Times Company
Reprinted by permission

First published in the U.S.A. by
The Dial Press, New York

First British Edition published 1980 by
Souvenir Press Ltd., 43 Great Russell Street London WC1B 3PA

ISBN 0 285 62450 4

Printed and bound in Great Britain by
Redwood Burn Limited
Trowbridge & Esher

TABLE OF CONTENTS

FOREWORD TO NEW EDITION

It is now some fifteen years since I walked into the Boston office of Dr. Benjamin Simon, a leading neuro-psychiatrist in the United States. I was there to track down a story which still leaves me baffled. As a reporter for *Look* magazine, a documentary film producer for the major networks, and a columnist for the *Saturday Review* at the time, I felt I had no business poking my nose into a story as strange as this one.

It involved flying saucers, a phrase which smacks of pseudo-mythology, and which I dislike intensely. I even have trouble accepting the sanitized synonym: Unidentified Flying Objects, or UFO's. I then knew little or nothing about them. In fact, I was extremely skeptical, a position shared exactly by Dr. Simon.

Simon's credentials were impeccable. A former lecturer at Harvard and Yale, he was a Rockefeller Foundation Fellow in neurology and president of his regional medical association. In addition to his private practice, he was director of one of the largest state mental hospitals in Massachusetts. He was as unfamilar with UFO's as I was.

The focus of our attention was on two of his patients: Barney and Betty Hill, of Portsmouth, New Hampshire. The couple had granted *Look* magazine and me permission to examine the records and tapes of their experience with a UFO in the White Mountains of New Hampshire a few years before.

Their story, which follows in these pages, is incredible. Yet the facts that emerge are hard, tough, and unassailable. They do not need to be extrapolated to arrive at the conclusion that this is either one of the most unusual cases in the history of psychiatry—or the possible historical event of the first extraterrestrial visit to be heavily documented in detail. Either way, the story is gripping and mind-boggling.

The conscious memory of the Hills themselves could not illuminate the story, except in fragments. The incident involved two hours of lost time for both of them, a concise slice of time that had been eradicated from their conscious minds. This strange trauma of sudden double amnesia came to them when they saw an enormous UFO come over their car on a lonely mountain road along the Vermont–New Hampshire border. They woke up two hours later, still in their car, but some thirty miles away from Canon Mountain, where the craft had originally approached them.

For two years, they tried to reconstruct what happened in those two missing hours. They developed serious anxiety symptoms as a result of the inexplicable twin amnesia. They were referred by their family physician to a psychiatrist, a consultant to the prestigious Exeter Academy. He diagnosed their mutual problem as traumatic anxiety from their experience and their amnesia. The only specific treatment for amnesia is skilled regression either by sodium amytal, sodium pentothal, or hypnosis to break down the threshhold that bars the memories from reaching the consciousness. The Hills in turn were referred to Dr. Simon.

As a chief of neuropsychiatry and Lt. Colonel in the United States Army at major installations during World War II, Dr. Simon was practiced in dealing with amnesia among soldiers whose battle experiences left them unable to function. Through regressive hypnosis, Simon enabled them to re-live—often painfully—their experiences so that their anxiety was lifted, and their health restored.

As part of the treatment, Dr. Simon regressed Betty and Barney Hill by hypnosis separately, once a week, for seven months. Every session was tape recorded. Two identical stories emerged, yet neither knew what the other was saying. The result: nearly forty hours of a dramatic re-living of being abducted by humanoid beings aboard a large UFO, given a physical examination, and returned to their car without a conscious memory of the event.

I had already visited the Hills before I went to see Dr. Simon. They impressed me with their sincerity, their frankness, and their intelligence. They were leaders in the Portsmouth Community and in the Unitarian Church they attended. Their I.Q.s were both over 130, high on the scale. They were as puzzled about the whole sequence of events as Dr. Simon and I were.

At Dr. Simon's office, I asked him: "How can you possibly account for this story?"

"There are many things to consider," he said. "Remember that I was treating them professionally for one specific purpose: to relieve their anxiety symptoms. In fact, that was almost my entire interest."

"But what about the UFO and the humanoid aspect?" I asked.

"That is entirely out of my area. I know nothing about UFO's, beyond what I learned in the course of treatment."

"Do you believe UFO's could exist?" I asked.

"I believe anything exists if I see enough hard, palpable evidence."

"Do you see that here?"

"I see an extremely interesting case of double amnesia, with the veil of amnesia lifted through careful regressive hypnosis."

"Do you think they are lying?" I asked.

"It is very difficult to lie under the pattern of regression I put them through. It is very difficult to lie under any properly-administered hypnosis. The barriers are down between the conscious and unconscious. It would be almost impossible for them to lie under such an intensive program covering seven months."

"Do you think they were hallucinating?"

"After careful examination of the tapes and the records, I do not think they were hallucinating."

I pressed the doctor further. "Do you think they are psychotic?"

"I do not see any signs of psychosis on the part of either Barney or Betty," Simon said.

"Then roughly speaking, you could say that it is unlikely that the Hills were lying, psychotic, or hallucinating?"

"That's too simplistic a question to answer," he said.

I tried to re-frame the question. "If they were not lying, or hallucinating, or psychotic—would that mean that this actually happened?"

"You said that," Simon answered. "I didn't."

I laughed. "I didn't say it," I added. "I *asked* it."

"You forget," Dr. Simon said. "I'm a scientist. I cannot accept anything that is not accepted scientifically, and UFO's, from what I know, have not been accepted."

"A reporter has the same responsibility as a scientist," I said. "We have to get facts, we have to understand them, and we have to present them accurately. That's my job here."

Dr. Simon smiled. "You are going to have your hands full with this story," he said. "There are many things that are unexplainable in this case. I threw many kinds of tests at them during the months of therapy. I couldn't shake their stories, and they were definitely not malingering. In fact—and this is interesting—they had a major medical insurance policy that covered part of the cost of their treatment. I believe it's the first time in history that an insurance company has approved and settled a claim on a UFO case."

Having been an insurance claims investigator in the deep past, I knew how interesting this was. It was also interesting that the Hills had paid a large part of the medical costs themselves, indicating that they were genuinely anxious to solve the riddle of their anxiety symptoms (reflected mostly by Betty's repetitive dreams and Barney's ulcers), the nagging doubts about their two-hour amnesic period, and the stark puzzlement about their vivid UFO encounter, which was to turn out to be a classic of the cases now referred to as "Close Encounters of the Third Kind."

I began my research by listening to over forty hours of the tape recordings of the regressive hypnosis sessions, recorded over a period of many months by Dr. Simon. I listened for several weeks, three nights a week with him, where the tapes were played on a stop-and-go basis, so that he could explain the technical aspects of the process, and so that I could ask question after question about them. The impact on hearing the tapes was shocking, startling, frightening. The Hills—in separate sessions —were not merely describing what happened. They were *living* the abduction on the lonely New Hampshire mountain road all over again, experiencing all the emotions of the events as they had happened.

At some points, the screams and shouting went beyond the capacity of the tape recorder to handle them. But beyond that was the consistency of the recall of the experience. Dr. Simon pressed hard, almost, but not quite hostile in his questioning. He would ask the same question in different forms, probing deeply into motives and possible fantasies. But the testimony held up over the months. With neither one of the couple knowing what the other was saying, their recall stayed firm and level throughout. The content of the material was substantially the same for both Barney and Betty, down to exact details except for point-of-view.

Following the long tape review with Dr. Simon, I spent many days and nights with the Hills, drawing from them every possible conscious recall of the journey and the encounter. I drove with them back over the route of their journey, asked them to reenact what had happened at specific points along the road, observing their actions and reactions as they did so.

One interesting thing took place at a point on the side of the road where they recalled stopping their car to get out to take a look at the strange object as it was approaching them over the mountains, across the state line in Vermont. Barney insisted that they stood beside a certain pine tree in a clearing, while Betty was certain they had stood about twenty paces away. After rather an intense exchange of words, Barney finally admitted that he was wrong—he was thinking of another stop they had made further down the road. This interested me, because if they had been trying to relate a pat and prearranged story, they would not have bothered to argue so intensely. They would have nodded and agreed completely.

Many months later, when I had finished the long, two-part story for *Look* magazine, I sat down with the editors and researchers to make sure that all the facts were correct and checked out. In a story as strange as this, accuracy and understatement are essential. There was no need for any dramatizations or extrapolation. The story itself was dramatic enough. The schedule date was set, and the story wrapped up. But it occurred to all of us that a final check should be made to make sure that facts stood up in the present, because the events had taken place several years before. It would be irresponsible journalism to present the two-part article to millions of readers without a last-minute affirmation under the same sort of controlled conditions represented by the medical regressive hypnosis that would confirm that the events still held up.

We decided to approach Dr. Simon and the Hills to allow a senior editor of *Look* and me to question them under hypnosis. In this way we could check their up-to-date conviction just before publication to make sure that nothing had eroded in either their conscious or unconscious minds.

Dr. Simon agreed and Barney Hill volunteered to do this. *Look* senior editor Gerry Zimmermann and I joined them for a session that would involve Barney going into deep hypnosis to review the journey in exact detail, and to allow either Zimmermann or myself to question him on details.

Barney sat comfortably in a chair in Dr. Simon's office, facing the three of us. The doctor gave him the instructions to enter into a trance state. Since Barney had been pre-conditioned for this during all his therapy sessions, it was a matter of moments before his eyes were closed, and his voice became somnambulistic.

On instructions from the doctor, Barney retraced the essential events of the journey, and the encounter with the unknown craft. Under deep hypnosis, he confirmed to us that there was no variation in his previous story whatever. As the session drew to a close, we asked Dr. Simon to press hard on the details of the abduction, to make especially sure that this incredible and important part of the story stood up under intensive inquiry.

Since this was not a medical or therapeutic treatment, the doctor was able to be more firm than ever in his questioning. Simon leaned forward in his chair, and assumed the tone of a trial lawyer at this point.

"What is your feeling now?" Dr. Simon asked. "*Were* you abducted or weren't you?"

Barney, his eyes still closed in trance, spoke in level, even tones: "I feel I was abducted."

Dr. Simon drove hard again. "*Were* you abducted?"

Barney's voice remained calm. "I don't want to believe I was abducted."

"But you're convinced that you were?"

"I said 'I feel'," Barney replied, in his trance "because this makes it more comfortable for me to accept something I don't want to accept that happened."

We were reaching a critical point in the questioning. I felt tense and nervous myself. In listening to the previous medical tapes, I had noted that it was impossible to anticipate what might happen next. Almost anything could trigger an intense emotional reaction.

Dr. Simon's voice remained cool and firm. "*What* would make it more comfortable?" he asked.

"For me to say 'I feel'," Barney said.

"You mean," Dr. Simon went on, "it would be worse to say 'I actually was abducted'?"

"It is not worse," Barney said, his voice continuing to be flat and expressionless.

Simon nodded. "More comfortable the other way?"

"I'm comfortable the other way," Barney responded.

The doctor now took another tack. "What are you uncomfortable about?"

Barney replied with a statement he had told me before in my general questioning: "Because it is such a weird story. If anyone else told me that this had happened to them, I would not believe them. And I hate very badly to be accused of something that I didn't do, when I know that I didn't do it . . ."

"What are you being accused of?" Dr. Simon jumped the gun on this question, because Barney had not yet finished his statement.

". . . or if I am not believed that I have done something, and I know that I have done it."

"Well," said Dr. Simon. "Suppose that you have just absorbed Betty's dreams?"

This was a theory Dr. Simon had been considering, in an attempt to make a rationalist's explanation for the case. The doctor felt there was a possibility that Betty had transferred her vivid dreams of the incident to Barney, so that he could re-live them as part of a real experience. But since this involved the acceptance of major thought-transference, it remained as strange as accepting the abduction as real. In Barney's recall under hypnosis, he had re-lived several painful parts of the purported abduction. In one instance, he had reported that he felt the humanoids placing an instrument on his genitals, ostensibly to draw semen out. He had reacted so violently, that Dr. Simon had had to take him temporarily out of his trance. There were many incidents like these, nowhere recorded in Betty's dreams, that made the dream transference-theory hard to apply as an alternate.

When Dr. Simon asked Barney if he might have just absorbed Betty's dreams, Barney replied with hestitation from his trance state: "I would like that."

The doctor pressed on. "You would like that?" Then he hesitated a moment, and added: "Could that be *true*?"

Barney answered with no hesitation. "No!"

"Why not?" the doctor said.

Barney suddenly began heavy breathing—deep, emotional, intense. I looked over at Gerry Zimmermann. He was as tense as I was. Barney was no longer in a calm trance. He opened and closed his hands, and began writhing. Then he almost yelled out:

"*Because I don't like them putting their hands on me!*"

Dr. Simon quickly cut in. "That's all right, Barney. You don't have to be upset. Take it easy!"

Barney was now crying openly. He continued twisting in his chair. "I don't like them putting their hands on me!" he repeated. "I don't like them *touching* me!"

I had to admit I was frightened. I admired Dr. Simon's coolness. "Okay, Barney," he said reassuringly. "They're not touching you now. They're not touching you. You can let that go . . ."

Barney calmed down almost instantly. Dr. Simon began gradually to take him out of his trance state. I looked down at my hands. They were sweating. Gerry Zimmermann took out a pocket Kleenex, and wiped his forehead. Then he leaned over to me and said quietly: "Okay. We'll run the story as scheduled."

*   *   *

The story of what happened at that session is recounted later in the book. It is of critical importance. Without confirmation of the validity of the experience under hypnosis, we were all prepared to scrap the story. There was too much at stake for a highly-respected doctor, the editorial integrity of *Look* magazine, the publishers of the book, myself as a journalist, and the Hills themselves, as respected members of their community. But the story was powerfully confirmed, in a most unusual and dramatic way.

*　　*　　*

The story did run in *Look* shortly after our session. It set an all-time high circulation record for the magazine. It was followed by the publication of this book, first published a decade and a half ago. It has been translated and published in many countries throughout the world as probably the first major "Close Encounter of the Third Kind". While the film of that title is fictional, the story of Barney and Betty Hill is real and unembellished.

Its reception has been varied. Some think that it is inalterable proof that we have been visited by aliens from another planet. Others think it is a fantasy. One thing is certain: the facts that have been put forth in the book have not been altered in any way whatever.

Several other important things have happened since the original publication. They are covered in the new epilog at the back of this edition. They can be appraised by readers, after they have absorbed the material in the book.

I have been often asked what I think, after sharing vicariously the Hills' experience over many months of research and writing. I'm inclined to go back to my first discussion with Dr. Simon. When I had asked him that if the Hills were not lying, were not psychotic, and not hallucinating—could these events actually had happened, his reply basically had been simply: "I am a scientist."

If the same question were put to me, I'd have to take a long deep breath, and say: "I am a journalist." Then I would leave it up to the reader to decide for himself.

John G. Fuller

Weston, Connecticut
September 25, 1979

xiv

INTRODUCTION

On December 14, 1963, Mr. Barney Hill presented himself at my office to keep his appointment for a consultation. It was like any other day. The appointment had been made in advance, and Mr. Hill had been referred for the consultation by another psychiatrist. At the time I knew nothing of Mr. Hill's problems, but when he introduced his wife, who is white, I wondered, fleetingly, if their interracial marriage might be involved in Mr. Hill's disturbance. At his request I saw the couple together and soon realized that both needed help.

A month after the "sighting" the Hills had been interviewed by Walter Webb, a lecturer at Boston's Hayden Planetarium and a scientific advisor to the National Investigations Committee on Aerial Phenomena. With a copy of Mr. Webb's report to NICAP as a basis, Mr. and Mrs. Hill unfolded the story which follows in Mr. Fuller's book.

At the time there was no indication that either the interracial marriage or the UFO experience bore more than a tangential relationship to the central problems which Mr. and Mrs. Hill presented—crippling anxiety, manifested by him in fairly open fashion and by Mrs. Hill more in the form of repetitive nightmarish dreams. Aside from its topical interest, the UFO experience was important because it presented for both Mr. and Mrs. Hill the focal point of the anxiety which had apparently impeded the psychiatric treatment Mr. Hill had been undergoing for some time. This point appeared to be a period of time in the course of their trip home from Canada in September, 1961. They were constantly haunted by a nagging anxiety centering around this period of several hours—a feeling that something had occurred, but what?

A treatment program was outlined for the Hills, and it was decided first to try to unlock the door to the hidden room (the amnesia), and that for this aspect of therapy, hypnosis would be used. Plans were made to begin treatment after the coming Christmas holidays, the first treatment session being set for January 4, 1964.

Apart from the unique quality engendered by the UFO story, treatment proceeded apace as might be expected with two very anxious and co-operative patients, and continued regularly until terminated at the end of June, 1964. During this time there was no portent of the unfolding drama which began on December 14, 1963, which was to extend back in time for two years and to extend forward to this moment exactly two and a half years later when I would be writing an introduction to the book which was to revive the whole drama—the unfolding of events of which I had had no hint during the whole period of treatment. It was a drama which culminated in Mr. Fuller's book and my introduction, which is rather unique in being an apologia for my presence on stage as a reluctant member of the dramatis personae.

The formal treatment program was terminated on June 27, 1964, and from then until late summer of 1965 the Hills and I maintained contact through reports of their progress by visits and telephone calls. I had no indication of the developing storm until the late summer of 1965 when I received a telephone call from a newspaper reporter who appeared to be aware of the Hill story, their treatment, and my part in it—including the use of hypnosis; he requested an interview with me—which I refused, informing him that I would not discuss the Hills' case without their written consent and that even with their written permission any discussion would have to depend on my judgment of its potential effect on their emotional health. A month or two later Mr. Hill, in considerable distress, called to say that the reporter had approached them for an interview—which they had refused. He (the reporter) claimed to have data on the case which he would publish without an interview with them if they refused to comply. It appeared to me that there was nothing that could be done on this basis. The question of giving an interview would be a matter for themselves to decide, perhaps with legal advice.

While I was attending professional meetings in Washington during the week of October 25, 1965, my office called that "All hell had broken loose." There were calls from Mr. Hill and calls from a great many strangers. All seemed to be connected with the appearance of a series of articles in a Boston newspaper. These were written by the reporter to whom I had refused the interview and, apparently, without permission from Mr. and Mrs. Hill. My associates and our office staff did the best they could with the calls pending my return. On my return Mr. Hill telephoned and expressed their great distress over this series of articles—which I had not yet seen. He felt that they distorted the truth and considered them a violation of his right of privacy. He wanted my advice, and I suggested that he seek legal advice. From Mr. Hill I also learned that I had been named in the articles, which explained the large number of calls coming to my office.

The nature of these calls gave me a fairly good clue to the way the articles were being interpreted by the general public. The callers could be classified into four major groups:

1. *The Despairing:* These were people who were apparently emotionally or mentally ill and who saw in hypnosis, as it was presented by the reporter, the magical solution to their problems.

2. *The Mystics:* People who were interested in clairvoyance, extrasensory perception, astrology and other related phenomena. Many of this group saw in the experience and the hypnosis support of their own ideas and beliefs.

3. *The "Fellow Travelers":* These were the self-appointed interviewers who knew the answers to the mysteries of life and saw in the Hills' experience and the hypnosis confirmation of their beliefs. Most of them seemed to be motivated by the wish to bring themselves to my attention as mutual supporters—perhaps for their gain.

4. *The Sympathizers:* A number of callers expressed sympathy for my "persecution" by the writer, who mentioned me either as a Boston or Back Bay psychiatrist, or by name, in all but one of the articles. The use of my name was quite subtle, and I was regularly credited with refusing to violate the doctor-patient relationship by discussing the case. Quite subtly, however, the total impression created in the articles was that some of the fantastic statements which were made came from revelations made under hypnosis, and in some way from me; hence my many phone calls and letters from the public.

After consultation with friends and their counsel, the Hills decided that the best way to handle the newspaper articles and any further forays into this field would be to publish the truth. At the time Mr. John Fuller had been investigating UFO phenomena in the New Hampshire area and was working on a book about incidents in the Exeter area. The Hills discussed the matter with me and asked me to make available to Mr. Fuller my records, chiefly the tape recordings of their treatment, so that they could present an authentic version of the true story as they had experienced it. Public interest, rather than abating, had been increasing, and there was danger that other stories might be published which would increase their distress.

For therapeutic purposes, all of the treatment under hypnosis had been recorded verbatim on a tape recorder. It was inevitable, I suppose, that Mr. Fuller would want to have this verbatim and incontestable material, and the Hills' request was understandable.

The physician's records are his property, but the contents of these records should be available in the interest of his patients. In this sense they are also property of the patients. I decided ultimately that the paramount issue, the emotional health of Mr. and Mrs. Hill, would best be served by releasing the recordings if I could be assured that they would be used honestly, and not detrimentally to them. It appeared that both Mr. Fuller and I had had the same idea and had checked each other's biographies in *Who's Who in the East* to our mutual satisfaction. Conferences with Mr. Fuller and the Hills ensued, and it was agreed that I would have the right to pass on all medical data in the book to prevent, as much as possible, the creation of false impressions and conclusions. It was also agreed that no information of a personal and intimate nature would be revealed if it was not relevant to the UFO experience and the period of amnesia. Mr. Fuller hoped to revivify the experiences and the emotional reactions which were so well expressed in the tape recordings—a difficult task indeed.

The decision to release the recordings created a corollary problem for me—the matter of my professional anonymity, one of the canons of our profession. In this I was already the victim of the newspaper articles in which I was mentioned without my consent. By now this was no longer a local matter involving only the city of Boston. I received calls and letters from other cities, and when I received a request for information from as far west as Wisconsin, it was obvious I no longer possessed any anonymity, and the disclosure of my participation could cause me to be identified with certain statements and conclusions by the reporter about the Hills' experiences, with which I strongly disagree. The mystique of hypnosis and my position as the mystical "Master" by the simple act of association with the statements in the story seemed to give them the quality of an authenticity quite at variance with the facts.

Though I have confined my active participation in this book to editorial supervision of medical statements, I feel that I should make clear the status of hypnosis because of public misconceptions which often envelop hypnosis with an arcane charisma, and the practitioner with the robe of Merlin. Hypnosis is a useful procedure in psychiatry to direct concentrated attention on some particular point in the course of the whole therapeutic procedure. In cases like the Hills', it can be the key to the locked room, the amnesic period. Under hypnosis, experiences buried in amnesia may be recalled in a much shorter time than in the normal course of the psychotherapeutic process. Nevertheless, there is little produced under or by hypnosis that is not possible without. The charisma of hypnosis has tended to foster the belief that hypnosis is the magical and royal road to TRUTH. In one sense this is so, but it must be understood that hypnosis is a pathway to the truth as it is felt and understood by the patient. The truth is what he believes to be the truth, and this may or may not be consonant with the ultimate nonpersonal truth. Most frequently it is.

In the exercise of my editorial rights over Mr. Fuller's book I have confined myself as strictly as possible to the medical data—my observations and records. I have tried to avoid loose speculation insofar as my own data is concerned without inhibiting Mr. Fuller's free expression of his own reasoning and conclusions as long as my data was not distorted. To me the story is the partial documentation of fascinating human experience in an unusual setting connected with what are popularly called "Unidentified Flying Objects." Their existence (the UFO's) as concrete objects is of less concern to me than the experience of these two people showing the cumulative impact of past experiences and fantasies on their present experiences and responses. To Mr. Fuller the former is understandably of greater concern. It follows that his reasoning and speculations are his own, based on his evaluation of my data, the Hills' statements, his past experience and his present convictions.

I have no doubt given him sleepless nights and many moments of despair. I am sure there have been times when he felt I was taking the life of his child; but he has always taken my criticism with good grace and has managed to remove the objectionable or restore the missing in a manner which would be acceptable to me, so that even I, who have lived through much of it, find the book good reading indeed.

Benjamin Simon, M.D.

June 14, 1966

THE INTERRUPTED JOURNEY:

CHAPTER ONE

September in the White Mountains is the cruelest month. The gaunt hotels, vestiges of Victorian tradition, are shuttered, or getting ready to be; motels and overnight cabins flash their neon vacancy signs for only a few fitful hours before their owners give up and retire early. The New Hampshire ski slopes are barren of snow and skiers, the trails appearing as great, brownish gashes beside the silent tramways and chair-lifts. The Labor Day exodus has swept most of the roads clear of traffic; very few vacation trailers and roof-laden station wagons straggle toward Boston or the New York throughways. Winter is already here on the chilled and ominous slopes of Mount Washington, its summit weather station clocking the highest wind velocities ever recorded on any mountain top in the world. Bears and red foxes roam freely. In a few weeks hunters in scarlet or luminous orange jackets will be on the trails, intent on deer or ruffed grouse, or anything legal in sight. The skiers follow later, their minds on powder snow and hot buttered rum, as they bring back the gay holiday mood of summer. Once again the White Mountains will take on a new life.

It was in the doleful mid-September period of 1961—September 19, to be exact—that Barney Hill and his wife Betty began their drive from the Canadian border down U.S. 3, through the White Mountains, on their way home to Portsmouth. It was to be a night drive, brought on by a sense of urgency. The radio of their 1957 Chevrolet Bel Air hardtop made it clear that a hurricane coming up the coast might cut in toward New Hampshire, an event that in previous years had uprooted trees and spilled high-tension wires across the roads. They had failed to bring along enough cash to cover all the extras of their holiday trip, and their funds had dwindled sharply as they had driven leisurely up to Niagara Falls, then circled back through Montreal toward home.

They had cleared through the U.S.-Canadian custom house at about nine that evening, winding along the lonely ceiling of Vermont's Northeast Kingdom, a section of the state that is said to have threatened to secede not only from Vermont, but from the United States as well. The traffic was sparse; few other cars appeared on the road before the Hills approached the welcome lights of Colebrook a half an hour later, an ancient New Hampshire settlement founded in 1770, lying in the shadow of Mt. Monadnock, just across the river from Vermont. The lights of the village, though a relief from the endless turns of the narrow two-way road they had been traveling, were few. A forlorn glow came from the windows of a single restaurant, and realizing that this might be the last chance for any bracing refreshment for the rest of the trip, they decided to turn back even though they had driven past it.

The restaurant was nearly deserted. A few teen-agers gathered in a far corner. Only one woman, the waitress, in the quiet restaurant seemed to show any reaction at all to the fact that Betty and Barney Hill's was a mixed marriage: Barney, a strikingly handsome descendant of a proud Ethiopian freeman whose great-grandmother was born during slavery, but raised in the house of the plantation owner because she was his own daughter; Betty, whose family bought three tracts of land in York, Maine, in 1637, only to have one member cut down by Indians. Regardless of what attention their mixed marriage drew in public places, they were no longer self-conscious about it. Their first attraction to each other, one that still remained, was of intellect and mutual interests. Together, they stumped the state of New Hampshire speaking for the cause of Civil Rights. Barney, former political action and now legal redress chairman of the Portsmouth NAACP, was also a member of the State Advisory Board of the United States Civil Rights Commission and the Board of Directors of the Rockingham County Poverty Program. Both he and his wife are proud to display the award he received from Sargent Shriver for his work. Betty, a social worker for the state of New Hampshire, continues after hours with her job as assistant secretary and community coordinator for the NAACP, and as United Nations envoy for the Unitarian-Universalist Church to which they belong in Portsmouth.

But what was to happen to them this night of September 19, 1961, had nothing whatever to do with their successful mixed marriage, or their dedication to social progress. Nor was there any hint of what was to happen as they sat at the paneled restaurant counter in Colebrook, Barney unceremoniously eating a hamburger, Betty a piece of chocolate layer cake. They didn't linger too long at the counter, just long enough for a cigarette and a cup of black coffee before they continued down U.S. 3 toward home.

The distance from Colebrook to Portsmouth is a hundred and seventy miles, with U.S. 3 remarkably smooth and navigable in the face of the deep mountain gorges it must negotiate. Further south, below Plymouth, nearly thirty miles of four-lane highway—more than that now— invite safe speeds up to sixty-five miles an hour. For the other roads, Barney Hill liked to drive between fifty and fifty-five, even if this should be a shade above the limit.

The clock over the restroom in the Colebrook restaurant read 10:05 when they left that night. "It looks," Barney had said to Betty as they got in their car, "like we should be home by 2:30 in the morning—or 3:00 at the latest." Betty agreed. She had confidence in Barney's driving, even though she sometimes goaded him for pushing too fast. It was a bright, clear night with an almost full moon. The stars were brilliant, as they always are in the New Hampshire mountains on a cloudless night, when starshine seems to illuminate the tops of the peaks with a strange incandescence.

The car was running smoothly through the night air, the road winding effortlessly along the flat ground of the uppermost Connecticut River valley, an ancient Indian and lumbering country, rich in history and legend. The thirty miles south to Northumberland, where Rogers' Rangers made their rendezvous after the sack of St. Francis, passed quickly. Betty, an inveterate sight-seer, enjoyed the brilliance of the moon reflecting on the valley and the mountains in the distance, both in New Hampshire to the east and over the river to Vermont in the west. Delsey, the Hills' scrappy little dachshund, was at peace on the floor by the front seat at Betty's feet. Through Lancaster, a village with a wide main street and fine old pre-Revolutionary houses—all dark now on this September night—U.S. 3 continues south, as the Connecticut River swings westward to widen New Hampshire's territory and narrow Vermont's. Here the smooth, wide valley changes to a more uncertain path through the mountains, with the serrated peaks of the Pilot Range, described lushly by one writer as "a great rolling rampart which plays fantastic tricks with the sunshine and shadow, and towards sunset assumes the tenderest tints of deep amethyst."

There was no sunshine or amethyst now, only the luminous moon, very bright and large, and a black tarvia two-lane road which seemed totally deserted. To the left of the moon, and slightly below it, was a particularly bright star, perhaps a planet, Betty Hill thought, because of its steady glow. Just south of Lancaster, the exact time she cannot remember, Betty was a little startled to notice that another star or planet, a bigger one, had appeared above the other. It had not been there, she was sure, when she looked before. But more curious was that the new celestial visitor clearly appeared to be getting bigger and brighter. For several moments she watched it, said nothing to her husband as he negotiated the driving through the mountains. Finally, when the strange light persisted, she nudged Barney, who slowed the car somewhat and looked out the right-hand side of the windshield to see it. "When I looked at it first," Barney Hill later said, "it didn't seem anything particularly unusual, except that we were fortunate enough to see a satellite. It had no doubt gone off its course, and it seemed to be going along the curvature of the earth. It was quite a distance out, meaning it looked like a star, in motion."

They drove on, glancing at the bright object frequently, finding it difficult to tell if the light itself were moving, or if the movement of the car were making it *seem* to move. The object would disappear behind trees, or a mountain top, then reappear again as the obstruction was cleared. Delsey, the dog, was beginning to get slightly restless, and Betty mentioned that perhaps they should let her out and take advantage of the road stop to get a better look. Barney, an avid plane watcher who sometimes liked to take his two sons (from a former marriage) to watch Piper Cub seaplanes land and take off on Lake Winnipesaukee, agreed, and pulled the car over to the side of the road where there was reasonably unobstructed visibility.

There were woods nearby, and Barney, a worrier at times, mentioned they might keep an eye out for bears, a distinct possibility in this part of the country. Betty, who seldom lets herself get concerned or emotional about anything, laughed his suggestion off, snapped the chain lead on Delsey's collar, and walked her along the side of the road. At this moment, she noted that the star, or the light, or whatever it was in the September sky, was definitely moving. As Barney joined her on the road, she handed Delsey's leash to him and went back to the car. She took from the front seat a pair of 7 x 50 Crescent binoculars they had brought along for their holiday scenery, especially Niagara Falls, which Betty Hill had never seen before. Barney, noting that the light in the sky *was* moving, was now fully convinced that it was a straying satellite.

Betty put the binoculars up to her eyes and focused carefully. What they both were about to see was to change their lives forever, and as some observers claim, change the course of the history of the world.

*   *   *

The holiday trip had been a spontaneous idea, originating with Barney. For some time now, he had been assigned to the night shift at the Boston post office, where he worked as an assistant dispatcher. He liked the job, if not the hours and the long commuting drive from Portsmouth to Boston each night—60 miles each way. The commuting was especially exhausting, with no train or bus available at the late-night hour he began work. The rigors of the daily 120-mile round trip had, Barney felt, been instrumental in causing his ulcer to kick up, a condition for which he was under medical treatment.

He began thinking about the idea for the trip while he was driving into work on the evening of September 14, 1961. Betty had a week's vacation coming up, a badly-needed one from her job as a child welfare worker for the state, handling a rather overwhelming case-load of 120 assignments at one time. With luck, Barney would be able to take some of his vacation leave and relieve some of the pressure while waiting for the results of some recent X-rays of his ulcer his doctor had taken. All during that night at work, the idea appealed to him more. It grew on him as he went through his usual routine, standing in front of some 40 clerks sorting mail, calling out numbers of towns or sections of the city of Boston. The clerks in turn would put the mail from designated slots onto a conveyor belt, where the mail handlers would carry the process on as the hampers moved to the elevators to be dispatched. Barney, with an IQ of nearly 140, could handle more complex jobs than this, but like so many post-office workers he found the frustration of routine work compensated for by the civil service advantages. Further, the steadiness of the job gave him ample time for his community service work which, he felt, was both demanding and rewarding.

He punched out of the Boston post office at 7:30 the following morning and drove toward Portsmouth in anticipation of surprising Betty. Just the idea of getting away relaxed him. Though the harsh realities of the New Hampshire winter would soon be on them, the roads would be free and clear now, and the traffic would be light—ideal for leisurely motoring.

They planned their trip that morning over a cup of hot coffee, Betty accepting the idea at once. But trip money was not in the budget. Barney's main regret was that his two sons couldn't join them, for they both had made a pleasing adjustment to the second marriage, with mutual affection springing up spontaneously between boys and Betty, a condition that Barney whimsically attributed to Betty's expert cookery.

The total adjustment to their mixed marriage had been remarkably smooth. Betty was as proud of her liberalism as she was of her long New England lineage. "In my family," she once wrote in a theme, "it seems to be a belief that the purpose of one's life is to bridge the gap between the past and the future; over this bridge flows all the past, good or bad, to influence the future, and the future of the world depends upon the individuality and strength of the bridge."

All through her family history, Betty points out, various members have fought for unpopular causes. The Dow branch of the family were Quakers in 1662, were attacked, beaten and driven out of Salisbury, Massachusetts, their property stolen and their homes burned. Just before the Civil War, they were active abolitionists, and were with John Greenleaf Whittier when his printing presses were burned by the townspeople of Amesbury, in the same state.

"The greatest day of my life," Betty once said, "was when I learned to read. My days of boredom were over."

She was a bright student in the one-room school that she attended in Kingston, New Hampshire. With one teacher for six grades, she was able to move ahead at her own rate. She can remember explaining long division to the fourth grade when she was in third, and won all of the contests, spelling bees, dramatic roles and prizes there were to be had. An energetic child, sometimes troublesome, she worked on constant projects to earn money—picking cowslips, wild strawberries, raspberries and blueberries, and selling them at a handsome profit. She was so voracious in her reading that her mother used to limit her to one book a day. When Betty was eleven, at the height of the depression, her mother threw away family tradition to work in a factory. At first, it was to be a temporary measure, part-time. Betty's father, the breadwinner, had become ill, savings had dwindled, and her mother's inheritance had been embezzled. But labor union organizers were moving into the New England mill towns, and her mother, a lady of rigid New England gentility, became enthralled. She helped to organize, led strikes, and became a member of the union's Executive Board. Betty was proud of her mother, watching her on the picket lines, worried about the possibility of attack by hecklers or arrest by police. During this time, the family table groaned not with food, but with arguments between an uncle who was helping to organize the CIO in Lynn, a family friend who was carrying out the same chore in Lawrence, and Betty's mother who was strictly A. F. of L. These were exciting scenes to young Betty, with the strikes, the elections and the celebrations. Her father, working for another uncle who owned a shoe factory, remained stoically neutral.

Betty's experience with colored people was limited. Not too many lived in New Hampshire, but at an early age she lived across the street from an interracial couple and absorbed the snide remarks of her classmates against the colored wife. Later, Betty's mother impressed her by saying that although some people did not like colored people, this was wrong because they were people just like everyone else. If Betty heard anyone talking against them, she should speak up without hesitation.

She did. As a sophomore at the University of New Hampshire, which Betty entered in 1937, a girl who was a Negro from Wilmington, Delaware, enrolled at the college—to the consternation of both the administration and the students. In the late 30's, integration was a problem even in the northern state universities. Betty would find Ann, alone in the corner of the smoking room, ignored by the other students. Betty would say nothing at the time, but seethed underneath. When Ann would leave, the other girls would suggest caustically that Ann should go back where she came from, and Betty would react strongly. On one such occasion, as Ann was leaving the smoking room, Betty went to her, and in front of the others, asked to see her room.

It was the beginning of acceptance for Ann, but not until after a long struggle. At times, Betty would almost physically restrain her from leaving the university. She fought with Ann to stop her from packing her luggage. Eventually, Ann graduated Phi Beta Kappa, went on to Harvard and now teaches on the faculty of a southern college.

Although the roots of Betty Hill's marriage to Barney may lie in the attitude expressed by this incident, their problems as an interracial couple are minimal. Barney, at times, shows concern about rejection in public places: hotels, restaurants or meetings. But in their private social life they are popular, accepted, and almost overactive. Their initial self-consciousness dissolved quickly. "It doesn't have any more meaning to me," Betty once told a friend, "than a person having blue eyes or brown eyes. Everyone wants to meet us; everybody wants to invite us places. We've even had to set up some kind of limits, or we would be going here, there, everywhere, constantly."

*   *   *

The planning of the trip that was to have such a profound impact on their lives was brief and relaxed. The shortage of immediate funds was partially compensated for by Betty's idea of borrowing a car-refrigerator from a friend. In this way, the expense of too many meals in restaurants would be reduced. Barney, momentarily ignoring the diet for his ulcers, drank a glass of orange juice, ate six strips of bacon and two soft-boiled eggs, as he plotted the course of the trip on a few Gulf road maps. They would drive leisurely, avoiding the throughways, pay a brief visit to Niagara Falls, then circle through Montreal, and back to Portsmouth. While Betty

9

shopped for food, Barney took a nap to recover from his all-night work at the Boston post office.

They finished most of their packing that afternoon, filled the car-refrigerator with food and put it in the deep freeze. By eight o'clock that evening they were in bed with the alarm set for four the next morning.

Barney, an inveterate early-riser, was up first, but in moments Betty had coffee percolating, and the last-minute packing process began. As he loaded the trunk, Barney shoved a bag of bone-meal fertilizer to one side, and packed the luggage around it. Betty had bought the fertilizer to work on the garden during the vacation; it was just as easy to let it stay in the trunk as to take it out. Later, they were to find this comfortably homey material creating an unusual inquiry and speculation.

It was a clear, crisp New Hampshire morning as they drove off, noting the mileage on the speedometer only to lose the slip of paper later—an ingrained habit of Barney's. They drove out Route 4, toward Concord, in a festive mood. Barney, at the wheel, burst into a hoarse version of "Oh, What A Beautiful Morning." Betty, who liked to hear Barney sing, smiled. Barney, who liked to please Betty, smiled back. There was no hint at all of what was about to happen later; nor could there be. No such event would be so thoroughly documented.

*   *   *

The object they saw in the sky near Route 3 four nights later, south of Lancaster, New Hampshire, continued its unpredictable movement as they passed through Whitfield and the village of Twin Mountain. They stopped briefly several times, and by now Barney was frankly puzzled. His only alternate theory, aside from that of a satellite, was that the object was a star, a theory he immediately discounted because they had proved that it was in movement, changing its course in an erratic manner. At one of the stops, a few miles north of Cannon Mountain, Betty had said, "Barney, if you think that's a satellite, or a star, you're being absolutely ridiculous."

With his naked eye, Barney could tell that she was right. It was obviously not a celestial object now, he was sure. "We've made a mistake, Betty," he said. "It's a commercial plane. Probably on its way to Canada." He got back in the car, and they continued driving on.

Betty, in the passenger seat, kept it in view as they moved down Route 3. It seemed to her that it was getting bigger and brighter, and she kept getting more puzzled and more curious. Barney would note it through the windshield on occasion, but was more worried about a car coming around the now frequent curves of the road. His theory that it was a commercial airliner headed for Canada soothed his annoyance at the fact that he might be confronted with some unexplainable phenomenon. The road was completely deserted; they hadn't seen a car or truck in either direction for miles now, which left them alone in the deep gorges late at night. Some natives of northern New Hampshire prefer never to drive through these roads at night, through long-standing custom and superstition. In winter, an informal group known as the Blue Angels patrols the roads for cars frozen or broken down. It is too easy to freeze to death in these lonely streches, and the State Troopers cannot possibly cover the wide territory frequently enough. Barney, his concern growing in spite of his comforting theories, hoped that he would soon see a trooper or at least another car driving by which he could flag and compare notes with.

Around eleven o'clock they approached the enormous and somber silhouette of Cannon Mountain, looming to the west on their right. Barney slowed the car down near a picnic turnout that commanded a wide view to the west and looked again at the strange moving light. In amazement, he noted that it swung suddenly from its northern flight pattern, turning to the west, then completing its turn and heading back directly toward them. Barney braked the car sharply, turning off into the picnic area.

"Whatever you're calling it, Barney," Betty said, "I don't know why, because it's still up there, and it's still following us, and if anything it's coming right toward us."

"It's got to be a plane," Barney said. They were standing in the picnic area now, looking up at the light which was growing bigger still. "A commercial liner."

"With a crazy course like that?" Betty said.

"Well, then it's a Piper Cub. That's what it is. With some hunters, who might be lost."

"It's not the hunting season," Betty said, as Barney took the binoculars from her. "And I don't hear a sound."

Neither did Barney, although he desperately wanted to.

"It might be a helicopter," he said as he looked through the binoculars. He was sure that it wasn't, but was reaching for any kind of explanation which would make sense. "The wind might be carrying the sound the other direction."

"There *is* no wind, Barney. Not tonight. You know that."

Through the binoculars, Barney now made out a shape, like the fuselage of a plane, although he could see no wings. There also seemed to be a blinking series of lights along the fuselage, or whatever it was, in an alternating pattern. When Betty took the glasses, the object passed in front of the moon, in silhouette. It appeared to be flashing thin pencils of different colored lights, rotating around an object which at that time appeared cigar shaped. Just a moment before it had changed its speed from slow to fast, then slowed down again as it crossed the face of the moon. The lights were flashing persistently, red, amber, green and blue. She turned to Barney, asking him to take another look.

"It's *got* to be a plane," Barney said. "Maybe a military plane. A search plane. Maybe it's a plane that's lost."

He was getting irritated at Betty now, or taking out his irritation on her because she was refusing to accept a natural explanation. At one time, several years before, in 1957, Betty's sister and family had described seeing clearly an unidentified flying object in Kingston, New Hampshire, where they lived. Betty, who had confidence in her sister's reliability and capacity for observation, believed the story of her sighting. Barney neither believed nor disbelieved; he was indifferent to the subject as a whole, had little interest in it. If anything, he was more skeptical of flying objects after hearing her story. He felt that Betty, for the first time in five years, was about to bring this subject up again. But she didn't mention it.

Beside them, the dachshund was whining and cowering. Betty gave the binoculars to Barney, took Delsey to the car and got in and shut the door. Barney put the glasses on the object again, again wishing that he could find some comfort from comparing notes with a passing motorist. He wanted above all to hear a sound: the throb of a propeller-driven plane or the whir of a jet. None came. For the first time, he felt he was being observed, that the object was actually coming closer and attempting to circle them. If it's a military craft, he was thinking, it should not do this, and his mind went back to a time a few years before when a jet had buzzed close by him, shattered the sound barrier, and cracked the air with an explosion.

Getting back in the car, Barney mentioned to Betty that he thought the craft had seen them and was playing games with them. He tried not to let Betty know that he was afraid, something he didn't like to admit to himself.

They drove on toward Cannon Mountain at not much more than five miles an hour, catching glimpses of the object as it moved erratically in the sky. At the top of the mountain, the only light they had seen for miles glowed like a beacon, appearing to be on top of the closed and silent aerial tramway, or perhaps on the restaurant there. They stopped again near the base of the mountain, momentarily, as the object suddenly swung behind the dark silhouette and disappeared. At the same moment, the light on the top of the mountain went out, inexplicably. Betty looked at her watch as it did so, wondering if the restaurant were closed. She could not read the dial very plainly in the dashboard light, and never did get an accurate reading. If there were people up there, she thought, they must be getting an exceptional view of the object.

As the car moved by the darkened silhouette of the Old Man of the Mountain, the object appeared again, gliding silently, leisurely, parallel to the car to the west of them, on the Vermont side of the car. It was more wooded here, more difficult to keep the object in sight as it glided behind the trees. But it was there, moving with them. Near the turnoff for The Flume, a tourist attraction, they stopped again, almost got a sharp, clear look at it, but again the trees intervened.

Just beyond The Flume they passed a small motel, the first sign of life they had seen for many miles. The tidy hostelry looked comforting, although Barney, his eyes alternately moving between the curves of the road and the object in the sky, barely noticed it. Betty noted a sign, beaming with AAA approval, and the light in a single, lonely window. A man was standing in the doorway of one of the cottages, and Betty thought how easy it would be to end the whole situation right now by simply pulling into the motel. She was thinking this—but she didn't say anything to Barney. Her curiosity about the object had now become overwhelming, and she was determined to see more of it. By now, Barney was beginning to irritate her by trying to deny the existence of the object. In fact, he was. He was still concerned about another car coming around a blind curve while he tried to keep one eye on the object as it moved around almost directly ahead of them on the road.

It was now apparently only a few hundred feet high, and it was huge. Further off, it had seemed to Betty that it was spinning; now it had stopped and the light pattern had changed from blinking, multi-colored lights to a steady, white glow. In spite of the vibrations of the car, she put the binoculars to her eyes and looked again.

She drew a quick, involuntary breath because she could clearly see a double row of windows. Without the glasses, it had appeared only as a streak of light. Now it was clear that this was a structured craft of enormous dimension, just how large she couldn't tell because both distance and altitude were hard to judge exactly. Then, slowly, a red light came out on the left side of the object, followed by a similar one on the right.

"Barney," she said, " I don't know *why* you're trying not to look at this. Stop the car and look at it!"

"It'll go away by the time I do that," Barney said. He was not at all convinced that it would.

"Barney, you've got to *stop*. You've never seen anything like this in your life."

He looked through the windshield and could see it plainly now, not more than two hundred feet in the air, he thought, and coming closer. A curve to the left in the road now shifted the object to the right of the car, but the distance remained the same. To the right, not far south of Indian Head, where another historic stone face surveys the mountains and valleys, he saw two imitation commercial wigwams on the site of a closed-down enterprise known as Natureland. Here, hundreds of youngsters swarm with their parents during summer visits. At this moment, it was silent and tomb-like.

Barney stopped the car almost in the center of the road, forgetting in the excitement any problem with other traffic. "All right, give me the binoculars," he said. Betty resented his tone. It sounded as if he were trying to humor her.

Barney got out, the motor still running, and leaned his arm on the door of the car. By now the object had swung toward them and hovered silently in the air not more than a short city block away, not more than two treetops high. It was raked on an angle, and its full shape was apparent for the first time: that of a large glowing pancake. But the vibrations from the motor jostled his arm, blurring his vision. He stepped to one side of the car to get a better look.

"Do you see it? Do you see it?" Betty said. For the first time her voice was rising in emotion. Barney, he admitted frankly later, was scared, perhaps as much because Betty rarely became excited as because of the nearness of this strange and utterly silent object defying almost any law of aerodynamics.

"It's just a plane or something," he snapped at her.

"Okay," Betty said. "It's a plane. But did you ever see a plane with *two* red lights? I always thought planes had one red and one green light."

"Well, I can't get a good look at it," he said. "The car was shaking the binoculars." Then he stepped a few feet away and looked again.

As he did so, the huge object—as wide in diameter as the distance

14

between three telephone poles along the road, Barney later described it—swung in a silent arc directly across the road, not more than a hundred feet from him. The double row of windows was now clear and obvious.

Barney was fully gripped with fear now, but for a reason that he cannot yet explain, he found himself moving across the road on the driver's side of the car, on to the field, and across the field, directly toward it. Now the enormous disc was raked on an angle toward him. Two fin-like projections on either side were now sliding out further, each with a red light on it. The windows curved around the craft, around the perimeter of the thick, pancake-like disc, glowing with brilliant white light. There was still no sound. Shaken, but still finding an irresistible impulse to move closer to the craft, he continued on across the field, coming within fifty feet of it, as it dropped down to the height of a single tall tree. He did not estimate its size in feet, except that he knew it was as big or bigger in diameter than the length of a jet airliner.

Back in the car, Betty was not at first aware that Barney was walking away from her. She was thinking that this wasn't a very smart place to park the car, in the middle of the highway, even though there were no curves nearby. The car was neither on the right nor the left—it was splitting the white dotted line down the middle of the road. She would watch, she thought, to see if any headlights appeared either in front of or to the rear of the car, and at least pull the car quickly out of the way if another should appear on the road. She busied herself doing this for several moments, and then suddenly became aware that Barney had disappeared into the blackness of the field. Instinctively, she called for him.

"Barney," she screamed. "Barney, you damn fool, come back here." If he didn't reappear in a moment, she resolved to go out after him. "Barney! What's wrong with you? Do you hear me?"

There was no answer, and she started to slide across the front seat, toward the open door on the driver's side of the car.

Out on the field, near a shuttered vegetable stand and a single, gnarled apple tree, Barney put the binoculars up to his eyes. Then he stopped very still.

Behind the clearly structured windows he could see the figures, at least half a dozen living beings. They seemed to be bracing themselves against the transparent windows, as the craft tilted down toward his direction. They were, as a group, staring directly at him. He became vaguely aware that they were wearing uniforms. Betty, now nearly two hundred feet away, was screaming at him from the car, but Barney has no recollection of hearing this.

The binoculars seemed glued to his eyes. Then, on some invisible, inaudible signal, every member of the crew stepped back from the window toward a large panel a few feet behind the window line.

Only one remained there looking at him, apparently a leader. In the binoculars, Barney could see appendages in action among the apparent crew at what seemed to be a control board behind the windows of the craft. Slowly the craft descended lower, a few feet at a time. As the fins bearing the two red lights spread out further on the sides of the craft, an extension lowered from the underside, perhaps a ladder, he could not be sure.

He sharpened the focus of the binoculars on the one face remaining at the window. His memory at this point is blurred. For a reason he cannot explain, he was certain he was about to be captured. He tried to pull the glasses away from his eyes, to turn away, but he couldn't. As the focus became sharp, he remembers the eyes of the one crew member who stared down at him. Barney had never seen eyes like that before. With all his energy he ripped the binoculars from his eyes and ran screaming back across the field to Betty and the car. He tossed the binoculars on the seat, barely missing Betty, who had just straightened up from getting ready to slide out of his side of the car, as she heard him running across the hard surface of the road.

Barney was near hysteria. He jammed the car into first gear, spurted off down the road, shouting that he was sure they were going to be captured. He ordered Betty to look out the window to see where the craft was. She rolled down the window on the passenger side, looked out. The object was nowhere in sight. Craning her neck, she looked directly above the car. She could see nothing whatever. The strange craft did not appear in sight. But neither were the stars which had seconds ago been so brilliant in the sky. Barney kept yelling that he was sure it had swung above them.

Betty checked again, but all she could see was total darkness. She looked out the rear window, saw nothing—except the stars, then visible through the window.

Then suddenly a strange electronic-sounding beeping was heard. The car seemed to vibrate with it. It was in irregular rhythm—beep, beep—beep, beep, beep—seeming to come from behind the car, in the direction of the trunk.

Barney said, "What's that noise?"

Betty said, "I don't know."

They each began to feel an odd tingling drowsiness come over them. From that moment, a sort of haze came over them.

*　　*　　*

Some time later, how long they were not sure, the beeping sound repeated itself. They were conscious only that there were two sets of these beeps, separated by a time span they had no idea about—as well as what had happened or how long it had taken.

As the second set of beeps grew louder, the Hills' awareness slowly returned. They were still in the car—and the car was moving, with Barney at the wheel. They were silent, numb, and somnambulistic. At first, they rode silently, glancing out at the road to see just where they might be. A sign told them they were somewhere in the vicinity of Ashland, thirty-five miles south of Indian Head, where the inexplicable beeping had first sounded. In those first few moments of consciousness, Betty remembers faintly saying to her husband: *"Now* do you believe in flying saucers?" And he recalls answering: "Don't be ridiculous. Of course not."

But neither can remember much detail, other than this, until they had driven on to the new throughway, U.S. 93. Not long after entering this highway, Betty suddenly snapped out of her semi-wakefulness and pointed to a sign reading: CONCORD—17 MILES.

"That's where we are, Barney," she said. "Now we know."

Barney, too, remembers his mind clearing at this point. He does not even recall being disturbed or concerned about the thirty-five miles between Indian Head and Ashland, about which he seemed to remember nothing.

They drove on toward Concord, saying little. They did decide, though, that the experience at Indian Head was so strange, so unbelievable that they would tell no one about it. "No one would believe it, anyway," Barney said. "I find it hard to believe, myself."

Betty agreed. Near Concord, they looked for a place to have a cup of coffee, but nothing was open, anywhere. Still groggy and uncommunicative, they ploughed on, now turning east on Route 4, swinging across the state toward the ocean and Portsmouth.

Just outside of Portsmouth, they noticed dawn streaking the sky in the east. As they drove through the streets of the slumbering city, no one was stirring. The birds were already chattering, though, and it was nearly full daylight when they reached home. Barney looked at his watch, but it had stopped running, and shortly afterward Betty looked at hers, which had also stopped. Inside, the kitchen clock read shortly after five in the morning. "It looks," said Barney, "like we've arrived home a little later than expected."

Betty took Delsey out on her chain for a morning airing, while Barney unloaded the car. The birds were in full chorus now, a background for Betty's thoughts of the night before, which still haunted her. Barney, too, was thoughtful. They said little. For a reason she couldn't pinpoint, Betty asked him to put the luggage in the back hall, instead of having it in the house. He complied, then went to clear out the rest of the car. Picking up the binoculars, he noticed for the first time an unusual thing: the leather strap that had been around his neck the night before was freshly and cleanly broken in half.

From Concord on down, during the silent drive, both Betty and Barney had looked to the sky at regular intervals, wondering if the strange object would appear again. Even after they went into the house, a red frame structure on a small plot in Portsmouth, they found themselves occasionally going to the windows to look up at the morning sky.

Both had a strange, clammy feeling. They sat down at the kitchen table over a cup of coffee, but not before Barney went into the bathroom to examine his lower abdomen, which for a reason he could not explain, was bothering him. After two years, he still could not recall what made him do this.

After he came out of the bathroom, they reviewed what had happened, and again resolved not to discuss it with anyone. The latter part of the trip was extremely vague; they couldn't recall much of anything about the drive from Indian Head to Ashland. They had some fragmentary recollections of going through Plymouth, just north of the second series of beeps. Barney was baffled and confused by the absence of sound in the craft. He tried to classify it as a known aircraft in spite of the completely foreign appearance, the other-worldly feeling it had created in them.

They remembered two distinct series of beeps. But the sandwich in between was puzzling to them. Betty, with the aid of a strong cup of coffee, could recall very faintly some of the things which had happened right after Indian Head. She could recall seeing a road marker that divided the towns of Lincoln and North Woodstock, but it was a flashing, fragmentary impression. She could remember passing a store in the town of North Woodstock, again an isolated impression. Both recalled very faintly a large, luminous moon-shape, which seemed to be touching the road, sitting on end under some pines. Betty, straining to remember, thought that Barney had made a sharp left turn from Route 3, but could not in any way identify where this might have been. When they had seen the moon-shaped object, Barney faintly recalled saying to Betty, "Oh, no, not again." Betty recalls her reaction to Barney's denial that it could have been an Unidentified Flying Object. She thought: That's the way Barney is. If something frightens him, or he doesn't like it, he just says to himself that it never happened. Barney, to a degree, will confess to this.

Both agree they regained full consciousnesses at the sign on U.S. 93 which indicated that it was seventeen miles to Concord. Before that, one other recollection came to their minds: a fragmentary image of the darkened streets of Plymouth, a half a dozen miles north of Ashland, where the second series of beeps took place.

"When we arrived at our house," Barney said later, "and Betty got out and took the dog on her leash to walk her around the yard, I got out of the car and began taking things out. Betty said she wanted me to throw the food from the refrigerator out, and to keep the rest of the things from the car out of the house. I could hardly wait until I was able to get everything from the car to the back porch so that I could go into the bathroom, where I took a mirror and began looking over my body. And I don't know, I didn't know why at the time, but I felt unclean. With a grime different from what usually accumulates on a trip. Somewhat clammy. Betty and I both went to the window, and then I opened the back door, and we both looked skyward. And I went into the bedroom and looked around. I can't describe it—it was a presence. Not that the presence was there with us, but something very puzzling had happened."

They collapsed into bed immediately after a breakfast snack and their sleep was undisturbed. They were hoping that the incident would fade quickly from their minds and remain only an interesting anecdote that someday they might tell someone about. They were unaware that it would affect their lives profoundly for many years to come.

CHAPTER TWO

It was nearly three that afternoon when they woke up. Their sleep had been dreamless, their relief considerable at being home again, bathed and well rested. Barney, lying in bed with his eyes opened, again began recalling the strange experience of the night before. Most of all, he was baffled and confused by the total lack of sound of the object all during the extended encounter, further puzzled by the absence of any characteristics that could be related to ordinary aircraft. He regretted deeply that neither a state trooper nor a truck had passed to share the experience with them. He still had the feeling that there was a presence around somewhere, a vague and totally indefinable presence. Somewhere, very faintly, it seemed that he had encountered a roadblock during the night. But this impression was blurred and indistinct.

The return of awareness after he had heard the strange electronic sound came back to him very slowly. Before his mind had fully cleared, he had another flash of insight—that he had turned from Route 3 on to Route 104 to approach the expressway to Concord. But the sign CONCORD—17 MILES remained both his and Betty's symbol of the return to normality. He felt, as he lay in bed awake on this afternoon, that the reason he and Betty said so little all during the latter part of the drive was because he, at least, had been in a mild state of shock. The figures he had seen aboard the craft he shunted quickly out of his mind. He did not want to think about them.

As Betty awakened, the thoughts of what had happened the night before crowded everything else out of her mind. She could not think beyond that trip home and the experience they had had. She was to go around the rest of the day, shaking her head in disbelief. One of her first acts that afternoon, on arising (why, she never fully knew), was to take the dress and shoes she had worn during the night before and pack them in the back of her closet. She has never worn them since.

Barney, on arising, went over to the clothes he had worn the night before and was a little startled to discover that his best shoes were severely scuffed along their shiny tops. Momentarily, he was puzzled by the numerous burrs around the cuffs of his pants and on his socks, until another flood of memory came to him of walking onto and across the lonely field at Indian Head. Barney, who pays special attention to good grooming, could not understand why it was the *tops* of his shoes that were so badly scuffed. He finally assumed that somewhere in that field he had dragged the top of his feet along some rocks, how he did not exactly know, and shrugged it off. Later he was to discover the possible cause.

The sudden recollection of the incident at the field near Indian Head prompted him to go to the back door and look at the sky again. He was expecting something—but he didn't know what it was. He strained to recollect what happened after he put the binoculars to his eyes and rushed back to the car, but was unsuccessful. He simply could not get beyond that point.

At their second breakfast of the day, he discussed it with Betty, who pressed him on why he had rushed to the car in such excitement and why he felt they were going to be captured. Also, why hadn't he heard her screaming for him to return to the car? Later, on one of the many trips they made back to the area, they discovered that it was difficult to hear anyone calling at the distance Barney estimated he had walked into the field. Beyond all this, Barney became aware of an unexplained soreness on the back of his neck.

Their resolution to keep the experience absolutely quiet began to waver during their afternoon breakfast session that day. Barney was trying to hold out completely, but Betty, in the light of her sister's experience with a UFO several years before, wanted to share it with her, at least. Barney grudgingly went along with the idea, although he felt strongly that the best thing to do was to try to forget about the entire incident.

Betty went to the phone and called her sister, feeling a measure of relief in getting the story off her chest to a sympathetic listener. Her sister, Janet Miller, lived in nearby Kingston with her husband and children, the husband being the local scoutmaster and an amateur astronomy buff. Trying to keep calm, Betty recounted the story of the night before. Janet, who had no reservations about the possibility of a UFO sighting because of her own experience, grew very excited and confirmed Betty's growing feeling that the car or their clothes might have in some way been exposed to radiation if the object had hovered directly over the car. Up to this point, Betty's floating anxiety about some kind of contamination had been instinctive; now she wondered if there were not some kind of basis in reality for the feeling she had. Janet reminded Betty that a neighbor of theirs in Kingston was a physicist, and that she would check him about what kind of evidence might possibly be extant if, indeed, the object had come in close proximity to the car. In a few moments Janet was back on the phone to tell Betty that the physicist said any ordinary compass might show certain evidence of radiation if the needle became seriously disturbed on contact with the car's surface.

Barney's skepticism, on overhearing Betty's part of the phone conversation, stiffened. As she rushed around looking for the inexpensive compass they had used on the trip, Barney was determined to be uncooperative.

"Where *is* it?" she asked Barney, in her impatience to find it and get out to the car.

"I put it in the drawer," he said.

"What drawer?" Betty asked.

None of this was helping Barney put the incident out of his mind forever. "I don't know. You'll have to find it," he said.

Betty was getting extremely aggravated. "Thanks," she said. "You're a big help."

"What do you need the compass for, anyway?" he said. "You don't really need it."

"That's your viewpoint," Betty replied. "Keep your viewpoint, but give me the compass."

Barney finally relented and got the compass for her. She rushed outside and found it raining. She ran the compass along the wet sides of the car. The needle did not react to any appreciable extent, but as she drew it near the trunk of the car, her attention was drawn to an unusual sight: a dozen or more shiny circles scattered on the surface of the trunk, each perfectly circular and about the size of a silver dollar. They were highly polished in contrast to the dimmer surface of the rest of the trunk and the car, as if the paint had been buffed through a circular stencil. She recalled at this point that the strange beeping sounds they had heard the night before came from the direction of the trunk, and in the emotional state she was in after talking to her sister, she was startled by the sight of the round, shiny spots in this vicinity.

Carefully she placed the compass on one of the spots. The needle immediately began wavering. She almost panicked, but got control of herself and placed the compass on the side of the car, where none of the shiny spots appeared. The needle reacted normally, remaining pointed in one direction. Quickly, she shifted the compass back to the shiny spot. Again, the needle went out of control. She ran quickly back to the house.

"Barney," she said, "you've *got* to come outside and look at this with me. There're these bright, shiny spots all over the trunk of the car, and the compass spins every time I put it anywhere near them."

Barney insisted that it was her imagination and didn't want to go out in the rain.

In the meanwhile, a couple renting an apartment from the Hills in the second floor of their house dropped down, and noting that Betty was getting quite upset by something, asked what the matter was. Betty, in her state of excitement, spilled out the story of the UFO sighting to them and told them that she wanted Barney to go out and look at the strange spots and the reaction of the compass. Barney then reluctantly went out with the other couple, while Betty called her sister to report the findings. Janet, in the meanwhile, had talked to the former Chief of Police of Newton, New Hampshire, who happened to be visiting that day, and he had immediately suggested that the Hills notify the Pease Air Force Base in Portsmouth, a Strategic Air Force Command installation that had been the recipient of a steady number of UFO reports in New Hampshire in recent months. The Police Chief had received instructions on this procedure in line with the rash of UFO sightings in New Hampshire.

Barney came back into the living room within a few minutes, just before Betty hung up from the second call to her sister.

"How did the compass act for you?" Betty asked.

"Just like any compass," he said. "Oh, it might have jumped around a little when it got near the tire in the trunk. Things like that."

Betty eyed him coldly. "Well—why did it jump around when you touched it to the trunk?"

"I don't know," Barney said.

"I can see why it might jump around if it were near the battery. But the spare tire? Really, Barney."

"Oh, I don't know," Barney said. "Maybe it has something to do with the metal. It acted perfectly all right to me."

"What about the shiny spots?" Betty said. "Did you see those?"

"Yes," said Barney.

"Well—what about them?"

"Oh, probably something dropped on the trunk."

Betty was convinced that he was simply denying all this experience to himself, and she didn't know why. (Later, Barney explained that the experience had been such a nightmare to him, so unbelievable, that he wanted desperately to put the whole thing behind him and forget it. At the moment he was getting very irritated with Betty for persisting in her exploration.)

He again refused to give in when she asked him to go out with her and recheck the compass and the shiny spots. And he urged her to forget it when she insisted on following Janet's advice to call the Pease Air Force Base.

"All right," he finally agreed. "But if you do call the Air Force Base, leave me out of it."

Betty was haunted by the thought that they might have been exposed to radioactivity, but at the same time she realized that this might sound ridiculous to the officers at the Air Force Base. However, she called the Air Police at the base, and after several transfers by the switchboard she finally found one officer who asked her for the details.

She gave him the facts in bare outline, because the officer's attitude was cynical and uncommunicative. Out of embarrassment or shyness, she skipped the details of seeing the double row of windows, feeling that this might make her the target for further cynicism. She did, however, report the fins apparently separating at the sides of the craft, with the two red lights on either side. The officer grew more interested in this, and when Betty explained that her husband had a better look at this part of the craft than she did, the officer asked to speak with Barney.

Barney was extremely reluctant to come to the phone, but he had simmered down a little by now, and finally agreed. He cooperated in giving out as many details as he could remember, but he sheepishly avoided mentioning the figures he had clearly observed on the craft. At one moment, the officer told Barney that he was cutting him in with another extension at the base, and that the call was being monitored. Neither Barney nor Betty was anxious to be involved in a bizarre situation. While Betty felt that the attitude of the officers was one of indifference, Barney disagreed, saying that they *were* intensely interested, that they were at no time impatient, and that they were intrigued by the fins with red lights. To the Air Force officers this was a new slant in the many UFO reports they had screened.

The conversation on the phone made a slight change in Barney's attitude. From his discussion with the officer, Barney learned of other reports, some similar to his, so that he no longer felt as self-conscious about the possibility of being considered irrational in reporting something that he couldn't explain. Both refrained, however, from telling about the shiny spots on the car, and Barney still held back on revealing the figures aboard the craft behind the curved window. This, he felt, might put him in the position of being doubted, and he had enough of his own doubts to contend with at this point. His main concern was not to appear foolish.

On the next day, some of his concern in this respect was reduced when the Pease Air Force Base called back for further information. This gave Barney more confidence in himself and his own experience, but he still did not give out all the details.

It was Major Paul W. Henderson, of the 100th Bomb Wing at the Pease Base who called back the next day, and he told the Hills that he had stayed up all night working on the report and wanted a few more details. He also indicated that he might be calling back later, although after the second conversation the Hills did not hear from him again. His official report to Project Blue Book, the name of the Air Force unit at Wright-Patterson Field, Ohio, which handles the thousands of UFO sightings from over the entire country, indicates that the Hills need not have had the concern about being laughed at when they made their faltering call to the Base after their experience.

Information Report No. 100–1–61

On the night of 19–20 Sept between 20/001 and 20/0100 Mr. and Mrs. Hill were traveling south on Route 3 near Lincoln, N.H. when they observed, through the windshield of their car, a strange object in the sky. They noticed it because of its shape and the intensity of its lighting as compared to the stars in the sky. The weather and sky were clear at the time.

A. Description of Object

1. Continuous band of lights—cigar shaped at all times, despite changes in direction. [Neither of the Hills recalls whether they mentioned the disc shape of the craft at close range.]

2. Size: When first observed it appeared to be about the size of a nickel at arm's length. Later when it seemed to be a matter of hundreds of feet above the automobile it would be about the size of a dinner plate held at arm's length.

3. Color: Only color evident was that of the band of lights when comparable to the intensity and color of a filament of an incandescent lamp. (See reference to "wing tip" lights.) [Barney, who felt impelled at this time to understate everything, shied away from giving his full impression of the size of the craft.]

4. Number: One.

5. Formation: None.

6. Features or details: See 1 above. During period of observation wings seemed to appear from the main body described as V-shaped with red lights on tips. Later, wings appeared to extend further.

7. Tail, trail or exhaust: None observed.

8. Sound: None except as described in item D.

B. Description of Course of Object

1. First observed through windshield of car. Size and brightness of object compared to visible stars attracted observers' attention.

2. Angle of elevation, first observed: About forty-five degrees.

3. Angle of elevation, at disappearance: Not determinable because of inability to observe its departure from auto.

4. Flight path and maneuvers: See item D.

5. How object disappeared: See item D.

6. Length of observation: Approx thirty minutes.

C. Manner of Observation

1. Ground—visual.

2. Binoculars used at times.

3. Sighting made from inside auto while moving and stopped. Observed from inside and outside auto.

D. Location and Details

(Here the report recounts the general details of the sighting, including the strange sound of the beepings, which the Hills described to the Air Force interrogator as "sounding like someone had dropped a tuning fork." Under the pressures of the formal phone call, many details were omitted, among them being the varicolored lights seen by Betty, and of course the figures Barney had observed but did not want to talk about.)

The report concludes: "During a later conversation with Mr. Hill, he volunteered the observation that he did not originally intend to report this incident, but inasmuch as he and his wife did in fact see this occurrence he decided to report it. He says that on looking back he feels that the whole thing is incredible, and he feels somewhat foolish—he just cannot believe that such a thing could or did happen. He says, on the other hand, that they both saw what they reported, and this fact gives it some degree of reality.

Information contained herein was collected by means of a telephone conversation between the observers and the preparing individual. The reliability of the observer cannot be judged, and while his apparent honesty and seriousness appears to be valid it cannot be judged at this time.

Struggling to find some correlation between fantasy and fact, Barney suggested to Betty that they each draw a sketch of their impressions of the object. Betty agreed. Sitting in separate rooms, they roughed out two sketches, which when compared were remarkably similar.

Even though Barney's lengthy conversation with the Air Force Major reinforced his confidence in his own sighting, he still wasn't a full believer in unidentified flying objects. He worried about his inability to justify what he actually saw with his conviction that such a thing could not be. Betty, too, was cautious in spite of her belief in her sister's sighting, and in the inexplicable actions of the object that had stayed so long in sight on Route 3. Barney told a friend that his reaction was one of a person who saw something he doesn't want to remember. Later, this dichotomy was to bother him, to reflect itself in the worsening of his ulcer condition that up to this point had been improving considerably.

Where Barney recoiled from the situation, Betty's curiosity was ignited. Two days later, she went to the library to find any possible information on Unidentified Flying Objects, which had, to her knowledge, been receiving rather cavalier treatment in the press. Like most intelligent people, she was of two minds about the subject. She had felt, prior to their own startling experience, that there had to be something to the phenomenon, but of any extensive facts about the subject she knew nothing. At the library, she discovered that background material was sparse. However, a book by Major Donald Keyhoe, *The Flying Saucer Conspiracy,* commanded her attention. She took it home to read it at a single sitting. Barney, although his viewpoint had softened since he talked with the Air Force Base, declined to read it. The lingering resistance he ascribed to his continued desire to avoid the painfulness of the shock he had encountered. He was not, he insists, trying to be arbitrary or stubborn.

Major Keyhoe's thesis in the book, Betty discovered, indicated that the Air Force was making a serious effort to discredit all UFO sightings, at the expense of open scientific inquiry. A former Annapolis graduate and Marine Corps Major, Keyhoe was instrumental in establishing an organization known as the National Investigations Committee on Aerial Phenomena in Washington to correlate and analyze every available UFO sighting in an attempt to find a solution to the mystery, and to prepare the public, if necessary, for the possibility that the objects may be extraterrestrial spacecraft of unknown origin. NICAP, as Major Keyhoe's organization has come to be known, arrived at the conclusion that there are basically only two explanations for the consistent, world-wide reporting of UFO's every year: (1) Widespread and presently unaccountable delusion on a scale so vast that it should be, in itself, a matter of urgent scientific study; (2) people *are* seeing maneuvering, apparently controlled objects in the atmosphere. Members of NICAP, many of whom are reputable scientists, professors, technicians, pilots and former high-ranking military officers argue that the second hypothesis is the more reasonable, and that it is grounded on empirical observations. In its carefully documented study *The UFO Evidence,* the organization analyzes 575 technical and other reliable reports from 46 states, Puerto Rico, Mexico, Canada, and other countries throughout the world. NICAP investigators, serving on a voluntary basis, are instructed to document each case in painstaking detail and to contest wherever possible any wild and irresponsible reports of sightings from the lunatic fringe that has so frequently seized on the subject for either self-aggrandizement or profit. Among the members of NICAP's Board of Governors are Dr. Charles P. Olivier, Professor Emeritus of Astronomy, University of Pennsylvania and President of the American Meteor Society; J. B. Hartranft, Jr., President of the Aircraft Owners and Pilot Association and former Lt. Colonel in the Army Air Corps; Dewey Fournet, former Major, U.S. Air Force in charge of the UFO investigation known as Project Blue Book; Professor Charles A. Maney, head of the Department of Physics, Defiance College, Ohio, and others.

On reading Major Keyhoe's book, Betty gained more confidence in her own experience. She lost little time in sitting down to write him a letter:

Portsmouth, N.H.
September 26, 1961

Dear Major Keyhoe:

The purpose of this letter is twofold. We wish to inquire if you have written any more books about unidentified flying objects since *The Flying Saucer Conspiracy* was published. If so, it would certainly be appreciated if you would send us the name of the publisher, as we have been unsuccessful in finding any information more up-to-date than this book. A stamped, self-addressed envelope is being included for your convenience.

My husband and I have become immensely interested in this topic, as we recently had quite a frightening experience, which does seem to differ from others of which we are aware. About midnight on September 20th [the choice of midnight could be either the 19th or the 20th; Betty Hill chose the latter], we were driving in a National Forest Area in the White Mountains, in N.H. This is a desolate, uninhabited area. At first we noticed a bright object in the sky which seemed to be moving rapidly. We stopped our car and got out to observe it more closely with our binoculars. Suddenly it reversed its flight from the north to the southwest and appeared to be flying in a very erratic pattern. As we continued driving and then stopping to watch it, we observed the following flight pattern: the object was spinning and appeared to be lighted only on one side which gave it a twinkling effect.

As it approached our car, we stopped again. As it hovered in the air in front of us, it appeared to be pancake in shape, ringed with windows in the front through which we could see bright blue-white lights. Suddenly, two red lights appeared on each side. By this time my husband was standing in the road, watching closely. He saw wings protrude on each side and the red lights were on the wing tips.

As it glided closer he was able to see inside this object, but not too closely. He did see several figures scurrying about as though they were making some hurried type of preparation. One figure was observing us from the windows. From the distance, this was seen, the figures appeared to be about the size of a pencil [held at arm's length], and seemed to be dressed in some type of shiny black uniform.

At this point, my husband became shocked and got back in the car, in a hysterical condition, laughing and repeating that they were going to capture us. He started driving the car—the motor had been left running. As we started to move, we heard several buzzing or beeping sounds which seemed to be striking the trunk of our car.

We did not observe this object leaving, but we did not see it again, although about thirty miles further south we were again bombarded by those same beeping sounds.

The next day we did make a report to an Air Force officer, who seemed to be very interested in the wings and red lights. We did not report my husband's observation of the interior as it seems too fantastic to be true.

At this time we are searching for any clue that might be helpful to my husband, in recalling whatever it was he saw that caused him to panic. His mind has completely blacked out at this point. Every attempt to recall leaves him very frightened. This flying object was at least as large as a four-motor plane, its flight was noiseless and the lighting of the interior did not reflect on the ground. There does not appear to be any damage to our car from the beeping sounds.

We both have been quite frightened by this experience, but fascinated. We feel a compelling urge to return to the spot where this occurred in the hope that we may again come in contact with this object. We realize this possibility is slight and we should, however, have more recent information regarding developments in the last six years.

Any suggested reading would be greatly appreciated. Your book has been of great help to us and a reassurance that we are not the only ones to have undergone an interesting and informative experience.

Very truly yours,

/s/ Mrs. Barney Hill
(Mrs.) Barney Hill

As Betty Hill's confidence increased through her study of the NICAP material, so did her willingness to reveal more of the details. For the first time in this letter she was willing to talk about Barney's description of the figures within the craft, although she did so with Barney's extremely reluctant approval. Betty's capacity for ventilating her feelings about the incident was helpful; Barney found himself envying her ability to do so, aware that suppressing the facts in his mind could be damaging.

Some ten days after the sighting, Betty began having a series of vivid dreams. They continued for five successive nights. Never in her memory had she recalled dreams of such detail and intensity. They dominated her waking life during that week and continued to plague her afterward. But they stopped abruptly after five days, and never returned again. In a sense, they assumed the proportion of nightmares. They were so awesome and of such magnitude that she hesitated to mention them to Barney, who was working those five nights and not with her when the dreams took place. When she eventually did mention rather casually that she was having a series of nightmares, Barney was sympathetic but not too concerned, and the matter was dropped. Betty did not press the matter further.

A few weeks later, another puzzling incident occurred that neither Barney nor Betty could explain. They were driving in the car through the countryside near Portsmouth, on a road in a sparsely populated area. Up ahead of them a parked car was partially blocking the road. A group of people were standing outside the car, and Barney began to slow down gradually to avoid an accident.

Suddenly Betty was overcome by fear. She could not explain it, even to herself. "Barney," she said. "Barney—keep going. Please don't slow down. Keep going, keep going!" And she found herself starting to open the car door on the passenger side, with an almost uncontrollable impulse to jump out of the car and run.

Barney was startled and tried to find out what was wrong. Betty was nearing a state of panic. Without asking any more questions, Barney speeded up as fast as was practicable with people partially blocking the road, and Betty recovered her equilibrium. What disturbed her most was that she was not at all inclined to be this emotional; she had never before or since experienced such a sensation. The impact of the unexplainable incident stayed with them for many days afterward, as well as the effect of the nightmares on Betty, that still persisted.

Realizing that Barney was attempting to put the UFO event out of his mind, Betty refrained from discussing the nightmares with him. But she began telling a few close friends, one of whom was a fellow social worker, who urged her to write down her dreams. Feeling that this might relieve her conscious preoccupation with them, she sat down at her typewriter and wrote.

Her dreams were unusual in subject matter and detail. They revealed that she encountered a strange road block on a lonely New Hampshire road as a group of men approached the car. The men were dressed alike. As soon as they reached the car, she slipped into unconsciousness. She awoke to find herself and Barney being taken aboard a wholly strange craft, where she was given a complete physical examination by intelligent, humanoid beings. Barney was taken off down a corridor, curving to the contour of the ship, for apparently the same reason. They were assured, in the dream, that no harm would come to them and that they would be released without any conscious memory of the strange happening.

Betty's written paper on the dreams was in complete detail, with full descriptions of the craft, the examination, and the humanoid beings.

It was to play a large part in what happened two years later, a part she could not anticipate now, in her bewilderment over the incident she and Barney had so recently experienced.

CHAPTER THREE

On October 19, 1961, Walter Webb, lecturer on the staff of the Hayden Planetarium in Boston, opened his mail to read a letter from Richard Hall, then secretary and now Assistant Director of the National Investigations Committee on Aerial Phenomena in Washington. As a Scientific Adviser to NICAP, Walter Webb occasionally investigated the more serious and puzzling UFO reports in the New England area, drafting a detailed document for Washington when the merits of the case warranted it. Hall's letter included a copy of the letter Betty Hill had written to Major Keyhoe and suggested to Webb that it might be worthwhile to drive the eighty miles north of Boston to Portsmouth to investigate the case.

Webb, who had joined the Smithsonian Astrophysical Observatory in Cambridge, Massachusetts, shortly after his graduation from college in 1956, had been interested in Unidentified Flying Objects since 1951, when, as a counselor at a boys' camp in Michigan, he had made a sighting while training campers in the use of a telescope. Although his work with the Smithsonian Satellite Tracking Program required months of photographing satellites against a star background from a volcanic mountain in Hawaii during the International Geophysical year, he had not personally observed any further UFO's since his experience at the boy's camp. His own sighting was totally convincing to him that such objects did exist, but his intense interest in the subject did not bloom fully until the summer of 1952, when a now famous group of sightings was made over Washington, recorded on several radar screens, and confirmed by competent visual observers both in the air and on the ground. Many details on this event were quickly hushed by the Air

Force, and further intelligent study of the phenomenon was rendered impossible. The sighting Webb had made with his nature study students at camp followed a pattern reported many times to NICAP. It was a clear summer night, and the three members of the group spotted a red-orange object traveling from east to west over the southern hills beyond Big Silver Lake in Michigan. At first they suspected that it might have been an ordinary aircraft, but its movements shattered all conventional aerodynamic patterns. The object moved in a strange, undulating manner, creating a perfect sine-wave course over the hills in the distance, a course in which the up-and-down dips described a smooth, bell-shaped pattern along the tops of the hills.

Webb's first reaction to Richard Hall's letter was reluctance. It was plain that this case involved a report of the movement of beings on the craft, and Webb was skeptical of this type of sighting. There had been in the past a rash of this sort of thing from highly irresponsible people, none of whom had provided any kind of rational documentation, and who insisted on talking about such incidents in the most exaggerated terms. Webb was determined not to become associated with any such irresponsible case.

He drove up to Portsmouth on October 21, 1961, with his skeptical attitude unchanged. In his mind were thoughts of the sensational nature of the claim, the possibility that the Hills might be seeking publicity, perpetrating a hoax, or suffering from a mental aberration. On the other hand, he felt that Betty Hill's letter was extremely literate, an honest and straightforward account of a frightening experience which had happened to two people. He would reserve judgment until after his interview, which, he resolved, would be thorough and painstaking with special attention to finding flaws in the story. As an interviewer with a scientific background, he was certain he could create a slip-up somewhere if the Hill's story was spurious, and he would not hesitate to crack the story if he could.

He arrived at the Hills' house at about noon. Barney was relieved to find an intelligent man, who would not ridicule or pooh-pooh the experience, showing a demonstrable interest in the event. Barney was at the point where he detested the term "flying saucer," although Webb's reference to UFO's was palatable to him. Further, he hoped that he could learn more about the subject from Webb, to give some kind of answer to the mystery which still burned in him underneath the surface.

To Betty, Webb appeared to be extremely professional, and obviously was skilled and experienced in interviewing people.

The interview began shortly after noon, and continued with little interruption until eight that evening. "I was so amazed, impressed by both the Hills and their account," Walter Webb later said, "that we skipped lunch and went right through the afternoon and early evening. During that time, I cross-examined them together, separately, together, requestioned them again and again. I tried to make them slip up somewhere, and I couldn't; I simply couldn't. Theirs was an iron-clad story. They seemed to me to be a sincere, honest couple driving home from vacation, late at night on a lonely road, when suddenly something completely unknown and undefinable descended on them. Something entirely foreign or alien to their existence."

During the interview, the Hills gave Webb their sketches, drawn independently, yet comparing so identically. As the interview drew toward a close, Barney found himself almost reliving the incident. He could see himself standing in the road confronted by the enormous object. "It was a long grilling," Barney describes the Webb interview. "He began asking us questions, going over in detail all the experiences. First, we had to recite the story. Then he would have us go back and regress to different periods of the experience, so that all the details would come out. Then I would come to this curtain—the moment I put the field glasses on the vehicle and saw this figure close up. And here—as with every other time I've tried to think it through—I could never get past this curtain in my memory. I could go no further, but I had the most eerie, chilling feeling, like watching a late show by myself at night. I get chills as the ghost walks around the old haunted house. And I continually got chills when I got to that point of thought, whether it was during the Webb interview or at other times. I would get chills, I would shudder and I would look briefly around in the room, though I was safely in the comfort of my own home."

Walter Webb had a map with him, and he carefully used it to fill in a complete timetable of the Hills' journey. For some reason, although the Hills explained in detail about the shiny spots on the car, they forgot to show them to him, and Webb forgot to ask to examine them. None of the three can explain this oversight, although Webb said: "I have tried to recall whether I saw those silvery spots they claim to have seen on the car immediately following the sighting. To this day, I can't. I am sure I did not go out and look at the car. I knew of the spots. This is just poor reporting on my part. Poor investigation. Maybe I just didn't think there was anything to these spots. In fact, in my initial report on the case, I reduced the spots and the beeping noises to a very low value. I mentioned them in an embarrassed way—well, here it is, but what is it? And I went on from there. I don't recall ever checking."

"If I recall it," Barney said, "there was so much detail we got into—

the position of the moon when we saw it, identification of the stars and weather conditions, things like that, that it slipped our minds to get Webb to check the spots."

At the close of the session, Webb suggested to the Hills that they drive back over the trip, trying to pin down the exact spots where varied events happened: the first notice of the object, the frequent short stops between Lancaster and Indian Head and the exact spot near The Flume and Indian Head where the closest encounter took place. The Hills agreed and Barney gave up most of his reluctance to review the case, as a result of Walter Webb's intensive cross-examination.

*   *   *

Driving back to Boston, Webb mentally reviewed the case. He was extremely impressed by it. His doubts about a hoax, about the Hills' competence, about an aberration, were dispelled. "I had read of such cases before," Webb said later, "but this is the first time I had come in contact with apparently reliable witnesses who claimed to have seen UFO occupants. Of course, we have to be very careful about such cases. Very careful. I was impressed that the Hills *underplayed* the dramatic aspects of the case. They were not trying to sensationalize. They did not seek publicity. They wanted me to keep this just to myself, confidential with NICAP. Barney's complete resistance to the idea of UFO's was most convincing. There were two different personalities here, in a way: Barney—the more careful, scientific, accurate person—and Betty, the talker. But at the same time, she didn't overdo it, either."

Five days later, Webb prepared his report for NICAP in Washington, reviewing the incident in the minutest detail, including compass directions, position of the moon and planets, weather, and detailed description of the object, including the sketches the Hills had given him.

He concluded his lengthy report: "It is the opinion of this investigator, after questioning these people for over six hours and studying their reactions and personalities during that time, that they were telling the truth, and the incident occurred exactly as reported except for some minor uncertainties and technicalities that must be tolerated in any such observation where human judgment is involved (that is, exact time and length of visibility, apparent sizes of object and occupants, distance and height of object, etc.). Although their occupations do not especially qualify the witnesses as trained scientific observers, I was impressed by their intelligence, apparent honesty, and obvious desire to get at the facts and to underplay the more sensational aspects of the sighting. Mr. Hill had been a complete UFO skeptic before the sighting. In fact, the experience so jolted his reason and sensibilities that his mind evidently could not make the adjustment. In his conversation with me (and with his wife since the sighting) a mental block occurred when he mentioned the "leader" peering out the window at him. Mr. Hill believes he saw something he doesn't want to remember. He claimed he was not close enough to see any facial characteristics on the figures, although at another time he referred to one of them looking over his shoulder and grinning and to the leader's expressionless face. However, it is my view that the observer's blackout is not of any great significance [later this was to be seriously challenged]. I think the whole experience was so improbable and fantastic to witness —along with the very real fear of being captured adding to imagined fears—that his mind finally refused to believe what his eyes were perceiving and a mental block resulted.

"Needless to say, neither Mr. Hill nor his wife are UFO doubters any longer. Both are now quite interested in the UFO subject and wish to know more about it and read as much as they can. Near the conclusion of the interview, I was asked many questions concerning the possible nature and origin of such objects. . . .

"It will be noted that there were no electromagnetic disturbances, such as engine and headlight failure [mentioned in other close-range UFO observations]. However, the code-like beeping sounds on the rear of the car (a 1957 two-door hardtop) are an unexplained feature of the case. Neither did the witnesses notice any physiological effects— warmth, burns, shock, or paralysis. The dog did not appear to be alarmed at any time during the whole sighting [the Hills at this point had forgotten to tell Webb about several instances of Delsey's odd behavior]. There were no other aircraft in the sky. Just for the record— not that there is any connection at all—the Hills' sighting took place a day before Hurricane Esther's rains and winds hit New England.

"The Hills live in Portsmouth, N.H. Barney, thirty-nine, is a clerk at a Boston, Mass., post office (South Station) and Betty, forty-one, is a child welfare worker employed at Portsmouth by the New Hampshire Department of Public Welfare.

"New Hampshire has furnished quite a number of UFO reports in recent years. For example, in 1960 NICAP recorded seven sightings, six of them in the White Mountains area, especially around Plymouth. Of particular interest were the red cigar-shaped objects seen during April—twice from Plymouth (on the 15th and 25th) and once from West Thornton (on the 28th). See NICAP Special Bulletin, May 1960, p. 4. Another "cigar" was observed in the same area, near Rumney, on August 24. See NICAP report form on case. . . .

"About eight years ago, Mrs. Hill's sister, Janet, was driving from Kingston, N.H., to Haverhill, Mass., on Route 125 and saw near Plaistow, N.H., a large glowing object in the sky with smaller objects flying around it. She ran to a house and got others to look at the strange apparition. They all saw the smaller objects fly into the larger one which then took off."

/s/ W. N. Webb
10/26/61

* * *

As a Scientific Adviser to NICAP, Webb had an extensive knowledge of the files of the organization and, of course, immediate access to them. Under the direction of Major Keyhoe, a graduate of the U.S. Naval Academy and former Marine Corps pilot, the organization constantly emphasizes that it avoids any preposterous claims regarding UFO's and instructs its area representatives to disprove cases before accepting the sighting as related. Wherever possible, NICAP concentrates only on those sightings by pilots, radarmen, police, engineers, technicians, and responsible and competent citizens. Major Keyhoe's battle with the Air Force has been going on for over a decade. In the course of its investigations, NICAP receives over forty thousand letters a year, many of which are fresh reports of new sightings that are constantly cropping up in this country and throughout the world.

Beginning in the spring of 1965, four years after the Hills' encounter, reports of low-level and near-landing UFO sightings increased so that the organization was overwhelmed with documentation on the phenomenon. The Oklahoma, Texas and New Mexico sightings during August of 1965 involved nearly forty members of the Oklahoma State Highway Patrol, with its teletypes clogged for three nights with UFO reports made by its officers and hundreds of reliable laymen—sightings corroborated by radar fixes from the Carswell and Tinker Air Force Bases. In Exeter, New Hampshire, two seasoned policemen encountered an enormous UFO at low-level, so low that one of the officers dropped to the ground and drew his gun. During the fall and winter of 1965–66, hundreds of other people in the area reported similar experiences documented by taped interviews and cross-examinations resulting in overwhelming evidence for the existence of the objects.

The Michigan sightings in March of 1966, involving policemen and hundreds of reliable witnesses, brought the subject to a head, including a demand by Republican House Leader Gerald Ford for a full-scale Congressional investigation. In announcing his findings as special consultant to the Air Force, Dr. J. Allen Hynek, Chairman of the Department of Astronomy at Northwestern University and director of the Dearborn Observatory was widely misquoted by the press regarding his statement that the sightings might be attributed to a spontaneous combustion of methane or marsh gas. What Dr. Hynek did say was that two of the sightings might be attributed to this phenomenon, but that these two cases by no means explained the hundreds of unidentified sightings by reliable people that were continuing to be reported throughout the world. In his press release he urged that a scientific panel be set up to study the subject in depth, a statement that was largely ignored by the press.

Back in 1961, when Walter Webb was trying to fit the pieces of the Hill case together, none of this recent and startling evidence was available. But there were thousands of other cases in the files, not as well known to the general public because of the reluctance of the press to cover them and because the challenge to Air Force secrecy had not become as strong.

Webb also was familiar with the findings and research of the Aerial Phenomena Research Organization in Tucson, Arizona, another conservative non-profit group, inclined to take more seriously the reports of intelligent beings associated with UFO sightings, where the craft hovered or landed. APRO, as the organization is known, is under the direction of L. J. Lorenzen, an engineer in the Kitt Peak National Observatory at Tucson. Among its advisers are Dr. Frank Salisbury, Professor of Plant Physiology at Colorado State University; Dr. R. Leo Sprinkle, Assistant Professor of Psychology at the University of Wyoming; H. C. Dudley, Chairman and Professor of Physics, University of Southern Mississippi; Dr. James A. Harder, Associate Professor in the College of Engineering, University of California, Berkeley, and others.

Dr. Dudley once said, "I recommend we use a bit of scientific curiosity to see whatever is the physics of the phenomena so many people are describing as UFO's. Ascribing the phenomena as due to psychological aberration is nonsense. There is a series of physical phenomena that needs explaining; let's get on with it in an open-minded, scientifically oriented manner. Then let the data provide the answer."

Dr. Harder, of the University of California, added: "I think the evidence for the reality of Unidentified Flying Objects is beyond a reason-

39

able doubt, and that the phenomena is deserving of scientific attention in spite of the existence of organizations on the lunatic fringe that have tended to discredit such attention."

Among the organizations to which members of APRO's advisory staff are associated are: The American Physical Society, the American Psychological Association, the National Science Foundation, the National Institute of Health and NASA.

Among the APRO reports (documented in the book by Coral Lorenzen, *The Great Flying Saucer Hoax,* William-Frederick Press, 1962) Walter Webb found an unusual series of sightings investigated by Dr. Olavo Fontes, in Brazil. Dr. Fontes, the APRO representative in that country, is a medical doctor, and First Vice President of the Brazilian Society of Gastroenterology and Nutrition. Webb discovered in Dr. Fontes' reports that the village of Ponta Poran, Brazil, had been the scene of a strange series of UFO experiences over a period of two and a half months, from December 1957 to March 1958. They interested Webb in relation to the Hill case because of the persistent tendency of the objects to trail and follow individuals and vehicles, much in the same nature as the object in New Hampshire had followed the Hills. For the most part, the objects in Brazil were Saturn shaped, a shape often described in UFO sightings, along with the saucer and cigar shapes more commonly noted. During this extended time period, the objects buzzed jeeps and cars, mostly along the lonely roads near Ponta Poran. The actions of the objects were interpreted as a probe to discover human reactions to their presence.

The incident near Ponta Poran, on the southwestern frontier of Brazil, a landscape consisting of a forest-covered plateau known as Mato Grosso, was the first one recorded. It was approximately 6:30 in the evening of December 21, 1957, when a farm woman, her driver and servant, and three young sons were driving toward the town in a jeep. Two glowing objects, flying side by side, approached them and glided along the side of the road, oscillating in a strange wobbling motion. They were described as metallic spheres, about fifteen feet in diameter, encircled by a rotating ring. The upper half of the objects was fiery red, the lower, silvery white. Each gave off a blinding glare, with variable intensity.

For two full hours the objects followed the jeep, darting ahead of it and around it in circles. In the two times the driver stopped the jeep, one of the objects came down to just above the ground, while the other hovered high in the air. When the jeep entered Ponta Poran, both objects climbed into the sky and disappeared.

On February 19, two sightings were made near the town, one of them at 4:00 A.M., the other at 10:30 P.M. The early-morning sighting involved the same family, this time with the object dropping down over the road and hovering in front of the jeep, its red glow dimming and turning to a silvery color. The people in the jeep were afraid—as Barney Hill had been in the field near Indian Head—that they were in imminent danger of being captured. The driver turned around and sped back to the village, where the object climbed to a high altitude and hovered over the town for half an hour longer. Six other witnesses were rounded up, and the group loaded into two jeeps to drive out to the lonely section of the road where the UFO had first been spotted. The object followed them, but remained at a distance, again climbing to a high altitude. It was not until 6:00 A.M. that it shot upward at tremendous speed and disappeared.

That night, four highly respected citizens of the town, including a professor, a law student, a notary and a tax clerk went to the location on the road where the object had first hovered so low. At 10:30 the brilliant reddish object approached them from the sky, oscillating from side to side. When another object appeared to join it, the group panicked and drove back to town.

On March 3 a similar incident took place, with the object finally hovering a few feet above the road in front of the jeep. When the driver tried to ram it, it shot straight up and disappeared. (Interestingly, over a dozen strikingly similar accounts to these were recorded in Exeter, New Hampshire, and many other locations in the United States in 1965-66.)

What interested Webb was that these stories, and many others like them in both NICAP and APRO records, were close parallels to the Hill case, yet they had occurred in different parts of the world, and none knew of the others' experiences.

On November 2, 1961, Webb wrote the Hills to thank them for their cooperation, indicating that he had submitted his extensive report to NICAP. None of the three knew at that time that there was to be another even more extensive report by Webb that would far exceed his first in interest and impact.

*   *   *

About a month before Webb filed his NICAP report, Robert Hohman, a staff scientific writer on both engineering and science for one of the world's most notable corporations in the electronic industry, and C. D. Jackson, a senior engineer for the same company, went to Washington to attend the XII International Astronautical Congress as part of their regular routine. Both had been deeply involved in work on the space program and were preparing a paper on three experimental scientists of

41

previous years: Nikola Tesla, David Todd, and Marconi, the acknowledged father of radio. Their paper was to examine the original data of these scientists in response to a rhetorical inquiry by the Office of the Director of Defense Research and Engineering: "What research is being done to keep abreast of the scientific advances of the past . . . to see that there is not needless duplication of effort?"

The paper presented evidence and deductive scientific reasoning to indicate that Tesla, Todd and Marconi observed laboratory data and related phenomena that suggested the possibility that they were monitoring interplanetary communications during the period of 1899 to 1924. They also noted that during the same period exactly, the Russian theorist Konstantin Tsiokovsky deduced a model of an intelligence existing independently of terrestrial influence. The paper examined the possibility of identical radio signals in this time span, emanating from Tau Ceti, a celestial body some 11.8 light years away.

As technicians working in advanced fields of science, both Hohman and Jackson were interested in the data being accumulated on the UFO subject by NICAP and arranged to have lunch with Major Keyhoe during the Astronautical Congress. Hohman happened to mention to the Major that he had not heard of many recent UFO reports and wondered if the entire phenomenon were dropping in frequency. Major Keyhoe brought up the letter NICAP had just received from the Hills, one of the organization's most interesting cases in many months. Hohman and Jackson were at once interested, but the story seemed so incredible that they were cautious in accepting it. On the other hand, if there were any truth to the story, they wanted to investigate it with an open mind.

They debated the idea for several weeks and finally got in touch with Walter Webb, who had just completed his report. He sent them a copy, and they studied it carefully. Knowing of Webb's reputation for accuracy, they were considerably impressed. His appraisal of the character and competence of the Hills led them to take immediate action. On November 3, 1961, they wrote the Hills:

Dear Mr. and Mrs. Hill:

This letter will introduce Mr. C. D. Jackson and myself. Our interest in writing you at this time concerns your recent experience of September 19–20, 1961. . . .

Your participation in this event was brought to our attention by Major Donald Keyhoe with whom we had luncheon during the recent XII International Astronautical Congress, Washington, D.C., on October 4–5, 1961, and more specifically, through Mr. Webb, NICAP representative in the Boston area.

Whereas our principal interest in this subject is concerned with the attempt to verify the origin of these vehicles according to existing scientific theory maintained by Professor Hermann Oberth, of Germany, there is, naturally, a similar interest in trying to determine as well, the meaning of the whole phenomenon. Your own recent experience might offer some help in this latter regard.

Mr. Jackson and I would like to visit with you at a time and place convenient to you. We are mature people associated with a major electronics and engineering corporation. Our discussion would be entirely objective. Having a close familiarity with most of the unclassified (military) literature dealing with this subject, and dating back to 1947, we would like to be of assistance in answering your questions, as well as continuing our own investigation on this subject.

For the purpose of scheduling, we would be able to visit in Portsmouth, New Hampshire, during the week of November 13, 1961, preferably the 18–19th of that week.

Sincerely yours,

/s/ Robert E. Hohman

Hohman and Jackson were not able to get together with the Hills at their home in Portsmouth until a week beyond their suggested date. But on November 25, they arrived to review the story of the strange experience. Visiting the Hills at the time was Major James McDonald, an Air Force intelligence officer who had just recently retired from active duty, and a close friend of the Hills. Later, in 1962, Barney and Betty Hill were to stand up for the Major when he was married to one of Betty's close friends and associates in her welfare work. Further, when NICAP made additional inquiry about the character and reliability of the Hills, Major McDonald was to give them an unqualified recommendation.

The group—Betty and Barney Hill, Robert Hohman, C. D. Jackson and Major MacDonald—conferred for another long session, beginning at noon and running almost until midnight.

The Hills were impressed by the businesslike and professional attitude of Hohman and Jackson, with Barney again reflecting surprise that so much attention was being directed toward a subject he still had lingering doubts about, in spite of his own traumatic experience.

Hohman and Jackson inquired about many facets in the case that puzzled Barney, particularly an inquiry as to whether there were any nitrates or nitrate derivatives in the Hills' car. "The only thing I could think of that possibly had some connection with nitrates," Barney later said, "was gunpowder. I did have about a dozen shotgun shells in the car, left over from a trip to the South when I had practiced shooting at tin cans on my uncle's farm, but aside from that, I couldn't think

43

of anything. The reason they were asking, they said, was that in several close UFO encounters, the people had been in rural areas where they were exposed to nitrates or nitrate fertilizer. Then it hit us: Betty had left the bone-meal fertilizer in the trunk of the car before the trip, and I hadn't bothered to take it out. Now who knows? Maybe it does have significance, maybe it doesn't. It was interesting that they should bring it up, when we had forgotten all about it. And they asked a lot of questions that started me thinking—questions like did we have anything new in the car, any new object, and had it disappeared? There had been reports, apparently, of people having close sightings, and something they had recently purchased, had disappeared. They asked if anything had disappeared out of our car, but this was two months later, and we had a lot of junk in there. I couldn't remember.

"One of the questions they did ask was: Why did we take the trip? This might seem to an unrealistic question. But in thinking on it, it's not too far-fetched. Number one, there was no preparation for the trip. I had gone to Boston that night and had worked and was returning to Portsmouth that day. I decided during work, well, I think I would like to go to Niagara Falls and then return via Montreal. Betty had the week off anyway, and I was able to call in and get an extension of the weekend for several days. So we packed our car that night."

Betty Hill's comments are similar: "This was how impulsive it was. The only money we had was in our pockets. Saturday the banks were closed so we couldn't even cash a check. I think the amount between the two of us was less than $70. So the questions they asked were interesting, mainly because we had never thought along those lines. They provoked a lot of thought in both of us, mentioning the remote possibilities of life existing on planets involved with Alpha Centauri or Tau Ceti, which was news to me. I don't think I've ever heard of them. Their questions were so far out that I just couldn't see what relationship they had to our experience. And this business of nitrates. At that time, I had all kinds of plants in the house. In fact, in the living room, I had an avocado tree that touched the ceiling. They walked around, looked my plants over and asked me what kind of fertilizer I used on them and things like this.

"And while they were here they were mentally reconstructing the whole trip. One of them said, 'What took you so long to get home?' They said, look, you went this distance and it took you these hours. Where were you? Well, when they said this, I thought I was really going to crack up. I got terrified, and I even put my head on the table. And I went back over the trip in my mind, recalling, or trying to recall

44

that vague moment when it looked as if the moon had been on the ground. They tried to reconstruct that time sequence, and they said, 'You couldn't have seen the moon on the ground at the time, because apparently at that period . . .' they knew what time the moon had set that night. And the moon had set fairly early. It just wouldn't tie in with this time business. They suggested that we check and find just where the moon sat at the time, because it apparently wasn't the moon that we saw—or thought we saw. Then this whole lapse of time business. I really became upset about that. . . ."

"I became suddenly flabbergasted," Barney added in his words, "to think that I realized for the first time that at the rate of speed I always travel, we should have arrived home at least two hours earlier than we did. Normally, for me to travel from Colebrook to here—we know we left at 10:05 that night—actually takes less than four hours, even figuring out the period of time we stopped on the highway—and at no time did we stop for more than five minutes. I was baffled as to what the reason was for us leaving Colebrook at 10:05 P.M. and arriving back here at dawn, somewhere around 5:00 A.M.—nearly seven hours instead of less than four. Even if I allowed more time than I know we took at those roadside stops, there still were at least two hours missing out of that night's trip."

To the entire group in the Hill living room that afternoon, the missing time period became a major mystery. The Hills tried but simply could not account for it. Nor could they account for the thirty-five miles between Indian Head and Ashland, during which their recollection amounted to almost nothing. They were now more puzzled and confused than ever. For the first time it fully dawned on them that they were facing a period of simultaneous amnesia, experienced by each of them at the same time, falling roughly between the first series of beeps that emanated from the back of their car and the second series of beeps they encountered somewhere near Ashland, thirty-five miles to the south. The thought that plagued everyone at the meeting was that while it was unusual enough for one person to be struck suddenly with a temporary period of amnesia, it was very strange for two intelligent people to experience it together under such fantastic conditions.

As a hard-headed former intelligence officer in the Air Force, Major James MacDonald groped for some kind of answer to the puzzle. UFO's are constantly being discussed in the Air Force, much more so than the laconic official statements from the Pentagon indicate. Officially, the Air Force position requires that no member of the force can report any incidents to the public; all information must be channeled through the

Foreign Technology Division at Wright-Patterson Air Force Base, Ohio, and in turn, any release of that information can only be made by the Office of the Secretary of the Air Force at the Pentagon. The fact remains that many Air Force pilots and radar men do talk, and those who have directly come in contact with the objects reveal stories of incredible speeds, right angle turns, and maneuvers that are impossible to duplicate by any aircraft known to the military. Even the most sophisticated weapons were said to have been used in an attempt to bring the UFO's down without success.

Major MacDonald had had no direct experience with the subject of UFO's in his Air Force career, but he had a profound respect for it. He felt that it was a subject to be viewed with an open mind, each case considered on its own merits, and that only firsthand accounts had any value. He was also aware that many reports of UFO's consisted of an observer's honest mistakes, perhaps by confusing shooting stars, Venus, shadows on a windshield, or St. Elmo's Fire, with unidentified craft. On the other hand, he was aware of the many cases involving technically qualified people of impeccable character whose close encounters with the objects were clearly observed and unexplainable in conventional aerodynamic terms. He realized the complete probability of the phenomena, that the valid reports were by no means unrealistic or absurd and that extraterrestrial life was not only possible but entirely probable. Space programs on the earth included impact landings on Venus and a soft landing on the moon—so why couldn't the reverse process be taking place?

He was fascinated by the probe that Hohman and Jackson were conducting, impressed by their attention to detail and their posing of interesting and imponderable questions. But most critical of all—what happened in the two hours when the Hills suffered double amnesia? What could have happened? What *did* happen?

When the discussion focused on this critical point, the problem narrowed down to finding a way of discovering what happened during the missing time period, a way to penetrate the unyielding curtain that began to descend when Barney Hill looked through the binoculars and came down completely when the first series of beeps sounded in the speeding car. What was missing was not only the two hours of time— but a distance of thirty-five miles, for which there was little accounting.

It was at this point in the informal gathering that Major MacDonald suggested the possibility of medical hypnosis.

He had, during his Air Force career, become somewhat familiar with the subject and was impressed with its valid use under controlled medical conditions. He was also aware of its dangers in the hands of stage hypnotists or other inexperienced people. He knew that hypnotherapy and hypnoanalysis had been used in cases involving amnesia, producing some strikingly dramatic results in the rehabilitation of servicemen suffering from war neuroses (sometimes described as "battle fatigue" or "shell shock"). In a sense, he reasoned, the Hills had experienced a violent trauma much like shell shock, a condition that often produced temporary amnesia—which had frequently been treated successfully by medical hypnosis.

When Major MacDonald suggested hypnosis, the group was immediately interested. Hohman and Jackson by now had no doubts about the character and competence of the Hills, but they were aware that this strange case needed further documentation. Major MacDonald, who had discussed the case many times with the Hills, was convinced of their sincerity and anxious to help them overcome the nagging doubts and fears. On several occasions, Barney had said to MacDonald, "Jim—how do I *know* that this thing happened? How do I *know* that I wasn't just seeing things? I'm in this terrible position where I really *do* know it happened, and I can't get myself to believe it. It's bugging me so seriously that my ulcers are kicking up, just at the point where they were getting better."

It was agreed that the idea of medical hypnosis was a good one, but the problem became one of finding the proper medical man to take the case, or if, indeed, he thought it was wise to do so. Obviously, the case should not be entrusted to any but the most competent psychiatric specialist, but no one immediately came to mind. Hohman, Jackson, and Major MacDonald agreed to make inquiries, and the Hills, both felt the idea had merit.

"I agreed with the idea wholeheartedly," Betty later said. "Because the moment they suggested hypnosis, I thought of my dreams, and this was the first time I began to wonder if they were *more* than just dreams. Then I really got upset over my dreams. I thought, well now, if I have hypnosis, I'll know one way or the other because this was, I thought—God, well maybe my dreams are something that really happened. I also thought about that strange experience while driving with Barney in the car— when he slowed down for the other car standing in the road. I really panicked at that time. And when hypnosis was suggested, I thought of this incident too. And I thought to myself, why did I react in this way? I've never done that before in my life."

"My reaction to the hypnosis idea," Barney added, "was, first, what are the effects of hypnosis? What is it about? The experience of it. What will I feel like going under? I was mildly reluctant, without saying so, to submit myself to such a thing, unless it was for someone I could have complete confidence in. But what overruled my apprehension about that was the thought: once and for all, for all times, this might clear up Betty and her nonsense about her dreams. I further thought that the hypnosis process might also explain the mental blockage I had at Indian Head— and that whole trip that seemed to be missing for the thirty-five miles from Indian Head to Ashland. So I felt that this could be something I would get a full understanding about, and of course it would clear up Betty's dreams to the point that for once and for all, I could say: 'Look, Betty —they are *dreams*. They have nothing whatever to do with the UFO sighting.'

"You see, Betty kept wondering about what happened between the two series of beeps. I didn't think anything happened between the two. All I thought was that it would get me beyond that point of standing on the highway, looking at these moving figures in the craft, the one that kept looking back at me with those eyes. He gave me the impression— and this was dim in my memory, but there just the same—that he was a very capable person, and there can be no nonsense here. We have business to attend to. These were all thoughts going through my mind. As to how this person was affecting me, I wanted to get beyond that point. And this was the reason that Jim MacDonald's suggestion appealed to me."

It was to be some time before the Hills were able to follow up the suggestion. In the meantime, the compulsion grew in both of them that they must return to the scene of the incident, as Walter Webb had suggested, and relive the experience trying to recapture the elusive shreds of memory.

CHAPTER FOUR

It wasn't until after the holidays that the Hills were able to think about returning to the scene of the encounter. The inevitable Christmas bustle helped suspend their lingering doubts and questions, if only on a temporary basis.

Finally, in February of 1962, a series of pilgrimages began that were to continue for many months, in all seasons. At first they would go two or three times a month; later, they were to skip many weeks at a time. But always with the same questions to answer: What happened during the inexplicable blackout? Where did Barney spin the car off to a side road? And, if he did, what happened?

The idea of hypnosis was temporarily tabled. Neither Hohman, Jackson nor Major MacDonald could suggest a psychiatrist, and Betty, especially, hoped that the return trips to the area might spark a chain of memory that would suddenly bring back their recall.

Again, Barney was ambivalent about taking the trips. Betty could overcome Barney's resistance by suggesting they look for a new and different restaurant on each trip, a particular weakness of his. They would often pack a lunch to economize on the trip up, so that they later could splurge at dinner.

Or they might leave Portsmouth at three in the afternoon on a Saturday, drive along Route 4 toward Concord, then swing northerly on the expressway, planning to reach Route 3 at dusk. They reasoned that after dark the area would be as it was the night of the encounter, the landscape more provoking to their senses if they were to discover the vaguely defined road that they half recalled from the limbo period of their amnesia.

On one occasion that winter, Betty, with a flash of insight, recalled a vague vision of a diner she thought they had passed near Ashland shortly after the second series of beeps had brought them back to their senses. They had pulled up beside it, since it was the first lighted place they had come across in many miles. It had turned out to be only a night light and their hopes for a cup of coffee had been jolted. They would drive along Route 3, on several back roads branching off the main road, but they could find no sign of a diner of any kind. They would bicker about where they might have traveled, or which of the byways off Route 3 they might have made a turn on. No clear recall came back to them.

At Cannon Mountain, Indian Head and Lancaster they would reenact their frequent stops, in the hope that the repetition of the process might stimulate their memories. There was even disagreement as to where they had made road stops before the amnesia set in, although the general areas were firm in their minds. They brought the binoculars with them but had only a faint hope that they would see the object again.

Most often, they would plan the reenactment systematically, winding northward up U.S. 3 to a point above Cannon Mountain, turning around, and beginning the trip back down to Portsmouth the same night. Even with frequent side excursions to find the lost road, they could not account for the inordinate length of time it took them to reach Portsmouth the night of the incident.

On one occasion they stopped by a small restaurant near Woodstock, where several residents told them of frequent sightings of the objects hovering over Route 3, sometimes remaining suspended over an hour. (The UFO's had been reported to the Air Force, but nothing further had been heard.)

The Hills had no fear, no apprehension on these trips, the challenge of the mystery overriding the shock of the experience. They would park on a turnout, with a sweeping view of the mountain valleys during a moonlit night, and sit and look at the stars and the sky, as if some clue might arise to bring back their memories.

"During one winter night," Barney recalls, "we found ourselves on a road that seemed to go nowhere, a lonely mountain road that I cursed myself for turning on. As we got deeper and deeper into the valley, the road deteriorated into a mass of snow. About midnight I found myself trying to turn the car around, hoping that I wouldn't get stuck in the snow, and furious with Betty for suggesting driving up into the mountains. I thought, why go through all this? Why not just forget the whole thing? Or if we can't forget it, why make such an effort to relive all this or to think we can bring back the two lost hours? I don't know why we weren't apprehensive, to tell the truth. Vaguely, I hoped to see the thing again, I think. I can't even say. I *did* want to see it again. What I found most interesting about all these trips was that we never seemed to agree, completely. We would bicker and become mildly quarrelsome. Betty would insist I should take a right turn, and I would insist on making a left. But what bothers me still is the question: Why did I have so much apprehension that night at Indian Head, and yet I had none on returning to the mountains, scheduling our time to be there late at night? I don't know what the answer to that is."

*   *   *

The return trips were fruitless. Always the same curtain of darkness for Barney after the critical moment at Indian Head. Always, the blind veil for Betty after the strange series of beeps as they drove frantically away from Indian Head, with Barney, apparently in great emotional distress, at the wheel. Always the blank between Indian Head and Ashland.

The idea of hypnosis was not dormant for long. As the Hills attempted to settle down to something like a reasonable routine, they occasionally discussed the incident with a few close friends, Betty still being haunted by her graphic and startling dreams. For Betty, talking it out with close friends was helpful. Barney continued to try to ignore the subject, except on those occasions of the trips. He continued to plead with Betty to forget the dreams.

On one day in March of 1962, Betty had lunch with Gail Peabody, a friend of hers who was a state probation officer and in whom Betty had full confidence. She mentioned the idea of hypnosis, and Gail responded promptly by recommending a psychiatrist she knew of who was medical director of a private sanitarium in Georgetown, Massachusetts, only about ten miles away from Portsmouth.

On March 12, 1962, Betty typed a letter to the doctor.

Patrick J. Quirke, M.D.
222 West Main Street
Georgetown, Mass.

Dear Sir:

We are seeking the services of a psychiatrist who uses hypnotism, and are wondering if it would be possible to make an appointment to see you on a Saturday morning? My husband and I are both employed, but our working hours are such that this would be convenient for us. If this is not possible we could make an appointment at your convenience.

We have a unique reason for requesting this interview. The enclosed bulletin of the National Investigations Committee on Aerial Phenomena,

51

briefly describes an experience that occurred to us last September 19–20, 1961. We have been interviewed by Mr. C. D. Jackson and Robert Hohman of (name of company withheld).

Many puzzling aspects remain, so it is believed that hypnotism could clarify these. We have handled this experience confidentially with the exception of NICAP and a few close friends.

We do have a complete story of the report written by Mr. Walter Webb, of the Hayden Planetarium, which we would be willing to send to you, for your review. If you do not have time available to see us, or would prefer not to do this, would you be willing to suggest another psychiatrist willing to undertake this.

Very truly yours,
Eunice and Barney Hill

The interview took place on March 25, 1962, at eleven in the morning.

The private sanitarium is known as Baldpate, formerly the inn that inspired the famous old play *Seven Keys to Baldpate*. It sits on the top of a mountain, with a sweeping view of the Massachusetts countryside. It has been converted into a retreat for psychiatric patients who seek a comfortable, home-like atmosphere for therapy. The Hills were impressed by the paintings, the fireplace and the cheerful atmosphere, not at all what they had expected.

"At no time did I feel uncomfortable," Barney said. "The doctor sat across from us at his desk, while we sat in comfortable chairs, and I felt relieved to talk to this man about our experience, particularly since he did not look at it as if it were two persons talking about an obvious hallucination—and he was giving his professional attention to it. He acknowledged that we had an unusual experience, but he felt that we might gradually begin to remember some of the missing things, since we had probably suppressed much of the experience as a protective device. He felt that at this stage it might not be a good idea to explore this block of mine and Betty's disturbing reactions, forcibly, at least."

The ultimate, mutual decision was to postpone any action at the time, but that if problems should persist, then therapy might be indicated. The Hills felt relieved that Dr. Quirke ruled out simultaneous hallucination, a matter that had been giving them both some concern.

*　　*　　*

The long commuting drive from Portsmouth to Boston, the night work schedule, the separation from his sons who were living in Philadelphia with his former wife, the doubts about the Indian Head experience and the problem with his ulcers all began to take their toll on Barney. His condition was further complicated by the recurrence of elevated blood pressure, creating a vicious circle whereby he could not successfully remedy the last condition without the removal of the other problems, and vice versa. Another disturbing symptom began at this time, more of an annoyance than anything else, but contributing to his general problem: a series of warts began to develop in an almost geometrically perfect circular ring in the area of his groin. While they were a minor problem, they added to his concern.

By the summer of 1962, Barney's exhaustion and general malaise prompted him to seek a psychiatrist for his overall condition, entirely aside from the traumatic experience he and Betty had had in the White Mountains. He did not, in fact, associate his need for therapy with the UFO incident, feeling mainly that the conflict over his father-son relationship was at the base of his problem, the long distance to Philadelphia making it impossible to be a devoted father.

The physician treating him for elevated blood pressure and ulcers recommended a distinguished psychiatrist in nearby Exeter, New Hampshire, Dr. Duncan Stephens, and the long process of therapy began during the summer of 1962.

At first, the incident at Indian Head was ignored altogether by Barney. He did not emphasize it in his talks with Dr. Stephens because it seemed to be only a minor part of his anxiety, a sidelight to the other conditions, and he concentrated on his general emotional and social problems, with the help of Dr. Stephens.

He indicated to Barney that there were many unusual and interesting facets to his case, including the circumstances of Barney's interracial marriage in a New England town, a sociological condition that could not be ignored. He pointed out that both Barney and Betty were making a remarkably good adjustment, that their inherent good will and honesty and contribution to community life were remarkable.

Barney found him probing back through his early life to explore the experiences of his early childhood, and helping Barney to work through the conditioning influences of his early days. During the therapy, Barney became more aware of the special conflicts and problems arising from being a member of a minority race.

All through his family background was a record of interracial relationships. His mother's grandmother was born during slavery, her father being a white plantation owner. Being fair of color, the maternal great-grandmother was raised in the owner's house and cared for by his sisters, even though she was legally a slave. When she married, the plantation owner gave her and her husband 250 acres of land, to be handed down to their children.

The farm became quite profitable over the years, passing down to Barney's uncle, who assumed the care of Barney and another sister and brother when his mother became ill in Philadelphia for many months. During this time young Barney grew to feel that his aunt and uncle were his own parents. When his mother finally recovered, it was painful for him to leave his aunt and uncle and the large farm in Virginia. The feeling was reciprocal, since the couple could not have children of their own, and they offered to raise Barney and assure him of a college education.

But he returned to his parents in Philadelphia, to the hot asphalt streets and the walled-in row houses of the city. His father, though poor, was a good provider. He, too, reflected a mixed marriage; his paternal grandmother was fair—the daughter of white and colored parents. His grandfather was a proud Ethiopian freeman.

During the dismal depression years, Barney Hill's family never went without food and shelter, though many of their neighbors did.

"One Christmas stands out vividly," Barney recalls. "My father said he didn't think Santa Claus would be able to visit us that year because the newspaper stated that Santa's sleigh had been damaged in a blizzard at the North Pole. With long faces and saddened hearts my brothers and sisters and I went to bed. I woke up around five in the morning and found that the door of my room leading to the hall was tied. I went through the adjoining door to my sisters' room, and that was tied, too. I was able to squeeze through, untie the door, and the four of us ran downstairs. There in the living room were all the toys we had wanted and asked for under a beautifully decorated Christmas tree. My father and mother came downstairs, pretending great surprise. 'What do you know?' my father said. 'Santa did come. It must have been the noise we heard last night on the roof!' My father and mother derived much pleasure in giving us surprises this way."

Although Barney's parents created an atmosphere of love in the family's home life, he knew the inevitable struggle and conflicts that the Negro unnecessarily suffers. "One time in Junior High School," Barney recalls, "when the time came to select our course, I told my school adviser that I eventually wanted to become a structural engineer. He advised me to select another course because there was no future for Negroes in that field. I was disheartened. My marks suffered. I thought there could possibly be a future for me in the military service, so when America began its peacetime draft, I decided to enlist in the Army. I have always felt that it's right and proper to defend against an aggressor at all times, an attitude instilled in me by my uncle."

This attitude came in handy in the turbulent streets of Philadelphia. On one particular day, Barney learned through a friend that a gang of boys threatened to beat him up if they caught him out of his own neighborhood. Within the hour, Barney was on his bike, pedaling to the home of one of the boys, where he knew they gathered. He marched into the backyard and said: "I understand you fellows are looking for me."

One of the boys advanced, and said, "Yes, we are."

A scuffle followed, with Barney soundly trouncing the youngster. When he finished, he turned to the others and said: "I'll fight all of you together—and separately. Because I plan to leave my street any time I feel like it!"

There was no more trouble in the neighborhood.

Barney served three years in the Army, running into a similar incident of bullying, in which he succeeded in trimming down to size a soldier, thirty pounds heavier than he, in a grudge boxing match. His son from his previous marriage, Barney, was born while he was serving during World War II; his younger, Darrel, after he had been discharged.

Both in and out of therapy, Barney increasingly examined these and other scenes of his background. And as he did, his curiosity increased as to why he reacted so violently to the object as it hovered over him in the sky at Indian Head. What confused Barney most about the incident was that he was never inclined to panic, never afraid of facing a traumatic crisis. This attitude was reflected when he walked steadily across the road and out onto the field toward the enormous object, carrying his binoculars, on that night of September 19, 1961. It was not until he put the binoculars to his eyes and focused on the craft that he panicked and ran back to the car. The unexplained panic, that he knew to be foreign to his general reactions, plagued him, in addition to the curtain of absolute blankness that descended at that moment.

For a full year, from the summer of 1962 through the following summer of 1963, Barney continued working through his problem with Dr. Stephens, but never emphasizing and only briefly considering the UFO incident. Barney felt at first, and the doctor seemed to agree, this was peripheral to the case, a side issue that could only be considered as a sudden shock in a recent period of his life, rather than a deep, underlying cause of his symptoms. Further, Betty was not experiencing as much distress as he was over the incident, aside from the vivid recall of her dreams that fired up her curiosity. They had both taken Dr. Quirke's suggestion to relax for awhile and, temporarily, to put aside the idea of hypnosis as means of clarifying their memories.

One evening in September 1963, the Hills were invited by their church discussion group to relate (for the first time at any kind of gathering) their experience with the UFO in the White Mountains. They had mentioned the incident to their minister, who along with others in the church had a growing curiosity about the subject in the light of increasing Unidentified Flying Object reports throughout New England, and especially in New Hampshire and Vermont. Because of these reports, Barney and Betty felt that people might be willing now to accept their story without the usual skepticism. They had mixed feelings about the idea, as usual, although Betty was now becoming convinced that their story should be told. If it should represent a landmark in the history of the phenomenon, did they have a right to confine it to themselves?

At the discussion group meeting was another invited speaker, Captain Ben Swett, from the nearby Pease Air Force Base, who was well known in that area for his study of hypnosis, a subject which together with the story the Hills would tell might make up an interesting evening.

"After the Captain listened to our story—as much as we could tell with the blanking out of memory that took place at that moment at Indian Head—he was interested that the account was cut off as if by a cleaver at that point," Barney recalls. "We mentioned the fact that Hohman, Jackson, and Major MacDonald had recommended hypnosis, and as a man well acquainted with it himself, the Captain agreed that this might be a good idea. Especially if it were conducted by a psychiatrist. As a layman, he didn't dream of doing it himself. We, too, were aware of the danger of indiscriminate hypnosis. But it did stimulate our interest in the idea, which had been dormant for a long time."

At his next session with Dr. Stephens, Barney brought up the subject. The doctor told him that even though the UFO incident might be a sidelight, they should leave no stone unturned in examining Barney's anxieties. Dr. Stephens also indicated to Barney that simultaneous hallucination, to say nothing of simultaneous amnesia, was highly unlikely, although there is a rare psychological phenomenon known as *folie à deux,* in which two people develop a psychotic condition in which their beliefs and delusions are similar. This also seemed unlikely, since most of the conditions for this phenomenon did not seem to be present. Except for the possibility of this one traumatic experience,

56

there were no particular symptoms mutually reflected in their constant, day-to-day relationships as husband and wife over the entire period they had been married.

Dr. Stephens found it advisable at this point to have the opinion of Dr. Benjamin Simon, a well-known Boston psychiatrist and neurologist. Dr. Simon is a graduate of Stanford University, with a Master's degree, and received his M.D. from Washington University School of Medicine in St. Louis. While an undergraduate at Johns Hopkins University, he became interested in hypnosis when he served as a subject in some experiments conducted by the Psychology Department there. During his psychiatric and neurological training, he developed proficiency in techniques and procedures. While on a Rockefeller Foundation Fellowship in Europe in 1937 and 1938, he further extended the knowledge which was to prove so useful a few years later.

In World War II, he found it a very useful adjunct in the treatment of military psychiatric disorders, first as Consultant Psychiatrist to the General Dispensary in New York, and later on a very extensive scale as Chief of Neuropsychiatry and Executive Officer at Mason General Hospital, the Army's chief psychiatric center in World War II.

The responsibility of bringing treatment to three thousand patients a month made necessary the use of all the varied types of treatment, especially those which could be used in briefer therapy and with groups. Hypnosis, and its companion therapeutic procedure, narcosynthesis (the so-called "truth serum"), fulfilled these requirements expeditiously and became well established as therapeutic agents.

When John Huston produced his outstanding motion picture documentary on psychiatric treatment, "Let There Be Light," at the Mason General Hospital, Colonel Simon served as adviser, and personally did the scenes involving hypnosis and narcosynthesis. For his work as Chief of Neuropsychiatry and Executive Officer, he was awarded the Legion of Merit and the Army Commendation Medal. Mason General Hospital and its personnel received the Meritorious Service Unit Award. After leaving military service in 1946, Dr. Simon maintained his interest in these special procedures, though their place in civilian psychiatric practice is much more restricted.

*   *   *

In his office on Bay State Road in Boston, Dr. Simon received a call from Barney Hill early in December of 1963. Since the referral was made by Dr. Stephens, Dr. Simon set up an appointment for a consultation on December 14.

Bay State Road in Boston is sometimes known as Doctor's Row.

Formerly composed of fashionable town houses for Boston's Back Bay Brahmins, many of the structures have now been converted into pleasing and comfortable medical offices.

Barney and Betty Hill left Portsmouth well before seven o'clock on the morning of December 14, driving in and parking their car near Dr. Simon's offices with a comfortable margin of time before their appointment at eight. They approached the consultation with mingled feelings of curiosity, nervousness, and some apprehension, although these feelings were tempered with the relief that comes from taking a decisive step and action in the direction they thought would help.

Betty's anxiety was of course based on her dreams. When Hohman and Jackson had pointed out the time discrepancy to them, her anxiety had grown markedly, and the thought that they might have been more than just dreams was critically upsetting to her. Although less emotional in her general reaction than Barney, and more stoic, her fear that the dreams might be based on reality was affecting her work as well as her equanimity. At one time, not long after Hohman's and Jackson's visit, she confided in her supervisor for the State Welfare Department, with whom she frequently had dinner after Barney had left for his night-shift work. "I gave her the description of the dreams I had written down," Betty recalls, "and we used to talk them over. This must have gone on over a period of a couple of months. And finally one night she said to me, 'How do you know these dreams are *not* real?' She said that every indication and reaction I was having pointed to the direction that all this might have been reality, and that I should be willing to accept that as a possibility, but after that I began to give it serious consideration. Going into Dr. Simon's office that day gave me some confidence that I could clear this up, to remove this thing that was eating at me all the time. To get some kind of confirmation—one way or the other."

Betty, who had never been in therapy, was faintly amused at the fact that she had often escorted some of her welfare cases into psychiatric clinics, and now the tables were about to be turned. Barney, whose therapy had been continuing for many months, was curious about the possibility that they might be going to undergo hypnosis; he was anxious to see if indeed he *could* be hypnotized and what sort of method would be used to accomplish this.

Barney, at a later date, recalled his impressions of the first visit: "Walking into his office where Dr. Simon holds his consultations, I found it very impressive. It was nicely carpeted with green, along with a green pad on his desk—it was comfortable and quiet. He completely captivated me to the point that I felt this was a person I could trust. It was an instantaneous thing with me that I immediately liked him. And this was also what was to help me overcome my anxiety. Betty and I were together, of course, at the first consultation.

Betty, too, thought that the office was attractive and the doctor impressive. "I had full confidence in him even before we met, because at a recent Child Guidance Clinic I looked him up in the *Biographical Directory of the American Psychiatric Association*. The entry there convinced me of his competence and professional standing. To me, this was so important because of the unusual nature of our case."

Dr. Simon, somewhat surprised to note the interracial marriage of his patients, began with a general history of their problems, highlighted, of course, by the incident at Indian Head two years before.

Dr. Simon was aware that Barney had been undergoing therapy for his anxiety state and that it was increasingly apparent that the experience with the Unidentified Flying Object was an important facet in his failure to respond adequately to his treatment. He was similarly aware of the nightmares leading to Betty's anxiety. It became quickly apparent that both Barney and Betty needed treatment. Treatment would be centered on their anxiety reaction with the apparent amnesia for part of the experiences in the White Mountains as the point of departure.

There were practical questions, too, for both of them. The matter of cost was something they could not ignore. Their combined income was reasonably comfortable, but with two of them in therapy, they realized, there would be a severe strain on the budget. And the job of psychiatric treatment could not be accomplished over a short period of time. In addition to the fees that a competent psychiatrist would set, there was the not inconsiderable cost of driving to Boston each week for a double session. This was serious business to them, not a whim or fancy, and they accepted it as such.

The Unidentified Flying Object aspect was a secondary matter to Dr. Simon, because his first and major job was to determine the treatment, and aid the patients in overcoming their psychiatric problems. The UFO experience fell within the limits of the material he had heard and the little he had read about the subject. This secondary aspect of the case *was* most interesting, and he foresaw a rather prolonged and intensive period of therapy that might be unique.

One of the major objectives, of course, was to open up the amnesia, and since this symptom responds particularly well to hypnosis, the doctor decided to use it to initiate the treatment.

The general attitude of Dr. Simon to UFO's was neutral, tempered by a hard-headed realism that such objects could exist, as experimental aircraft or foreign reconnaissance craft not yet announced to the layman —or simply mistaken aircraft or stars. He had no personal interest in the subject and was willing to accept whatever authoritative sources said about it. He didn't realize the amount of controversy involved, even among the scientific community, nor was he familiar with the National Investigations Committee on Aerial Phenomena, whose report the Hills brought with them to give the doctor a full background on their experience, as documented by Walter Webb.

At the consultation that morning, Dr. Simon evaluated their cases and gave an outline of his treatment plan. Because the purported amnesia was a central factor in their distress, he planned to begin by using hypnosis to penetrate the amnesia, if this is what the condition turned out to be, and to proceed according to the developments. Dr. Simon also decided to record the therapeutic sessions on tape, both for an accurate record and for probable use to bring the material into consciousness under controlled conditions.

During hypnosis, the incidents described in the trance can be wiped from conscious memory. Conversely, on instruction from the doctor, they can be recalled. For the most real reproduction of the trance experience, the patient can listen to his own voice on tape and analyze it with the doctor, step by step.

The reality or non-reality of the dreams was of course foremost in Betty's mind. For nearly two years now, the answer to this question had been gnawing away at her. For Barney, as he had already told Betty, he was hoping that for once and for all she would accept the fact that her experience in regard to an abduction was no more than an intense series of dreams. The trauma of the low-level sighting on Route 3 was enough for Barney; to carry the incident on to the possible abduction—just the thought of it—was more than he cared to think about. To the doctor, the uniqueness of the story remained nothing more than the background against which he would have to work.

Barney and Betty Hill, like most laymen, had only a smattering of knowledge about hypnosis. Dr. Simon explained to them that the process was a close relationship between the doctor and the patient, in which the Hills would be brought into a condition like sleep. There would be no danger of harm to them—they should have nothing to fear.

In a lecture some years ago to the New York Academy of Medicine, "Hypnosis: Fact and Fancy," Dr. Simon covered the entire field of hypnosis and its function in medical and psychiatric practice, pointing out that only in the last several decades has hypnosis received significant attention as a medical practice.

Who can hypnotize? Who can be hypnotized? Who cannot be hypnotized? [Dr. Simon asked in the lecture]. Any intelligent adult with appropriate knowledge of technique can hypnotize. Any intelligent adult and most children above the age of seven can be hypnotized; in fact, children are more easily hypnotized than adults. Very psychotic individuals and the mentally retarded are very resistant to hypnosis. Most of these cannot be hypnotized. . . .

Ninety-five percent of hypnotizable persons can attain the first stage, but only about 20 percent can be brought to the third or somnambulistic stage. . . .

Will plays no part whatever in hypnosis, and the belief that hypnotizability is a manifestation of a weak will is false. The factors which influence hypnotizability are the intelligence of the individual, his conscious willingness, and the degree of unconscious resistance or submissiveness. The latter are not always manifest on the surface. . . .

Contrary to the common fears of the public, termination of the hypnotic state is not generally a problem. Universally, the suggestion for waking results in waking. There need be only the added suggestion of feelings of comfort and freedom from anxiety. In the rare instances where the subject does not wake on suggestion, if left alone he will fall into a natural sleep and wake up in a matter of hours. . . .

Sometimes drugs—such as sodium amytal or pentothal—are used to facilitate induction of the hypnotic state where the patient is unduly resistant. Under these conditions, the waking period will be delayed by the effect of the drug, but the suggestions given during the induction will be carried out as post-hypnotic suggestions. The two aforementioned drugs are of some value in difficult inductions and will help relax the apprehensive patient and increase his suggestibility.

There are generally described three stages of hypnosis: light, medium, and heavy. In the light stage, catalepsy of the eyelids [inability to open the eyes at will] can be produced on suggestion, and a certain degree of general suggestibility is present. Post-hypnotic suggestions may be given, and a great deal of treatment can be accomplished. . . .

In the medium stage, paralysis of volitional control of the larger muscles of the body may be produced—major catalepsy. In this stage, analgesia, insensitivity to pain, may be successfully suggested. . . .

In the third stage, or somnambulistic stage, almost any phenomenon can be produced, and the patient will be amnesic unless he is definitely told to recall the trance state. [This was to play an important part in the treatment of the Hills.] Positive or negative hallucinations may be induced, and post-hypnotic suggestions given in this somnambulistic stage will be very effective. Activity of the autonomic nervous system manifested by blushing, constriction of skin vessels, and slowing of the pulse can be produced. There is conflict among authorities on this matter, but there are reports of actual blistering by the suggestion of intense heat. . . .

Dr. Simon closed the lecture by stating his conviction that hypnosis should not be used in any field beyond research, medical practice and dentistry. He also added:

Hypnosis has gone through many periods of enthusiastic acceptance and then ensuing rejection as have some of our "modern trends" in psychiatry. There is no doubt that these symptoms [those removed by hypnosis] tend to recur or to be replaced by more distressing symptoms, unless the underlying emotional conflict [of which the symptoms are manifestations] is resolved. Unless the physician can be sure that he will be able to continue treatment of the patient after the removal of the symptoms, the symptoms should not be removed by hypnosis. . . .

Many question whether a forceable breakthrough of resistance [such as that which is provided by hypnosis] is a desirable approach. In a variety of conditions, hysterical, psychosomatic and others, hypnosis may help to shorten the time of therapy by facilitating the approach to unconscious conflicts, as has been described. Hypnosis has dangers and yet it is not dangerous. The essential dangers lie in its use by those not bound by a professional code of ethics, and who are not adequately trained.

As the Hills were to discover, they were in cautious, medically conservative hands. With the doctor's basic attitude neutral to the UFO subject, if not prejudiced against it, they were to run into a stiff test of whatever beliefs they now had as a result of their experience at Indian Head. Betty, in spite of her growing interest in the phenomenon, was willing to accept the truth of the matter, whatever it was. Barney, hopeful to clear up the anxiety symptoms that were seriously disturbing his life, was at the point where he wanted above all for the truth to come out, regardless of what it was.

None of them were to realize that the truth was so elusive, even with the desire and the most advanced means to find it.

CHAPTER FIVE

With the Hills' story and Walter Webb's six-page report in hand, Dr. Simon found himself interested in the uniqueness of the case and the unusual data accompanying it. The story, to all appearances, seemed reliable and valid. He noted that Webb's detailed opinion was based on an interview shortly after the incident, and the impact of it on the Hills was still evident two years later. While Dr. Simon's concerns were centered around the problem of the Hills' anxiety symptoms, he was aware that the Unidentified Flying Object aspect might add a new dimension to the case. As far as the existence or nonexistence of the phenomenon itself, the doctor took a neutral position.

Since hypnosis is the method of choice for the rapid opening of an amnesia,* and may be, as Dr. Simon expresses it, the key to the locked room, he planned to use it as a part of the therapeutic procedure. The sighting of the unidentified object had built itself into one of tremendous importance to the Hills, and the condition of aroused and concentrated attention produced by hypnosis might throw some additional light on their experience.

At eight in the morning, on Saturday, January 4, 1964, the Hills

---

*During World War II, hypnosis and narcosynthesis (narcoanalysis) were used rather extensively and often interchangeably in the treatment of acute psychiatric disorders. Hypnosis was most effectively used where there was a "point of departure" like an amnesia. Narcosynthesis was used most frequently to release the anxiety associated with mental conflicts below the surface of consciousness where a focal point was not so clearly apparent. This was accomplished by the slow injection of a drug, usually sodium amytal or sodium pentothal, the so-called "truth serums." They were neither sera nor did they necessarily produce the inviolable truth. They did, as did hypnosis, help in the discharge of repressed or suppressed emotional conflicts.

arrived at the doctor's office on Bay State Road for their first regular visit after the initial consultation. It was to be the first of three sessions in which the doctor would repeatedly induce hypnosis, as a conditioning process.

During these sessions, both of the Hills responded well, and the doctor was satisfied that they would be good subjects, able to attain the depth of trance desired. The repetition of the process over the three-week period would serve to reinforce the induction and to establish specific post-hypnotic cue words to replace future induction procedures. In this way the subsequent inductions would be quick and sure. In exploring the amnesia both the doctor and the patients would be going up a blind alley, and the reinforcement of the hypnosis would make it possible to maintain good control in the face of possible emotional disturbances that can arise in such an exploration.

Barney's nervousness increased somewhat as he prepared to undergo hypnosis for the first time. Dr. Simon stood him by the large desk in the office, placed his hands at his side, and stood near him, in front of the desk and just in front of a comfortable chair.

"Dr. Simon began talking to me," Barney described the process, "telling me that I was relaxing, and he had me clasp my hands together, and that they would be tight, tight, very tight, that I couldn't open them no matter how hard I tried. And I was standing there feeling very, very foolish, because I thought if this is hypnosis, there is nothing to it. I'm just humoring the man. I didn't want to hurt his feelings. I think he stopped and placed his hands over my eyes so that they would close. I said to myself that I wasn't really hypnotized, and when he told me that I couldn't pull my hands apart, I knew that all I had to do was open my fingers, and I could do it. But I just didn't feel like opening my fingers. I didn't even feel I was asleep, but then I was aware that he was waking me up and asking me how I felt. And I felt very, very good, very calm and comfortable. And I no longer then had any fear of hypnosis."

As so often happens, the patient feels he is humoring the operator, pretending to be cooperative, and without his knowing it, he moves into a deep trance with no knowledge or memory of what happened, unless the operator tells him he can remember.

The two, simple cue words creating rapid induction were repeated several times during the early sessions, along with tests to check the validity and depth of the trance. These are some of the customary tests used for this purpose: instructing that the patient's arm be stiff as a bar of steel (it remains so); testing for insensitivity to pain (when it is suggested, the patient does not react to the stimulus given); instructing the patient that the operator's finger will feel like a hot poker when it touches (the subject will pull his hand away in pain, even though the pain is only suggestion); and others.

Since the time of Mesmer the use of hypnosis in medicine has gone through many cycles of popularity. Breuer found that his patients were able to recall specific traumatic events through hypnosis. In part because he found that not everyone could be hypnotized, Freud developed the psychoanalytic method. The present medical attitude is reflected by Lewis R. Wolberg, M.D., Medical Director of the Postgraduate Center for Psychotherapy, New York City, and Clinical Professor of Psychiatry of the New York Medical College. He has described hypnosis as a state of being suspended like a hammock between consciousness and sleep. It should be used in a treatment plan, particularly when a patient is unable to verbalize freely, or when strong repressions bottle up highly charged material. "When a patient has repressed traumatic memories," he once told a medical symposium, "he may seal these memories off so effectively that it may not be possible to get to them with traditional techniques. Sometimes with hypnosis one can cut through repression enough to bring up traumatic memories."

With Barney and Betty Hill, this aspect of the hypnotic process would be important. The opening up of amnesia requires the use of time regression, wherein the patient's memory becomes vivid and exact —details long forgotten to the conscious mind emerge sharply. It is not unusual for person in hypnosis to recall the name and color of the eyes of everyone at his fifth birthday party if so requested, even if that might have taken place decades before. There is also the tendency to relive, re-create and reenact the time segment being recalled, so that the subject again goes through emotions involved in the original experience, a process referred to as abreaction. The physician must always be cognizant that in bringing to light unconscious memories and feelings, these may be intolerable to the patient and could lead to serious after-reactions. At times, the subject may emerge from the trance if he feels threatened, he may refuse to go further, or as in Barney Hill's case, he may plead to be taken out of the trance without emerging on his own. Often, when the emotional release, or abreaction, comes, the patient feels measurable relief. The doctor's control of the patient during hypnosis is essential. This was to be demonstrated later as the sessions continued.

Barney Hill, in spite of some apprehension, was fascinated by the process.

"After the first test," Barney Hill recalls, "a curious thing happened. As I got ready for the induction into hypnosis, I looked at my watch. It must have been five minutes after eight. And he gave me the key word, and I was hypnotized. And as far as time was concerned, I thought he was waking me immediately. But I looked at my watch, and it was after nine. I must have been without consciousness for an hour, and yet it seemed no time at all. I recalled also, just at the beginning of what must have been the trance, that he had poked my hand with something that felt like the bristle of a brush. I asked him if I could see this done. So the doctor put me in a trance again, and told me to open my eyes in the trance and that I would remember this part of it. Then he took a needle-like instrument and pushed it against my hand and there was no pain associated with this, except perhaps like a bristle of a brush. In fact, he put considerable pressure on it, and I could feel no pain at all. And I was amazed at that, because I looked at my skin, and the needle that had penetrated my skin, and there wasn't any blood. So I began to realize that there were two things that could happen here: One, I could be hypnotized and made to forget that I had been hypnotized so that I would awaken and would assume that I hadn't been hypnotized at all; two, I could be hypnotized and if I was told I could remember, I would retain a knowledge of all that had taken place under hypnosis."

In spite of Barney Hill's excellent response to the initial induction, Dr. Simon resolved to stay with his plan of two more sessions, during which Barney and Betty would become more reinforced in the process so that a deep trance would be reached quickly and the hypnosis could continue without interruption.

As with Barney, the doctor found that Betty Hill was also an exceptionally good subject. She would, he found, go into a deep trance easily and respond completely both to the trance and to the post-hypnotic suggestions without faltering.

With both subjects clearly responding to the induction, the doctor could now continue with future sessions simply by stating the established cue words that would produce the trance. He would, however, play safe by repeated deep trance inductions.

The doctor further tested the Hills during the three preliminary sessions with various posthypnotic suggestions, such as asking them, three minutes after they were awakened, to smoke a cigarette which would taste so bad that they would have to crush it out. They would be offered another and told that it would be fine, which of course it was. He instructed them (always separately, because this would be the method he would be using in the later sessions) that they would not remember anything whatever they revealed under hypnosis, unless they were directed to. Until Dr. Simon had the whole story and could assess its emotional effect, he was careful to make sure that the amnesia was reinstated after each session. This also had the desirable effect of preventing communication between the Hills after the sessions that were to follow, avoiding distortions that might arise from their discussing the material revealed under hypnosis. Later the memory of what came out under hypnosis would be made available to both, through tape recordings or by directing them to remember at a time when this would be therapeutically desirable.

The doctor planned to take Barney first, regress him to the night of September 19, 1961, and have him reveal every detail of the trip down from Canada to Portsmouth. Since the trance would provide details of marked clarity there was a reasonable expectation that Barney would bridge the amnesic gap under hypnosis, the blocking off of his memory after each session would permit Betty to give her own story in later sessions without being influenced by Barney.

Frequently, when a subject is in a deep trance, he cannot recall what has happened during the session when he is brought back into consciousness at the direction of the operator. However, he can recall the material if he is instructed by the operator to do so.

With the tests and induction period over after the third session, the Hills looked forward to the start of the therapeutic sessions, with the hope that once and for all the mystery at Indian Head would be cleared up. They were both comfortable and relaxed about the whole hypnotic process now, in fact they almost enjoyed its after effects.

"I can just describe it," Barney recalls, "as if it were like getting into a hot tub of water and soaking, as if every nerve in my body would be pleasant and tingling. It was something I had never been able to achieve before. Just a tingling, pleasant glow, just like a rubdown."

But both of them knew that the serious business was about to begin —that a long job lay ahead of them in their search for an end to the anxieties that had been upsetting their lives for so many months. The Hills arrived at the usual early morning hour at Dr. Simon's office on February 22, 1962, Betty realizing that she would merely be going to have her induction reinforced, and Barney ready to make his excursion into the unknown.

The doctor's procedure was clear for this session: after he reinforced Betty (the simple process of rehypnotizing her so that she would maintain her capacity for the deep trance state, when the time for her sessions came later), he would have Barney go back to the night of the journey and retrace it in detail. A psychologically-determined amnesia is commonly the loss of memory for painful ideas or experiences that serves to keep them out of consciousness. Through the concentration of attention brought on by hypnosis, the opposite of amnesia is often created—hypermnesia, or superlative memory. In this session, it was hoped that not only would the forgotten material be recalled, but that the accompanying emotions would be reexperienced. To bring back the recall without the emotions would not serve adequately from the therapeutic point of view.

For the tape recording of the sessions, Dr. Simon used a Revere M-2 Automatic cartridge-loading recorder at 1 7/8 IPS. The cartridges were not only longplaying, but they could be stacked ahead of time so that there would be a minimum of interruption during the sessions. Where an interruption was necessary, the procedure was simple: the doctor would simply tap Barney on the head, tell him that he would hear no sound whatsoever during the intermission period, and then tap him on the head again to continue. A subject under hypnosis has such accuracy of recall and retention that he will continue at the exact point left off, even if he is in the middle of a sentence. The recall and reliving not only approaches the accuracy of a tape recording, but it may be turned on and off at will at the instruction of the operator.

Further, the subject will take the instructions and questions of the operator in a literal sense. If asked a question: "Did you talk to this man?" the subject may respond by saying, "No, I did not talk to this man, I whispered to him." The preciseness of the response is marked.

*　　　*　　　*

Barney took his seat in front of the doctor's desk. He started to reach for a cigarette, but on the cue words from Dr. Simon, his eyes closed, and his head nodded. His hands were folded across his lap—he looked like anyone who had dozed over his morning paper while he sat in an easy chair. The deep trance was induced, and satisfying himself that Barney was fully in the trance state, the doctor began the session.

DOCTOR

(He is completing his reinforcement of the trance.)

You are deeper and deeper asleep. Deep asleep. You will remember everything now, and you will tell me everything.

BARNEY

Yes.

DOCTOR

And I want you to tell me in full detail *all* your experiences, *all* of your thoughts, and *all* of your feelings, beginning with the time you left your hotel. Were you in Montreal?

BARNEY

(His voice on the tape is now amazingly flat, monotonous, and trance-like in contrast to his animated tones of normal conversation. He responds to the doctor's questions with bluntness, with little inflection, in a curious monotone, and with measured preciseness.)

We did not stay in Montreal. We stayed in a motel.

DOCTOR

You stayed in a motel. What was the name of it?

BARNEY

In another city.

DOCTOR

Yes, where did you stay?

BARNEY

I can't seem to remember.

DOCTOR

It was near Montreal?

BARNEY

It was approximately 112 miles from Montreal.

(The attention to detail here is interesting—linking the word approximately with such an exact mileage figure.)

DOCTOR

Is there any reason why you can't remember it?

(There must be some reason. In such a deep trance, a subject usually recalls many details.)

BARNEY

We arrived at night at this motel, and I did not notice any name in the motel.

(The reason comes out, as expected.)

DOCTOR

I see. Do you know what the city was?

BARNEY

It was not a city; it was out in the country. We had been driving from Niagara Falls through Canada.

DOCTOR

Keep right on. Tell me about your arrival there.

BARNEY

We arrived in this small area, we did not see any town marks, and my car was making a lot of noise. It was Betty's car that we were driving. I was driving the car.

(The precision, the almost cumbersome exactness of the phrase is typical of the deep trance state.)

And I stopped at a service station and they told me the car had not been properly greased. And so they greased the car and this eliminated the noise that the car was making. We then decided we could not continue to Montreal and that we should look for a place to sleep overnight. And that's when I saw this motel, and did not pay any attention to the name.

(He is again explaining why he could not remember the name. He has also been instructed to relate all his thoughts as well as his actions.)

The thoughts that were going through my mind were: Would they accept me? Because they might say they were filled up, and I wondered if they were going to do this, because I was prejudiced . . . .

DOCTOR

Because *you* were prejudiced?

BARNEY

. . . because *they* were prejudiced.

DOCTOR

Because you were a Negro?

BARNEY

Because I am a Negro.

DOCTOR

You've run into that before, I take it?

BARNEY

I have not actually run into being denied a place of accommodation.

70

You mean you just worry about it?

BARNEY

But I do know that this does happen, and I was concerned because I was getting tired. And when I went to this place, they immediately accepted me. It cost us $12 for the two of us, and we stayed overnight.

DOCTOR

Did you express your concern to your wife? Does she share it?

BARNEY

She does not share my concern about this matter.

DOCTOR

Did you express it to her, or did you keep it to yourself?

BARNEY

I do express them to her.

DOCTOR

Did you on that night?

BARNEY

I did not. I never express them to her when we are seeking a place.

DOCTOR

I see. All right. Go on.

BARNEY

We had a little dog with us, and we were told it was a nice little dachshund-type dog, and we could have her in the motel unit.

(He is, of course, referring to their dog Delsey, describing her in literal terms.)

The next morning we got out bright and early, and there was a restaurant across the street. And we decided to eat breakfast. I had my grapefruit, ham, eggs, coffee. We then are driving along this wide highway. It's a new road, it's a beautiful road. It's four lanes in certain sections.

(Again, the desire shows itself to fill in every detail, inconsequential or not.)

I am coming into Montreal, and I do not particularly like the thoughts of staying here.

Why not?

BARNEY

It's a big city, there's much confusion, there are a lot of trucks on the road. There's quite an amount of traffic. It's building up, and I don't want to stay in Montreal with all this traffic. I have difficulty in keeping the highway route number I want . . . traffic is everywhere. And I decide that we should find a motel if we are going to stay overnight. To my chagrin, all motels are located quite a distance, or to me I think, a distance from the city. And I am riding, we are riding around, and I see a few Negroes, and I am amazed. I had not realized there were Negroes in Montreal. And I am quite a distance away from the downtown section, and all the buildings have wrought iron, like stairways, on the outside of the buildings. And I pull over to a service station, and I ask how I can get back to my route. And he doesn't understand me, and I realize he doesn't understand English.

(Barney speaks in the present tense, an indication of the full reexperiencing of the events, rather than the recounting of them.)

So I put two dollars worth of gas in the car and drive off. I locate a policeman directing traffic . . . .

DOCTOR

Why did you put two dollars worth of gas in the car instead of filling it?

BARNEY

I did not want gas when I stopped to ask directions.

DOCTOR

In other words, you felt you ought to repay them, is that it?

BARNEY

I felt I should do something. And I pull over to the side, and I ask the policeman: "How can I find, I keep thinking Route 3," and he does speak English very haltingly over the strong accent, but he does give me direc= tions. I'm passing a beautiful school, its a Catholic school. I see the priest out there. Beautiful rolling grounds, it's sitting on a hill. It's a very beautiful school in Montreal. And again, I miss my turn . . . .

(Barney continues describing the detail of the trip across Canada, and the upper part of Vermont.)

One fourteen! It's dark—it's not a good road—but it's a short distance to New Hampshire and I see the signs of Colebrook—and it is welcome. I feel alert. I feel that my trip is over and I'm on Route 3 and I see Route 3 going to the left and to the right from straight ahead, and I become confused, and I realize I want to go straight and not to the left. I decide to stop and check my map, and I turn around and go back to a restaurant I have passed—and I park—and we go in. There is a dark-skinned woman in there, I think, dark by Caucasian standards, and I wonder—is she a light-skinned Negro, or is she Indian, or is she white?—and she waits on us, and she is not very friendly, and I notice this, and others are there and they are looking at me and at Betty, and they seem to be friendly or pleased, but this dark-skinned woman doesn't. I wonder then more so— is she Negro and wonder if I—if she is wondering if I know she is Negro and is passing for white. I eat a hamburger and I become impatient with Betty to not—to drink her coffee so we can get started, and the clock and my watch say five minutes after ten, and I know I should be in Portsmouth, I think, by two o'clock.

DOCTOR

Didn't you say just a while ago it was 1:10 or 1:15?

BARNEY

I said *Route* 114.

DOCTOR

I see. All right, go on.

BARNEY

I see dark, very dark. No traffic and Betty has asked me to stop the car and let Delsey out—she's the dog.

DOCTOR

Why is she named Delsey?

BARNEY

I think the people that owned her before called her Dolce (he gives an Italian-like explosive pronunciation) — Dolce — and Betty called her Dolce—and this became her name.

DOCTOR

Go on, you stopped to take Dolce out.

BARNEY

My thoughts keep going back to Canada. I stop in Coaticook, Canada.

DOCTOR

Yes . . .

BARNEY

I can't park close to this restaurant, so I park on the street and we must walk to the restaurant. And everybody on the street passing us by is looking. And we go in to this restaurant, and all eyes are upon us. And I see what I call the stereotype of the "hoodlum." The ducktail haircut. And I immediately go on guard against any hostility. And no one says anything to me . . . and we are served.

DOCTOR

Now this other restaurant you were in—was that in Canada?

BARNEY

That was in Colebrook, New Hampshire.

DOCTOR

How is it your thoughts go back to Canada? Is this a memory you're having again?

BARNEY

I just went back. I went back because when Betty was telling me to stop the car when we left Colebrook, New Hampshire, and we are now in the country part, I was thinking that I should get hold of myself, and not think everyone was hostile, or rather suspect hostility, when there was no hostility there. It was a very pleasant restaurant. The people were friendly. And I wondered why was this so important to me? And why was I ready to be defensive—just because these boys were wearing this style of haircut.

DOCTOR

Just your thoughts went back to Canada?

BARNEY

Yes. I was thinking of that when we were in New Hampshire. When she asked me to stop and let the dog go for a walk. That's when my thoughts went back . . .

(Here, shortly before the sighting, Barney reveals again his apprehension, his ambivalence with respect to his acceptance by others, his need for reassurance. The seemingly unfriendly waitress pressed him to seek a reassuring one. Colebrook, the unfriendly, perhaps by clang association—a psychiatric term involving similar sounds which conjure up associations—invoked Coaticook.)

BARNEY

(He continues to describe the drive down U.S. 3. In the vicinity of Lancaster, New Hampshire, in his recall, he first brings up the object in the sky.)

I look up through the windshield of the car, and I see a star. That's funny, but I said, Betty, that's a satellite. And then I pulled over to the side of the road, and Betty jumped out her side with the binoculars. And I got the chain, and I hook it to the dog on her collar, and I say come on, Delsey, let's get out. And she jumps out . . . .

(Barney is mixing present and past tenses now, varying probably with the intensity of his feelings.)

And I look towards the sky, and I look back to Delsey, and walk her around to the trunk of the car. And I'm saying, hurry up, Betty, so I can get a look. And Betty passes the binoculars to me. And I see that it's not a satellite. It is a plane. And I tell Betty this, and give the binoculars back to her. And I am satisfied.

DOCTOR

What kind of plane was it?

BARNEY

I look—and it is to the right. And it does not go where I thought it would go. It does not go past me to the right, my right shoulder. I think it will pass my right shoulder, off in the distance, going to the north. I am facing west, and my right is to the north. And it does not go to the north.

(There is a faint trace of amazement beginning to come into his voice. From his tone, you can feel him reliving, not retelling, the story.)

DOCTOR

Does it have propellers?

BARNEY

And I think this is strange. I cannot tell. I cannot hear a motor to know if it has propellers.

DOCTOR

Was your engine running?

BARNEY

My engine was running.

75

DOCTOR

How about the noise that it had been making before you had your car greased?

BARNEY

It was not making this noise. And I did not pay attention to my engine running. I was concerned that it would not cut off while I was standing here with all the lights on in the car, and the battery runs down. And I was concerned, and I looked at the exhaust, and could tell that smoke was still coming from the exhaust.

DOCTOR

From the exhaust of . . . .

BARNEY

My car.

BARNEY

So I did not concern myself too much after that. And this object that was a plane—was *not* a plane. It was—oh, it was funny. It was coming around towards us. I looked up and down the road. And I thought: how dark it is. What if a bear was to come out? And I worried. I returned to the car and said, let's go Betty. It's nothing but a plane. And they're coming over this way. They're changing course. Probably it's a Piper Cub.

DOCTOR

A Piper Cub would have only one or two windows, wouldn't it? You saw windows in this plane?

BARNEY

This is what I said, and this is what I saw when I returned to my car. A Piper Cub.

DOCTOR

You saw a Piper Cub?

BARNEY

And I drive, and Betty is still looking. And she said, "Barney, this is not a plane. It is still following us." And I stop and I look and I see it is still out there. Off in a distance. So I search for a place to pull off the road. And I see a dirt road to the right of the main highway. And I think this is a good place where I can pull off. And if any car comes, it won't strike me. And I get out of the car, and I am thinking . . . this is strange.

(His tone reflects the strangeness, now. Ominously.)

76

'Cause it is still there. And Betty said—*I think* she said, I am mad with her. I say to myself, I believe Betty is trying to make me think this is a flying saucer.

DOCTOR
(The tape recorder needs a minor adjustment, and he must interrupt.)

All right. Let's stop right there for now. Until I speak to you again, you will not hear any sound here. You will be comfortable and relaxed. Just rest comfortably until I speak to you again.

(The doctor adjusts the equipment, then:)

All right. You may proceed.

BARNEY
And I am wondering why doesn't it go away. And I stop and I look again. And I see where it has gone up ahead of us on Cannon Mountain. And I think when I get past Old Man of the Mountain . . .

(The stone formation that has become the symbol of New Hampshire . . .)

It will be in a good area to look and see this thing. And I am going to report it.

DOCTOR
Do you still think it was a Piper Cub?

BARNEY
I am wondering why these pilots are military. And they shouldn't do that. They shouldn't do that. They will make some person have an accident by flying around like that. And what if they dive at me. And the military should not do that.

DOCTOR
Was it a single engine plane?

BARNEY
I do not know.

DOCTOR
You still saw no propellers anywhere?

BARNEY
(Still in his dead, level voice.)
I saw no propellers.

77

DOCTOR

Was it light enough to see?

(Throughout the entire interrogation, the doctor is checking, double checking, challenging.)

BARNEY

It was just a light moving through the sky. And I heard no noise. And I think this is ridiculous. And—

(He speaks as though Betty were with him.)

Betty! This is *not* a flying saucer. What are you doing this for? You want to believe in this thing, and I don't.

(Now he returns to his level monotone.)

And it is still there. And I *wish* I could pass a state trooper or someone, because this is dangerous.

DOCTOR

What was the danger?

BARNEY

I am thinking of bathing in French Creek, with my two boys. And this plane came overhead, and dove straight for us, and pulled up just a few inches from the state park.

(The movement of the object in the sky brought to Barney's mind a similar incident with a plane some time before in which he had a strong emotional reaction. It is interesting how related reminiscences of the past are recalled with the vividness and clarity of the original experience.)

DOCTOR

In French Creek?

BARNEY

In Pennsylvania. French Creek, Pennsylvania.

DOCTOR

Was it a Piper Cub?

BARNEY

It was a jet plane. A fighter plane. And I feel it in my chest. The explosion when it went up in the air again. And my ears, they feel like bursting.

78

And I think of that. And I become angry with this plane that is flying around, that it might do that. And it is a frightening sound, the boom.

(He is referring to the sonic boom of the jet breaking the sound barrier at French Creek. He is apprehensive of this happening again here in the White Mountains.)

DOCTOR

The jet?

BARNEY

Yes. French Creek.

DOCTOR

If there is any sound from what you call a Piper Cub, you can hear it now.

(The subject may "hear" the sounds of his past experience.)

BARNEY

I can't hear any sound.

DOCTOR

No sound whatsoever?

BARNEY

(Almost plaintively.)

I want to hear a *jet*. Oh, I want to hear a jet so *badly*. I want to hear it.

(He is referring to the sound of the motor, not the sonic boom. He is anxious to relate this mysterious object to reality.)

DOCTOR

Why? Why do you want to hear a jet?

BARNEY

Because Betty is making me mad. She is making me angry because she is saying: "Look at it! It is strange! It is not a plane! Look at it!" And I keep thinking, it's got to be. And I want to hear a hum. I want to hear a motor.

DOCTOR

How far away was it?

BARNEY

It was—oh—it wasn't far. It was about 1000 feet, I guess.

DOCTOR

A thousand feet?

BARNEY

One thousand feet.

DOCTOR

If it were a Piper Cub, do you think it would have been silent at this distance?

BARNEY

(Who is a practiced plane-watcher.)

I do not. I—I *know* it is not a Piper Cub.

DOCTOR

(Pressing hard for facts and inconsistencies.)

How do you happen to know so much about Piper Cubs?

BARNEY

I thought it was a Piper Cub, because I had seen Piper Cubs landing on the water at Lake Winnipesaukee. And I have seen them [with ski landing gear] landing on the ice. And I stopped my car, and Betty and I said, "Look, there's another one." And we enjoyed watching these planes. And I knew I was in the mountain area where I had seen Piper Cubs flying, and I thought this was a Piper Cub.

DOCTOR

All right.

BARNEY

But it was not. It was too fast. It moved too fast. It would go up and down. It could go back so fast . . .

(More amazement in his voice, as if he is watching the object do this.)

It could go away—and come back.

DOCTOR

Did it go back and forth, or did it go in circles?

BARNEY

It would—go toward the west. And without looking as though it turned, it would come straight back. It would go like a—

(He gropes momentarily for a simile.)

I think of a paddle and a ball and a rubber band tied to it. And you hit the ball, and the ball goes out and comes straight back, without a circle. And I think only a jet could fly that fast. And I am hoping I can find a good place where I can stop and really see this thing—whatever it is. And I see a wigwam, and I recognize this place, and I feel safe. And I feel—in the barren hostility of the wooded area . . .

(He is referring to a commercial trade wigwam, closed now for the season, but in the summer selling souvenirs of Indian Head at that time.)

DOCTOR

What is this place?

BARNEY

It is Indian Head. I had been there before. And I feel comforted that I see a familiar place. And I think I will get a good look at this thing because Betty was very annoying. She was annoying by telling me, "Look!" And I can't look. I had to drive the car.

DOCTOR

Did you think she was serious?

BARNEY

I knew she was serious.

DOCTOR

Was she excited?

BARNEY

And I know Betty only becomes excited rarely. She does not become—she does not get involved, like I do, emotionally as quickly. And so, this angered me, because I knew she was excited. It would have to be something, making her this excited.

DOCTOR

You said you thought she was trying to make you believe this was a flying saucer. Had you talked about flying saucers?

BARNEY

No.

(He is not sure about the doctor's question, so he asks for an explanation.)

Is this ever—or when?

DOCTOR

Ever.

Yes. We talked about flying saucers. And no one ever said anything conclusive except that they might exist. Betty said she believed in them.

DOCTOR

Did she believe in, them?

BARNEY

I felt—it wasn't that important. I didn't believe in them.

DOCTOR

But she did?

BARNEY

Yes, Betty did believe in flying saucers.

DOCTOR

Did she have any reason for believing in them?

BARNEY

Her sister. I am thinking of visiting her mother and father in Kingston, New Hampshire. And they live in a nice, quiet area. Only three houses —her two sisters' and her mother's houses are located there. And at night you can look at the sky and see millions of stars. And I think how beautiful this is. And we were talking about satellites. The Russians had sent up Sputnik. And her father was talking about, and how you could see some satellites from here at certain hours. And we talked about flying, we talked about life on other planets. And then Betty's sister said she had seen an object flying, long and cigar-shaped, and smaller objects coming to it and flying away from it.

(NICAP files record scores of this kind of report.)

I listened—and I did not criticize. But I thought nothing. I just listened and was indifferent to the conversation. So we did talk about flying saucers. But I have not talked about flying saucers since 1957, when we were talking about Sputnik. And this was 1961.

DOCTOR

Well, we're back in 1961 now. And you are looking for a place where you can stop and observe this. And Betty has been constantly egging you on.

BARNEY
(Sharply and suddenly.)

I want to wake up!

(This is an indication that the subject may be about to experience a painful recall, a memory that he cannot face even in the trance. Dr. Simon is alerted at this point to the likelihood of a strong emotional reaction.)

DOCTOR
(Firmly.)

You're not going to wake up. You're in a deep sleep. You are comfortable, relaxed. This is not going to trouble you. Go on. You can remember everything now.

BARNEY
(He is now becoming measurably excited.)

It's right over my right! God! What is it?

(His voice begins to tremble.)

And I try to maintain control, so Betty cannot tell I am *scared. God,* I'm scared!

DOCTOR
(His voice is calm, very calm, and firm in the face of Barney's mounting emotion.)

It's all right. You can go right on, experience it. It will not hurt you now.

BARNEY
(Breaks into breathless sobbing, then screams.)

I gotta get a weapon!

(He screams again in his chair, his sobs becoming uncontrollable. The doctor is faced with a hard decision now: to impose an amnesia and bring him out of the trance, or to keep him moving through the experience for the abreaction (discharge of feeling). Further, the amnesic period would appear somewhere in this area, and it has not yet been penetrated.)

DOCTOR
(Very firmly.)

Go to sleep. You can forget, now. You've forgotten.

(He provides Barney with momentary relief.)

You're calm now. Relaxed. Deeply relaxed. You do not have to make an outcry.

(Now he brings him back again to the experience. Barney's violent reaction subsides slightly, but he is still breathing heavily.)

But you can remember it now. Keep remembering. You feel you have to get a weapon.

BARNEY

Yes.

DOCTOR

This is going to harm you, you felt.

BARNEY

(He speaks in great excitement.)

Yes. I open the trunk of my car. I get the tire wrench . . . part of the jack. And I get back in the car.

(Again, his panic is rising.)

DOCTOR

All right. Just keep reasonably calm.

BARNEY

And I keep it by me. And then I get out with the binoculars.

(Now with quiet terror.)

And it is *there*. And I look. And I look. And it is just over the field. And I think, I think—I'm *not* afraid. I'm *not* afraid . . .

(But his voice is in terror.)

I'll fight it off. I'm not *afraid!* And I walk. And I walk out, and I walk across the road. There it is—up there! Ohhh God!

(He again breaks into a scream.)

DOCTOR

(His voice very calm and firm.)

It's there. You can see it. But it's not going to hurt you.

BARNEY

(Intensely emotional.)

Why doesn't it go *away! Look* at it!

(An especially loud gasp.)

There's a man there! Is—is—is he a Captain? What is he? He—he looks at me.

84

Just a minute. Let's go back a little now. You said it was there. Did you say a thousand feet away?

(The doctor is referring to the last time Barney mentioned the distance. In the space of time covered by Barney's recall, the object has now moved to slightly more than treetop level, and not more than a few hundred feet away from Barney, he later recalled, as he stood in the field.)

BARNEY

Oh, no.

DOCTOR

A thousand yards?

BARNEY

No, it doesn't look that far. It's very big. And it's not that far. And I can see it tilted toward me!

DOCTOR

What does it look like now?

BARNEY

(Very hesitantly, as if he is studying the object above him in the sky; but much calmer now, much more objective.)

It—looks—like a—big—pancake. With windows—and rows of windows, and lights. Not lights, just one huge light.

DOCTOR

Rows of windows? Like a commercial plane?

BARNEY

Rows of windows. They're *not* like a commercial plane. Because they curve around the side of this—this pancake. And I say to myself: My God, *no!* I have to shake my head. I've got—I've got—this can't be true. This *isn't* here.

(Sighs heavily, almost a moan.)

Ohhh, it's still there.

(There is a fatalistic resignation in his voice.)

And I look—up and down the road. Can't somebody come? Can't somebody come and *tell* me this is not there? It *can't* be, but—

85

DOCTOR

You're still safe. You can see it all clearly.

BARNEY

(With complete resignation.)

It's there.

DOCTOR

(Perhaps Barney is dreaming this. The doctor will press this point.)

You'd had no sleep that evening?

BARNEY

I pinch my right arm . . . it's not my right arm, it's my left arm. I'm confused.

DOCTOR

You're clear now. Relaxed.

BARNEY

(With more fatalism in his tone.)

It's still there.

(As if an idea strikes him.)

If I let my binoculars fall and dangle from my neck—and start over again, maybe it won't be there.

(Resigned, as he seems to go through this maneuver, a magical defense ritual, like crossing his fingers.)

But it is.

(Now with incredulity.)

Why? What do they want? What do they *want?* One person looks friendly to me. He's friendly-looking. And he's looking at me . . . over his right shoulder. And he's smiling. But . . . but . . .

DOCTOR

Could you see him clearly?

BARNEY

Yes, I could.

DOCTOR

What was his face like? What did it make you think of?

86

BARNEY

It was round.

(Pauses for a moment, then:)

I think of—I think of—a red-headed Irishman. I don't know why.

(Another pause, then:)

I think I know why. Because Irish are usually hostile to Negroes. And when I see a friendly Irish person, I react to him by thinking—*I* will be friendly. And I think this one that is looking over his shoulder is friendly.

DOCTOR

You say looking over his shoulder. Was he facing away from you?

BARNEY

Yes. He was facing a wall.

DOCTOR

You saw him through this window? You said there was a row of windows?

BARNEY

(He takes care to be extremely precise.)

There was a row of windows. A huge row of windows. Only divided by struts—or structures that prevented it from being one solid window. Or then—it would have been one solid window. And the evil face on the—

(He starts to say "leader.")

He looks like a German Nazi. He's a Nazi . . .

(There is a questioning tone in his voice.)

DOCTOR

He's a Nazi. Did he have on a uniform?

BARNEY

Yes.

DOCTOR

What kind of uniform?

BARNEY

(With a small amount of surprise.)

He had a black scarf around his neck, dangling over his left shoulder.

(He gestures in his trance.)

DOCTOR

You pointed it out as if it were on you.

BARNEY

(Half to himself.)

I never noticed that before.

DOCTOR

He had a black scarf around his neck?

(Another sharp probe:)

How could you see the figures so clearly at that distance?

BARNEY

I was looking at them with binoculars.

DOCTOR

Oh. Did they have faces like other people. You said one was like a red-headed Irishman.

BARNEY

(Describing the scene very slowly and carefully.)

His eyes were slanted. Oh—his eyes were *slanted!* But not like a Chinese—Oh. Oh.

(Quite abruptly.)

I feel like a rabbit. I feel like a rabbit.

DOCTOR

What do you mean by that?

BARNEY

(He recalls a scene from his earlier days, a scene that flashed through his mind as he stood in the dark field at Indian Head, an example of reminiscent recall showing the persistent impact of early experience on the present when similar in emotional significance.)

I was hunting for rabbits in Virginia. And this cute little bunny went into a bush that was not very big. And my cousin Marge was on one side of the bush, and I was on the other—with a hat. And the poor little bunny thought he was safe. And it tickled me, because he was just hiding behind a little stalk, which meant security to him—when I pounced on him, and threw my hat on him, and captured the poor little bunny who thought he was safe.

(Pauses a moment, in quiet reflection.)

Funny I thought of that—right out there on the field.

(Repeats the phrase as if to himself.)

I feel like a rabbit.

DOCTOR

What was Betty doing all this time?

BARNEY

I can't hear her.

(Later, in one of their many trips to the scene, the Hills checked this to find that it was very difficult to hear at the estimated distance Barney was from he car.)

DOCTOR

Did you make any outcry to her the way you did to me?

BARNEY

I—I can't remember—I don't know.

(An effort to avoid under hypnosis but he must also remember, and he speaks again as if he realizes this.)

I did not.

DOCTOR

You would remember if you did.

BARNEY

(His thoughts seem to be on the craft, and not on what the doctor is saying.)

I did not. I know this creature is telling me something.

DOCTOR

Telling you something? How? How is he getting it to you?

BARNEY

I can see it in his face. No, his lips are not moving.

DOCTOR

Go on. He's telling you something.

BARNEY

(His voice begins to rise in emotion again. Strong emotion.)

And he's looking at me. And he's just telling me: Don't be afraid. I'm not a bunny. I'm going to be . . . I'm going to be safe. He didn't tell me I was that bunny.

DOCTOR

What *did* he tell you?

BARNEY

(As if he's quoting what he was told.)

Stay there—and keep looking. Just keep *looking*—and stay there. And just keep looking. Just keep looking.

DOCTOR

Could you hear him tell you?

BARNEY

Oh! I got the binoculars away from my eyes. 'Cause if I don't, I'll just stand there.

DOCTOR

Did you hear him tell you this?

BARNEY

Oh, no. He didn't say it.

(More tremor in his voice.)

DOCTOR

You *felt* he said it?

BARNEY

(Very firmly.)

I *know*.

DOCTOR

You know he said it?

BARNEY

Yes. Just stay there, he said.

(Now his voice breaks in extreme terror.)

It's pounding in my head!!

(He screams again.)

I gotta get away! I gotta get away from here!

DOCTOR

(Quickly, firmly.)

All right. All right. Calm down.

BARNEY

(Still breathless.)

Gotta get away.

DOCTOR

Calm down. How can you be sure he was telling you this?

BARNEY

(He speaks now with awe.)

His *eyes!* His *eyes.* I've never seen eyes like that before.

DOCTOR

You said they were friendly.

BARNEY

Not the leader's. I said the one looking over his shoulder.

DOCTOR

How did you know the other one was the leader.

BARNEY

(In careful, level tones again.)

Because everybody moved—everybody was standing there looking at me.
But everybody moved. These levers were in the back . . . or they went to
a big board, it looked like a board. And only this one with the black, black
shiny jacket and the scarf stayed at the window.

DOCTOR

He had slanted eyes. What did that make you think of?

BARNEY

I don't know. I've never seen eyes slanted like that.

*(He gestures with his hands carefully, in an attempt to describe the
eyes.)*

They began to be round—and went back like that—and like that. And
they went up like that. Can I draw it?

DOCTOR

You want to draw it?

91

BARNEY

Yes.

DOCTOR

(He hands him the materials.)

I'm giving you a pad and a pencil. You can open your eyes, and you can draw whatever you want. You can draw it now. Go ahead.

(Under deep hypnosis, the subject can open his eyes without in any way disturbing his trance. He will have no memory of the event when he is awakened, unless the operator tells him he can. Barney Hill is no artist, nor does the trance state enhance his ability. He draws a crude, but graphic sketch, and hands it back to the doctor. Then he continues the story.)

BARNEY

I'm driving.

DOCTOR

You're back in the car now?

BARNEY

Yes.

DOCTOR

You put down the binoculars, did you?

BARNEY

I put them down.

DOCTOR

Yes. And you got into the car. Did you speak to Betty?

BARNEY

I'm getting a hold on myself. I'm saying to myself, "Remember, you've got fortitude. You can drive a car." And I told Betty to look out—and the object was still around us. I could *feel* it around us. I saw it when we passed by the object. When I got in the car, it had swung around so that it was out there. I—I *know* it was out there.

(With conviction.)

Yeah—it's out there. But I don't know where.

(With genuine surprise.)

That's funny.

92

Yes—speak a little louder.

BARNEY

(He complies. The puzzlement is now mounting in his voice considerably.)

I know Route 3.

(Now another emotional crescendo.)

Oh, those eyes! They're in my *brain!*

(Very plaintively.)

Please can't I wake up?

(This is a plea to relieve him of anxiety.)

DOCTOR

(With reassurance.)

Stay asleep a little longer. We'll get through this now.
(Barney is showing signs of more emotion.)

All right. All right. You'll get through this all right. Follow your feelings. Tell me. They won't upset you so much now.

BARNEY

(Now his voice becomes dreamy and musing.)

They're *there.* Isn't that funny—all the woods. That crazy dog. She stays in the car all the time. Isn't that funny? She stays in the car!

DOCTOR

She doesn't bark at anything?

BARNEY

(Surprised at Delsey's lack of response.)

She just stays there.

DOCTOR

What about Betty?

BARNEY

(The quiet amazement in his voice is growing now, but his fear has subsided.)

I don't know.

DOCTOR

Isn't she saying anything?

BARNEY

(He is intense, reliving the scene. He doesn't seem to hear the doctor.)

I—I—don't understand. Are we being robbed? I—I—I—I—I—I don't know.

DOCTOR

What makes you think you're being robbed?

BARNEY

(A significant pause, then:)

I know what's in my mind, and I don't want to say it.

DOCTOR

Well, you can say it to me. You can say it now.

BARNEY

(In total awe.)

They're—*men!* All with dark jackets. And I don't have any money. I don't have anything.

(Now with great puzzlement.)

I don't know.

(Now back to awe again.)

Oh—oh, the eyes are there. Always the eyes are there. And they're telling me I don't have to be afraid.

(Now, as if he's peering ahead on the road.)

Is that an accident down the road? What's the red? The bright red?

DOCTOR

Bright red?

BARNEY

Yes. Orange and red.

DOCTOR

What is that? Where is that?

BARNEY

Right down the road.

DOCTOR

Down the road?

BARNEY

(Again living with the scene more than responding to the doctor.)

And I don't have to be afraid. But they won't talk to me.

DOCTOR

Who won't talk to you?

BARNEY

The men.

DOCTOR

In the vehicle?

BARNEY

No. They're standing in the road.

DOCTOR

There are men standing in the road?

BARNEY

Yes. They won't talk to me. Only the eyes are talking to me. I—I—I—I don't understand that. Oh—the eyes don't have a body. They're just eyes.

(He speaks now as if he were moving into another state of consciousness, almost catatonic. As if his eyes were fixated, concentrated completely on another pair of eyes. Then, very suddenly, he speaks with tremendous relief.)

I know. I *know.*

(He muses to himself.)

Yes, that's what it's got to be.

(He laughs very flatly, very self-reassuringly, and quietly.)

I know what it is. It's a wildcat. A wildcat up a tree.

(The relief indicated here is intense, as if he were finding something that had a basis of reality, as if he were searching for some explanation for an imponderable phenomenon. Then, he is not so sure:)

No. No. I know what it is. It's the Cheshire cat in *Alice in Wonderland.* Ah, I don't have to be afraid of that. It disappeared too, and only the eyes remained. That's all right. I'm not afraid.

DOCTOR

You didn't see this . . .

BARNEY

No, I saw it.

DOCTOR

You saw it. You're still seeing this man?

BARNEY

(Again in his own thoughts.)

The eyes are telling me, "Don't be afraid."

DOCTOR

That's the leader's eyes?

BARNEY

I don't even see the leader.

DOCTOR

The other eyes.

BARNEY

(With certainty.)

All I see are these eyes.

DOCTOR

The eyes now.

BARNEY

I'm not even afraid that they're not connected to a body. They're just *there*. They're just up close to me, pressing against my eyes. That's funny. I'm not afraid.

DOCTOR

Now—what's happened to this vehicle?

BARNEY

I don't see any vehicle.

DOCTOR

It's gone?

BARNEY

It's there. No. It's not gone. But I don't see it. I'm just there.

(This is, of course, puzzling to the doctor, but he must stay with the patient, live with his thoughts and statements, and try to draw out from him what the patient is seeing and experiencing, without leading him too much and permitting free expression.)

96

DOCTOR

And where are you? Are you in the car?

BARNEY

No. I'm just suspended. I'm just floating about.

(His voice is now relaxed, relieved.)

Oh, how funny—floating about. Just floating. I—I—want to get back to the car. Just floating about.

DOCTOR

You're really floating about—or is that just the way you feel?

BARNEY

That's just the way I feel.

DOCTOR

You're still outside the car?

BARNEY

No.

DOCTOR

You're in the car?

BARNEY

I'm not in the car. I'm not near the car. I'm not in the woods. I'm not on the road.

DOCTOR

Well—where are these men?

BARNEY

I don't know.

DOCTOR

On the road?

BARNEY

I don't know.

(He persists airily.)

I'm just floating about.

(Now he seems to be suspended. He speaks his thoughts at this point as if he's speaking directly to Betty.)

Heh, heh, Betty. That's the funniest thing, Betty. The funniest thing. I never believed in flying saucers but—I don't know. Mighty mysterious. Yeah, well, I guess I won't say anything to anybody about this. It's too ridiculous, isn't it? Oh yes, really funny. Wonder where they came from? Oh, gee, I wish I had the—I wish I had gone with them . . .

DOCTOR

You wish you had gone with them?

BARNEY

Yes. Oh, what an experience to go to some distant planet.

(A pause as he reflects, then:)

Maybe this will prove the existence of God.

(Another brief pause.)

Isn't that funny? To look for the existence of God on another planet?

(Now directly as if to Betty:)

Were you scared? I wasn't. No, I wasn't afraid. I wasn't afraid, anyway. Ridiculous, just you and I here talking about it.

(Now his tone changes, as if considerable time has elapsed—something very disturbing is being passed over—this hints strongly at the amnesia gap.)

Well—it looks as if we're getting into Portsmouth a little later than I expected . . .

(His voice trails off. The doctor waits a moment, decides that this should wait for an evaluation of the effect of the session thus far.)

DOCTOR

All right. We'll stop there. You will be calm and relaxed. You will forget everything that we have had in this period together, until I ask you to recall it again. You will forget everything we have talked about until I ask you to recall it again.

(The repetition is intentional, to reinforce the command.)

It will not trouble you, it will not worry you. You will not be concerned. You will remain comfortable and relaxed and have no pain, no aches, no anxiety.

(The doctor then reinforces the cue words for future sessions.)

You will recall what I want you to recall, do what I tell you to do. You will forget what has transpired here until I ask you to recall it again. You're comfortable and relaxed now. No aches, no pains . . . no anxiety . . . All right, Barney, you may wake up now. You'll be comfortable and relaxed.

(Barney opens his eyes, a little groggy now. But he comes to full consciousness quickly.)

98

BARNEY

(Looks at his wristwatch.)

Wow. Nine-thirty. Didn't you bring me in here at ten minutes after eight?

DOCTOR

Yes.

BARNEY

Where was I?

DOCTOR

Right here with me.

BARNEY

Where are my cig—was I about to reach for a cigarette?

DOCTOR

Looked that way. Go ahead and have one.

BARNEY

I thought I was coming in here, and you asked me to take this seat, this chair, then I was going to reach for a cigarette. I never reached for it.

DOCTOR

(He is studying Barney's reactions to assure himself that Barney is fully out of the trance.)

How do you feel?

BARNEY

I feel fine.

DOCTOR

Good. Know what happened here?

BARNEY

You put me into a trance. I know the purpose of it, but—

(There is a pause.)

DOCTOR

That's all right. We'll continue this next week. A week from today . . .

* * *

The first probe into the unknown had been made. But the amnesic veil had scarcely been pierced. What was to follow, none of the three knew—and at this point, only the doctor was aware of what had been uncovered.

All through the session, Betty had been waiting, with some apprehension, in the waiting room. She made the pretense of fingering through a copy of the *New Yorker* and *McCalls,* but with little success at reading them. The waiting room is down the hall from Dr. Simon's office. Even though the offices are soundproof, Betty was aware of the emotional outbursts Barney had made at the crucial points. Anticipating that this could happen, the doctor had scheduled the Hills at a time when the offices were free of other people. Since the building was empty of all sounds, Barney's two major outbursts were intensified by the silence and Betty's own close attention to what might be happening.

"It hit me with such force that I sat there and cried all the time," Betty Hill recalls. "And I sat there wondering what kind of condition Barney would be in when he came out of the doctor's office. There were two big outbursts, the second not as loud as the first. The rest of the time it had been fairly quiet. So I waited—waited for him to come out. And when he did, both he and the doctor were smiling—pleasant, and I was quite surprised. So I didn't think I should say anything to Barney at all about my crying and things. I just played it by ear, and asked him what happened. I asked him if he was upset, and he said no, he wasn't. There was nothing to be upset about, he said."

Barney had no true recall about what had happened in the session except for some vague and fleeting impressions. It did not seem to him that he had been under hypnosis for more than a few minutes. He felt no discomfort at all, and only his watch indicated to him that over an hour and a half had gone by.

He was insatiably curious about what had happened during the session, but of course there was no way whatever of knowing until the doctor would give him the instruction to remember. There was no feeling associated with the lost time period.

On the way back to Portsmouth, they stopped by the International Pancake House, a splashy, chrome restaurant on Route 1 leading up to New Hampshire, near Saugus.

They ordered a heaping breakfast, Barney at that time unaffected by the strains of his session. Betty was pressing Barney for details about how he felt, and though she had been in hypnosis for the test sessions, she was anxious to find out Barney's full reaction to the therapeutic session. Barney reassured her that there wasn't anything upsetting about it, and Betty continued to withhold from Barney the fact that she had been in tears most of the time he was in the doctor's office.

Barney felt fully relaxed until they got back to their home in Portsmouth. He then began to have an overwhelming fear of something—something entirely vague and undefinable, something that he felt he should feel guilty about. He was very frightened about this feeling, as if he had a tremendous pressure in his head. He didn't relate it particularly to the hypnosis. He describes it as something buried in his unconscious, trying to work its way up to his conscious. He got upset enough to start to call the doctor about it, then decided to wait. The thought flickered through his mind that he might not want to go through with the rest of the program, or at least that he ask the doctor to take Betty on next, and give him a rest. But his fears gradually left him, and the anticipation and urge to know, to penetrate the mystery, took over.

CHAPTER SIX

When Barney Hill left the office after the first session that Saturday morning, Dr. Simon picked up the microphone of his tape recorder, and dictated:

> During the explosive parts of the patient's discussion, he showed very marked emotional discharge. Tears rolled down his cheeks, he would clutch his face, his head, and writhe in considerable agony. When he first described the eyes, he drew circles in the air which were in the shape of the eye that he ultimately drew. He actually drew a curve representing the left side of the face, and drew the left eye on it, without any other detail. When asked which eye this was, he showed some confusion. Then he drew the rest of the shape of the head, and also drew in the other eye and the cap and the visor. And then, as an afterthought, he drew in the scarf. Mrs. Hill was induced by post-hypnotic suggestion for reinforcement in anticipation of the time when she will be interviewed. She was in the waiting room for the entire period.

It was obvious in this first step of the procedure that Barney had only partially gone beyond the threshold that had blocked his conscious memory on that night. There was still only a vague and disconnected, dream-like description of the enormous object approaching him, the eyes of the figure aboard the ship, a bizarre floating sensation, an apparent accident down the road, and figures in the road with no explainable motive. All through the conscious period of the event, Barney's description was sharp and clear, with attention to the minutest detail. Then at the point he reexperienced Indian Head, his description became vague and fragmented—detached. There seemed to be two resistance points, one at the moment he raised the binoculars to his eyes, just after he had driven off and the object moved over the car, and the other at some point farther down the road, a roadblock. Here the account Barney gave leaped to a comment about arriving home at Portsmouth later than he had expected.

All through the account under hypnosis, Barney had indicated his deep-set resistance to the idea of Unidentified Flying Objects. As Barney later said, the likelihood of the object being a product of wishful thinking on his part seemed very slim, indeed. His strong objections to the existence of the phenomenon were deeply set, although his ambivalence about the experince was puzzling.

Dr. Simon was orienting his treatment to the recall of the patients' experiences and their accompanying thinking, and feeling—not to the establishment of the reality or nonreality of unidentified objects. Whether the experiences were true in the absolute sense was far less important to the doctor than their existence as a part of the patients' past or present mental life. Throughout the investigation, tests to establish reality were, of course, in progress, but no preliminary conclusions were possible at this time. A great deal of evidence remained to be obtained, particularly from Betty Hill, who had not yet been heard from.

The incident had little or no precedent. The roadblock, the figures Barney recalled in the road, and the strange reactions Barney had in the latter part of the session would need further exploration, as well as any possible distortion or fantasy.

Barney's pleas to Dr. Simon to let him wake up came at those moments when emotions were resurgent and memories were probably painful. Many recorded cases indicate the subject's resistance to the operator as he attempts to push past the block holding back the conscious memory. Only the operator's patient persistence can overcome the resistance.

The doctor's decision to keep Barney in the trance in spite of the intense abreaction, or emotional outburst, was based on the doctor's judgment of how much he could be safely permitted to endure.

*   *   *

On February 29, 1964, the Hills arrived punctually for their appointment, Betty being reinforced again, and Barney remaining in the office for his second therapeutic session. Before putting him in the customary trance, Dr. Simon asked him a few questions in review.

DOCTOR

Well—how have you been, Mr. Hill?

104

BARNEY

I've been fine. Physically, I've been fine, at least. But I have been upset . . .

DOCTOR

Tell me about it.

BARNEY

Well, last week after I left your office, I began having what I thought was remembrance of what had taken place in the office, and this became quite disturbing to me.

DOCTOR

And what did you remember?

BARNEY

I remembered "eyes." And I thought these "eyes" were telling me something. And I became alarmed because I thought my very sanity was in jeopardy. I considered calling you after reaching home, but I did not. And my wife and I went out to visit friends, and that relieved the tension.

DOCTOR

Is that the only thing you remember?

BARNEY

Basically, yes. Another interesting thing that seemed to happen, I began to pick out little details about my trip, which I thought was interesting, because I never thought of these things before. I had given no thought to them. Such as stopping in New York State and buying a six-pack of beer and Betty and I taking it to a motel. I thought of how when we were told we could take the little doggie in, and I put her in the bathroom and tied her with a long chain because the bathroom was tiled. In case she made an accident, it wouldn't soil the rug. And these things seemed to come back to me . . .

DOCTOR

They seem to be things you hadn't told me, but of course you wouldn't remember that. But I had told you to remember *everything*. And these seem to be things that you skipped.

BARNEY

Oh. I see.

DOCTOR

Because when you are in a trance you are told to remember everything. And these seem to be irrelevant details. But you hadn't mentioned them, the ones you mentioned now, so maybe you felt a little guilty that you hadn't although they are probably, irrelevant. Speaking of that, had you had much to drink on this trip?

BARNEY

That was the only thing.

DOCTOR

The six-pack? The two of you?

BARNEY

Yes. We each had a can of beer Sunday evening, and then we retired. And we brought back the four cans left.

DOCTOR

I see. You hadn't been doing much drinking on the trip at all?

BARNEY

No.

DOCTOR

Did this anxiety fade away as the week went along?

BARNEY

It more or less did. Yes, it did. It became sharpened last night. Last week, Saturday morning, when I got up I felt a little nauseous as if in anticipating, in anticipation of this. Last night, this occurred again.

DOCTOR

You are quite concerned about this experience. You'll begin to feel all right about that. You'll be all right. You won't have to worry about your sanity.

(This reassurance may have hypnotic force since repeated contact with the doctor at times increases suggestibility. Here was a warning that the repressed material would have to be dealt with carefully. It was threatening to break through prematurely in the absence of the doctor. He would make future instructions for amnesia more compelling until things had been worked through to a greater extent.)

But tell me—what do you think about this "eye" business? What do you think of? Does it connect up with anything? Does it suggest any thoughts to you?

106

BARNEY

No, it doesn't. Well, yes—I might say the only connection it does have is a foreboding type of effect. Of betraying. Of having been given a warning. This is the only kind of effect it has on me.

DOCTOR

You feel you have been given a warning?

BARNEY

Yes.

DOCTOR

Ever have that thought or feeling before?

BARNEY

No, I've never had anything like that before.

DOCTOR

About hypnosis—do you feel the eyes play a part in that?

BARNEY

No, I don't think so.

DOCTOR

Well, you wanted me to take Betty, and take you off the hook for a while. Is that it?

(The doctor refers to a brief mention of this Barney had made as he entered the office.)

BARNEY

Well, that's what I thought.

DOCTOR

Do you recall the eyes as part of the session we had? Or was it something that just hung over with you?

BARNEY

The eyes just seemed to hang over from that.

DOCTOR

Well, that was the last thing we got to. It was last Saturday, and it did carry over a bit. I'll see to it that you don't have that anxiety. We'll resume.

(He is now preparing to put Barney in the deep-trance state again.)

You don't remember now where we left off. We'll go back and I can probably take some of that over again. Let's go back a bit before the eyes came into the picture.

107

*(The doctor gives the cue words. Barney's eyes close immediately,
and his head nods forward on his chest.)*

You are deeper and deeper and deeper asleep. Fully relaxed, and deeper
and deeper and deeper asleep. You are in a deep sleep. You have no fear,
no anxiety. And now you will not be troubled by anything you remember.
But you will remember *everything*. You will remember everything. All
your feelings and all of your actions. They will not trouble you now, because they are here, with us. They will not trouble you, and I am here.

*(The repetition is to reinforce the instruction. It may or may not be
needed.)*

Your sleep is deeper and deeper, you are completely relaxed. Far, far
asleep. Deeper and deeper asleep. . . . Now you will remember everything that we have gone over about your trip from Montreal. You will go
back a bit, *before* you had the experience with the eyes. And you can
begin to tell me about the experience with the unidentified object. You
can start a little before we left off. Wherever you feel you freshly remember something.

BARNEY

(His voice is again flat and colorless; he is fully in trance.)

I'm remembering being in the woods, parked. And I have Delsey. And
I'm walking her around the back of the car. And Betty had asked if I
would leave Delsey out. And Betty is standing off to the left of the car
with the binoculars, and she is looking at this unidentified flying object.
And I am standing there looking up and down the highway, because I
am looking for other cars. And I give Betty the dog's chain, and I ask
her to let me see with the binoculars. And I only see a plane, flying in
the sky. And I tell her this is a plane, and it is on its way to Montreal,
where we just left. And I want to hurry and get back to the car and
return to Portsmouth. And Betty gets into the car, and she says, "Isn't
that strange?" And I'm driving along, and she said, "It's still out there."
And I think it's strange, and think it must be a Piper Cub. And it's not
making any sound. And I want to hurry up and get away, because this
is *strange,* this strange thing flying around. And I believe very strongly
that it can see us. And it is late at night, and I feel I am exposed.

DOCTOR

In what way do you feel exposed?

I feel I am in an exposed situation where my car lights are very bright. And it's dark where I am. And I know this object is flitting around in the sky. I think of a fly flitting aimlessly in the sky, with no pattern, as it is hovering over something it is about to light on. And I think this thing out there is just hovering around. And Betty is telling me to stop again. And I do. And I said, "Betty, what are you trying to do? Make me see something that isn't there?" And I became very angry with her. Because I think this is a plane, something that we can explain. And I believe, rather feel, that she is trying to make me think it is not. And this irritates me.

(In his normal conversation, Barney seldom starts his sentences with and. *Yet here, he seems to do so constantly, almost in Biblical style.)*

DOCTOR

What was her reply to this?

BARNEY

Betty's reply was, "Well, why is it doing what it is doing? Why doesn't it go away? What is it doing?"

DOCTOR

Now this will not upset you. You can tell me your feelings, but you will not be upset about it. Go ahead.

BARNEY

I said, "Betty it can't—I was thinking—I did not say that to Betty. I was thinking, my mind was thinking, it cannot be a plane.

(Note the concern for truth and accuracy here, making sure that he does not make any misstatements to the doctor.)

This is why I became upset because Betty was telling me it wasn't acting like any type of conventional flying craft. I somehow knew this and did not want to be told this.

DOCTOR

Did you feel that it wasn't acting like a conventional flying craft?

BARNEY

Yes, I did.

DOCTOR

In what ways?

BARNEY

Well, it flew very peculiarly. It did not fly in a definite straight line. It would go up suddenly . . .

(This is a very common UFO report.)

DOCTOR

Just rise vertically.

BARNEY

Just rise in a very straight-up position, and then fly for a short while horizontally. And then it would dip down. And as it did this, I noticed that the row of lights on it seemed to tilt and level off, as I imagined the body of this thing, of the position of this thing would be in.

DOCTOR

As if it were banking?

BARNEY

As if it were banking. But banking didn't fit, it doesn't seem to fit what I'm trying to describe. Because if it had banked, I could think of a plane, and know it would be a plane. It just tilted. It did not bank in a swooping bank. It just, from a horizontal line, became a vertical line.

(Another common UFO report.)

DOCTOR

How would you describe the shape of it?

BARNEY

I could not outline the shape.

DOCTOR

An ordinary plane, even a Piper Cub, has to be somewhat cigar-shaped. Even big helicopters.

BARNEY

Yes. The row of lights was like a row in a cigar-shaped pattern, only that it was a straight line that I saw, and it was elongated.

(Many reports of UFO's in the Air Force and NICAP files indicate a cigar-shaped object in the distance, but as it draws nearer, it becomes discernible as the lateral profile of a large disc.)

110

DOCTOR

You didn't surmise that this thing was round, like a so-called flying saucer?

BARNEY

No, I didn't see that.

DOCTOR

It did have some resemblance to ordinary planes, then?

BARNEY

At this time, yes.

DOCTOR

You imply that it changed shape later?

BARNEY

Yes. As I continued down the highway, I had a peculiar feeling that it was spinning.

DOCTOR

Like a top?

BARNEY

Like a top.

DOCTOR

Now, when you spoke of this before, you spoke of some lights down the highway. Red lights, I believe. Does that ring any bells? Lights down the highway—as if some men were working down there?

BARNEY

Yes. But that is further on.

DOCTOR

I see. Go on then, in your own way.

BARNEY

So I continued to look, and I would stop and leave and go. And Betty would insist that I stop. And we did this several times.

DOCTOR

Was this all to stop and look again?

BARNEY

To stop and look. And when I can see the tramway on the mountain up ahead, and I knew where I was, and I knew I would eventually pass by the Old Man of the Mountain. And the object seemed to have speeded

111

up, and to go to the right side of the Old Man of the Mountain. And I was going around the left side of the base. And when I got to where the Old Man of the Mountain figure was, I stopped again and got a good look. And I knew that this object still seemed to be out there. And it was stopped when I stopped. I thought this was strange.

(His voice becomes more and more intense as if he were watching what he describes.)

And it moved—oh, I did not see it move. I started driving the car, and Betty said it is moving behind the mountains again. And I was approaching a clear spot where I saw two wigwams on my right. And I knew I was close to Indian Head. And I saw this object far off even as I approached this spot by slowing down and looking. And then I returned to looking down the road to drive, and Betty became very excited. She said, "Oh, Barney, you must stop the car. Look what it is doing!"

(The doctor is encouraging the repetition of the story, to check for inconsistencies.)

And I became slower in my driving. And I looked through the windshield. And on her side the object looked as if it were right out there in front of the windshield, only I had to look up to see it. And I must have been driving five miles an hour, because I had to put the car in low gear so it would not stall. And I said, "Oh, this is funny." I thought of all the thoughts I had back since I first saw this thing. I thought it was a Piper Cub, I thought it was an airliner, I thought it was a military craft and that the military was having fun with us. And I came to a complete stop, and I reached down on the floor of the car to my left and picked up the tire wrench and kept it in my hand.

DOCTOR

You had already got the wrench from the trunk of the car?

BARNEY

Yes. And I kept hold of it and stuck it through my belt. And I got out of the car with my binoculars, and I stood with my arm on the door, and my right arm partly on top of the hood, the roof, of the car. And I look. And before I could get the binoculars up to my eyes, even as I did get them up there, the car was vibrating from the motor running. So I stepped away. And the object shifted, in an arc. And I thought, "How remarkable, it was a perfect arc." But it continued to have a

112

forward look, facing me, as if it swung and did not move from a position, but just swung from a position with the front facing me.

(Again, a typical pattern of many low-altitude UFO reports.)

And it moved to my left. And I continued to look and begin walking across the highway, shaking my head and blinking my eyes that this was just some kind of something that I could not explain.

(He is now at the moment when he reached his emotional crisis in the first session. But he is calm now, not at all as he was then, partially due to the doctor's suggestion in the trance induction.)

And I hoped if I looked down the highway and looked back, it would be gone. And I continued to walk across the highway toward the front of my car down the road. And I continued to look with my binoculars each time I would stop, and look up. And I would walk further toward it, and stop and look up. And I thought, "How interesting, there is the military pilot, and he is looking at me." And I looked at him, and he looked at me. And there were several others looking at me, and I thought of a huge dirigible, and I thought of all the men lined up at the window of this huge dirigible and were looking down at me. Then they moved to the back and I continued to look at this one man that stood there, and I kept looking at him and looking at him.

(The contrast in his description here, steady and unemotional, compared to the previous session is marked.)

Is this the man you call the leader?

BARNEY

He was dressed differently. And I thought of the Navy and the submarine, and I thought the men that moved back were just dressed in blue denims. But this other man was dressed in a black shiny coat, with a cap on.

DOCTOR

When you spoke of the hoodlums back on your trip, did they wear these black, shiny coats that they often do?

BARNEY

No, they did not.

(The doctor is checking to see if there was any influence on Barney's mind from the Montreal experience. Could the echo of the hoodlums Barney saw be reflected in what he pictures here? Both represent potential danger, resulting in fear, the common denominator.)

113

DOCTOR

There is no resemblance between them and this leader?

BARNEY

No. These Canadian men in Montreal were dressed in conventional dress, but the hair was in duck-bill style. And I thought of them as hoodlums because of their hair style.

DOCTOR

You can get back to this leader.

BARNEY

I looked at him, and he looked at me. And I thought, "This is not going to harm me." And I wanted to get back to Betty and discuss this interesting thing we were looking at. And I kept looking and he looked at me, and then I came back to the car. And Betty was flopping in the front seat. And I said, "Betty, were you excited?" And she said, "Why didn't you come back? I was screaming for you to come back. I could not understand why you were going out across the road."

DOCTOR

You hadn't heard her scream?

BARNEY

No, I did not hear her scream. And I just thought she was flopping on the seat. But she said she had leaned down across the seat so that she would be able to be closer to open the door and holler for me to get back in the car.

(The reassurance at the beginning of the trance appears to have reduced the terror of this recollection.)

I returned to the car and began driving down the highway. And I drove quite a few miles and noticed I was not on Route 3. . . .

(Here, for the first time, the door to the forgotten time period begins to swing open. His block had always been on the field at Indian Head, followed by blurring of consciousness after he had begun to drive away from the object. Betty, also, had never been able to bridge this point, except, she thought, the possibility that her dreams might be reality.)

114

And I could not understand that, because it is a straight highway. And I looked and I was being signaled to stop. And I thought, I wonder if there has been an accident. I do have the tire wrench. I'll put it near my hand. . . .

DOCTOR

Let me interrupt again: What was it you saw down the highway?

BARNEY

I saw a group of men, and they were standing in the highway. And it was brightly lit up, as if it were almost daylight, but not really day. It was not the kind of light of day, but it was brightly lighted. . . .

(Another description typical of many low-altitude UFO reports, including those of police officers and technical men.)

And they began coming toward me. And I did not think after that of my tire wrench. And I became afraid if I did think of this as a weapon, I would be harmed. And if I did not, I would not be harmed. And they came and assisted me.

DOCTOR

Who assisted you?

BARNEY

These men.

DOCTOR

They assisted you out of the car?

BARNEY

I felt very weak. I felt very weak, but I wasn't afraid. And I can't even think of being confused. I am not bewildered, I can't even think of questioning what is happening to me. And I am being assisted. And I am thinking of a picture I saw many years ago, and this man is being carried to the electric chair. And I think of this, and I think I am in this man's position. But I'm not being carried to the electric chair. And I think of this, and I think I'm in this man's position. But I'm not, but I think my feet are dragging, and I think of this picture. And I am not afraid. I feel like I am dreaming.

(This again, is a denial of fear. Later, when Barney listened to the playback of the tapes, he likened this event to the feeling he had when he went into hypnosis with the doctor. The questions have since been on his mind: If this is true, was he being put into hypnosis by these "men," and if so, was his amnesia caused by this?)

115

DOCTOR

Are you asleep at the time?

BARNEY

My eyes are tightly closed, and I seem—disassociated.

DOCTOR

Disassociated? Is that what you said?

BARNEY

Yes.

DOCTOR

(Checking Barney's definition.)

What do you mean by that?

BARNEY

I am there—and I am not there.

DOCTOR

Where is Betty through all of this?

BARNEY

I don't know. I'm trying to think, where's Betty? I don't know.

DOCTOR

Are these men part of your dream?

BARNEY

(Firmly, and with conviction.)

They are there, and I am there. I know they are there. But everything is black. My eyes are tightly closed. I can't believe what I think.

DOCTOR

Is there anything else that you think that you haven't told me?

BARNEY

Yes.

DOCTOR

You can tell me now.

BARNEY

I am always thinking of mental pictures, because my eyes are closed. And I think I am going up a slight incline, and my feet have stopped bumping on the rocks. That's funny. I thought of my feet bumping on the rocks. And they are not going up smoothly. But I'm afraid to open my eyes, because I am being told strongly by myself to keep my eyes closed, and don't open them. And I don't want to be operated on.

DOCTOR

You don't want to be operated on. What makes you think of an operation?

BARNEY

I don't know.

DOCTOR

Have you ever been operated on?

BARNEY

Only for my tonsils.

DOCTOR

Does this feel like that time?

BARNEY

I think like that, but my eyes are closed, and I only have mental pictures. And I am not in pain. And I can feel a slight feeling. My groin feels cold.

DOCTOR

Is that like any feeling with the operation?

BARNEY

I'm not being operated on. I am lying on something, and I think of the doctor putting something in my ear. When I was a boy. The doctor put something in my ear, and I looked up at it, and he explained to me that you could peek into the ear and light it up with this thing. And I think of that. . . . And I feel like the doctor did not pain me, and I will be very careful and be very still and will cooperate, and I won't be harmed.

(He pauses.)

DOCTOR

Yes. Go on.

BARNEY

I can't remember.

DOCTOR

You were thinking about this when you were on the road?

BARNEY

I was thinking about this when I was lying on this table.

117

DOCTOR

Where were you lying down?

BARNEY

I thought I was inside something. But I did not dare open my eyes. I had been told to keep my eyes closed.

DOCTOR

Who told you that?

BARNEY

The man.

DOCTOR

What man?

BARNEY

That I saw through the binoculars.

(He speaks matter-of-factly, as if the doctor should certainly know all about this.)

DOCTOR

Was this one of the men in the road?

BARNEY

No.

DOCTOR

These men in the road—what part did they play?

BARNEY

They took me and carried me up this ramp.

DOCTOR

Carried you up the ramp?

BARNEY

I know I was going up something, and my feet were dragging. And this man spoke to me, and I knew I had heard his voice, and he was looking at me when I was in the road.

DOCTOR

This happened after you were in the road?

BARNEY

This happened after I was in the road at Indian Head. I thought I had driven quite a distance from Indian Head when I got lost and found myself in the woods.

118

DOCTOR

You got lost after Indian Head, is that it?

BARNEY

I was not on Route 3, and I couldn't understand why.

DOCTOR

Was Indian Head before or after you saw this object?

BARNEY

I don't understand the question.

DOCTOR

Well, was it after you were at Indian Head that you saw this object?

BARNEY

It was at Indian Head that I saw the object standing in the sky. And it is after Indian Head. I have driven several miles, I think I have driven a lot of miles. And the road is not Route 3. But is in a heavily wooded area. But it is a road. And this is when I am flagged down.

DOCTOR

You are flagged down?

BARNEY

Yes.

DOCTOR

These men flagged you down?

BARNEY

Yes.

DOCTOR

How many were there?

BARNEY

I thought I saw a cluster of six men. Because three of them came to me, and three did not.

DOCTOR

How were they dressed?

BARNEY

I was told at that time to close my eyes. And I closed my eyes.

DOCTOR

But before you closed your eyes, didn't you see them?

119

BARNEY

They were all in dark clothing. And they were all dressed alike.

DOCTOR

Were they white men?

BARNEY

I don't know by the color. But it did not seem that they had different faces from white men.

DOCTOR

Were they in a uniform of any sort?

BARNEY

I thought of a Navy pea jacket, just before I closed my eyes.

DOCTOR

Did they say anything else besides "Close your eyes?" Did they tell you why they were stopping you?

BARNEY

They didn't tell me anything. They didn't say anything.

DOCTOR

Was there any vehicle around?

BARNEY

I didn't see any.

DOCTOR

You didn't see any vehicle?

BARNEY

I was told to close my eyes because I saw two eyes coming close to mine.

(The fragment in the first session where he thinks of a wildcat, or the Cheshire cat, perhaps.)

And I felt like the eyes had pushed into my eyes.

DOCTOR

Were these the same eyes of the leader that you saw from the binoculars?

BARNEY

Yes.

DOCTOR

Do you think it was the same man?

I didn't think of anything. I didn't think of the man in the sky in the machine that I saw. I just saw these eyes, and I closed mine.

(His voice becomes rather awed each time he mentions the eyes.)

And I got out of the car, and I put my left leg on the ground and two men helped me out. And I did not walk. I felt like I was being supported. And I did not go very far, I thought, before I felt I was going up, going up a ramp of some kind. My eyes were tightly closed, and I was afraid to open them.

(Another pause, then:)

Oh, that doesn't say what I mean.

DOCTOR

Well, try again.

BARNEY

I didn't want to open them. It was comfortable to keep them closed.

(Barney reflects the desire to shut out the experience.)

DOCTOR

Were these men holding you?

BARNEY

They were by my side, and I had a funny feeling, because I knew they were holding me, but I couldn't feel them.

DOCTOR

Is this what you mean last time when you spoke of floating?

BARNEY

I felt floating, suspended. I am thinking of getting out of the car, and I had not thought that these men when they helped me out of the car—I could not feel them. And I only became aware that I could not feel them when we were going up an incline. And then I felt I could not feel them. My arms were in the position of being supported. But I was not walking. And I want to peek. I want to look. I want to look.

(This was the feeling in the first session, now clarified.)

DOCTOR

Yes, go on. This won't trouble you now. You can tell me.

BARNEY

I opened my eyes.

DOCTOR

You opened your eyes. What did you see?

BARNEY

I saw a hospital operating room. It was pale blue. Sky blue. And I closed my eyes.

DOCTOR

Do you remember the operating room when you had your tonsils out?

BARNEY

I remember the hospital, and I was in there because they thought I had appendicitis. And I stayed there for thirteen or fourteen—No, it was thirteen days.

(Again, the insistence on absolute literal accuracy, even on irrelevant details.)

And I used to walk down the corridor and peek into the operating room. And I thought of that. It wasn't when I had my tonsils out.

DOCTOR

Was that operating room in the hospital blue?

BARNEY

No. It was bright lights.

DOCTOR

Bright lights?

BARNEY

Bright lights. Like electric bulbs. But this room was not like that. It was spotless. I thought of everything being so clean. And I closed my eyes.

DOCTOR

Did you feel you were going to be operated on?

BARNEY

No.

DOCTOR

Did you feel you were being attacked in any way?

BARNEY

No.

DOCTOR

Did you feel you were *going* to be attacked in any way?

122

BARNEY

No.

DOCTOR

You said your groin felt cold . . .

BARNEY

I was lying on a table, and I thought someone was putting a cup around my groin, and then it stopped. And I thought: How funny.

DOCTOR

Speak a little louder, please.

BARNEY

I thought how funny. If I keep real quiet and real still, I won't be harmed.
(Again the magical ritual.)

And it will be over. And I will just stay here and pretend that I am anywhere and think of God and think of Jesus and think that I am not afraid. And I am getting off the table, and I've got a big grin on my face, and I feel greatly relieved. And I am walking, and I am being guided. And my eyes are closed, and I open my eyes, and that is the car. And the lights are off, and the motor is not running. And Delsey is under the seat. And I reached under and touched her, and she is in a tight ball under the seat, and I sit back. And I see Betty is coming down the road, and she gets into the car, and I am grinning at her and she is grinning back at me. And we both seem so elated and we are really happy. And I'm thinking it isn't too bad. How funny. I had no reason to fear. And we look and I see a bright moon. And I laugh and say, "Well, there it goes." And I'm happy.

DOCTOR

You mean this object was gone?

BARNEY

Yes.

DOCTOR

It had gone?

BARNEY

It was going.

DOCTOR

Going. Could you still see it?

BARNEY

It was a bright, huge ball. Orange. It was a beautiful, bright ball. And it was going. And it was gone. And we were in darkness, and I put on

123

the lights of the car and looked down the road. And I thought there is a bend in the road. And we begin driving, and I could see a slight incline, and then I drove and came back to Route 3, because I was on a cement road. And I thought, oh boy, if I could only find a restaurant and get a cup of coffee. And Betty and I feel, I feel real hilarious, like a feeling of well-being and great relief.

DOCTOR

What were you relieved about?

BARNEY

I am relieved because I feel like I've been in a harrowing situation, and there was nothing damaging or harmful about it. And I feel greatly relieved.

DOCTOR

And the flying object was gone?

BARNEY

Yes.

DOCTOR

And it didn't come back?

BARNEY

Betty is giggling, and she said, "Do you believe in flying saucers now?" And I said, "Oh, Betty, don't be ridiculous. Of course I don't." And we heard a beeping and the car buzzed, and I kept silent.

DOCTOR

You heard a beeping.

BARNEY

It was a beeping sound. Beep—beep—beep—beep—beep.

DOCTOR

Was your radio on?

BARNEY

No. My radio was not on. It was so late, and I did not think I could get a station. So when I left Canada, I cut my radio off. I played my radio in Quebec, because I thought it was funny, humorous to get the Canadian stations, and every word was spoken in French. And the music sounded different to my ears. When I left Montreal I became determined to drive home, and I cut my radio off. I don't play my radio when I am driving.

124

DOCTOR

Now these beeps. You heard these beeps again. Did they sound like some of these beeps you get on a radio, when you have code signals? Or what did they sound like?

BARNEY

(Rapidly and sharply.)

Beep—beep—beep. They sound like beeps.

DOCTOR

Well, what did you do? What did you think about them?

BARNEY

I thought it was strange, the beep—beep—beep. And at the first beep or two, I touched the steering wheel with my finger tips, because I thought I felt a vibration when I heard the beep. And as it continued, Betty looked to the back, and I slowed the car down and stopped. And I said to Betty, "Is there something shifting in the car?"

DOCTOR

Did she say anything about hearing the beeps?

BARNEY

She said, "What is that noise?" And we looked in the back, and Delsey had climbed up on the back seat, and her ears were popped up, and the beep, beep, beep. And we said, "Oh—oh, do you think that thing is still around?" I called it a thing, Betty called it a flying saucer. And we had no answer, and we both thought, how strange. And I thought, that's very peculiar. I wonder if I can make the car do that. So I drove the car fast, and then would decelerate, rapidly. And I swerved over to the left of the highway and back to the right. And I came to a complete stop and accelerated rapidly. But I could not seem to get that sound. And we drove down the highway. And I saw the road for the expressway: 17 miles to Concord. And I drove to Concord and down Route 4.

DOCTOR

Did the beeping follow you there?

BARNEY

No. I did not hear any more beeps.

DOCTOR

After you got on the Concord road, is that it?

No, I did not hear any beeps quite a distance before I reached the main highway. Because Route 3 was also concrete, where I heard the beeping. And I heard it two times: when I got into the car, and when I returned to the car and started down the highway. And I thought, "What is that, Betty?" And we did not hear it anymore.

(He is referring back to Indian Head.)

DOCTOR

But she heard it too?

BARNEY

She heard it, too. And we did not hear it again until after we had been in the woods and had returned to Route 3. And she asked me, did I believe in flying saucers? And I did not want to say what I really believed.

DOCTOR

What did you really believe?

BARNEY

I believed that we had seen and been a part of something different than anything I had ever seen before.

DOCTOR

You mean also with the experience with these men in the operating room?

BARNEY

Yes.

DOCTOR

Did you fear you had been kidnapped?

BARNEY

I didn't use that word. I can only use that word intellectually. I did not feel that I had been kidnapped. But I think of kidnapping when you are being harmed.

DOCTOR

And you weren't harmed?

BARNEY

No.

DOCTOR

You had no idea why this was done?

BARNEY

I was anxious to get home and look at my groin.

126

You wanted to look at your groin. Afraid that they had done something harmful?

BARNEY

I wanted to look. I thought, this is proof that something happened to me. And I was unsure. And I would waver, feeling that it can't be. And then I would think, but it did happen. And I would think when I get home and look at my groin, I will touch whatever touched me, and see if there is a mark. And this is what I thought.

(But this thought was completely gone when he reached full consciousness. When he arrived home, he did examine himself, but had no memory whatever of the reason he did so.)

DOCTOR

All right. Go on.

BARNEY

I drove home and I walked into the house. And I was too tired to bring in the luggage. And Betty got out of the car, and she took Delsey, and she let her relieve herself on the grass and brought her in. And I went into the bathroom and examined myself and saw nothing wrong. And I went into the bedroom, and I kept thinking that something is around me. I went to the window, and I looked up into the morning sky, and I went to the back door and opened it and looked at the sky. And I thought, something is around, somewhere. And Betty and I retired, talking. Wasn't that strange, whatever happened. And I could not remember anything that happened except that I was at Indian Head. And I went to bed. And when we woke up, we decided we would not ever tell anyone. And would only talk about it to each other. And I said, "But Betty, will you draw a picture of what you think you saw? And I will." And we drew pictures, and they were identical. And Betty called her sister and told her sister.

DOCTOR

You mentioned something about spots on the car.

BARNEY

Betty came away from the telephone, and she said, "Where is the compass, where is the compass?" And when Betty does that to me, I immediately get angry. And I said, "I don't know what you're talking about, Betty." And she said, "The compass! The compass! Where's the compass?" And I said, "In the drawer, where it always is." And she got it, and I was irritated because when she got excited like this, she didn't think to open the drawer and find it. And she went out of the house, and I went to the bedroom window, which is the front window of our house, and I thought, this thing is getting the best of Betty. And we'd better forget this as soon as possible. And stop remembering it. And she stormed into the house, and said, "Barney! Come here! Come here, quick!" And I walked out, and I looked at the compass when she placed it by the car. And I said, "Oh, this is ridiculous, Betty. After all, the car is metal, and any metal will attract and cause a compass to react this way." And she said, "Look what it does. And look at the spots on my car!" And I looked, and there were large spots, shiny spots, on the trunk of the car. And I thought, what caused that? And I started to wipe one off, and she said, "Don't touch it!" And I said, "How can you know if it isn't anything?" And then I put the compass close to it. And the compass would spin and spin, and I could move the compass a few inches to a spot, to a part of the trunk and that did not have a spot, and the compass would drop down. And I could not understand this. And I knew I did not know anything about compasses. And I told Betty , "It is nothing at all. The compass is a cheap compass. It is nothing to get alarmed about."

DOCTOR

What gave her the idea of getting the compass?

BARNEY

I did not know at that time.

DOCTOR

What did you find out?

BARNEY

She told me later that while she was talking with her sister, her sister had suggested that she get a compass and check and see if the car was magnetized or something or other. And this why she . . .

DOCTOR

You say these spots made a compass needle spin?

BARNEY

When we would place a compass anywhere but on the spots, the needle would just flop down.

DOCTOR

You say these were shiny spots. What did you mean by that? Were there changes in the color of your car, or dust removed, or what?

BARNEY

Highly polished.

DOCTOR

As if the car had been highly polished?

BARNEY

Yes, in those spots.

DOCTOR

How big were they?

BARNEY

About the size of half dollars, silver dollars.

DOCTOR

Did you try to remove them? Or did you try to wipe the rest of the car off?

BARNEY

I never bothered with the spots.

DOCTOR

Was the rest of the car dusty?

BARNEY

Yes, it was.

DOCTOR

And you didn't try to polish it out and see if it would duplicate those spots?

BARNEY

There had been a rain . . .

(It rained the afternoon and evening after they arrived back in Portsmouth.)

and where the rain had washed some of the dust off, the shiny spots were still there, and I didn't try to dust them off.

DOCTOR

Could these spots have been caused by the rain drops hitting and taking the dust off?

BARNEY

No. The spots were shiny and in perfect circles.

DOCTOR

Well, what did you do? Just leave the spots?

BARNEY

I did.

DOCTOR

Did you wash or polish your car at some reasonable time afterward?

.BARNEY

That was Betty's car, and she washes her car. I suppose she did. I didn't pay any more attention.

DOCTOR

You don't know. How long did those spots stay, then?

BARNEY

I shut them out. I don't know. I just stopped thinking about those spots.

DOCTOR

You don't know when they disappeared—or did they?

BARNEY

Yes, they're gone.

DOCTOR

All right. We'll stop with this now. You will no longer think about what we talked about today, until I ask you to recall it. It will not trouble you at all. The eyes will not trouble you. You will not even think about them. Everything is comfortable, everything is relaxed. No need for anxiety, and nothing to worry about. Is that clear?

BARNEY

Yes.

DOCTOR

You are comfortable, aren't you?

BARNEY

Yes, I am.

DOCTOR

And relaxed. And you are not worrying, and you will not worry. Everything will be quite all right. And you and Betty will come back a week from today, just as you did today. You feel all right, now?

(The doctor is doubly assuring that Barney will not have the same problems he had during the week before.)

BARNEY

Yes, I do.

You are very comfortable. You will not worry at all. It is not going to affect your mind. It's an experience we'll talk about more, get it all cleared up. So you will have no fear, no anxiety. You will not think about this; it will not come to you any more. Anything we talked about in these sessions, you will not think about; it will not trouble you. You'll be comfortable and relaxed. No pains, no aches, no anxiety. You'll be all right.

BARNEY

Yes.

DOCTOR

You may wake now.

(Barney immediately wakes, feeling calm and refreshed. He has no memory whatever of what has gone on during the session.)

* * *

At the start of this session on February 29, Barney was not certain if the doctor was going to go along with his request to take Betty and give him a rest after the reaction he had had to the first session. In fact, he half expected, at the moment he went into the trance, that the doctor was merely doing it for the purpose of reinforcing him for further treatment. When he looked at his watch at the end of the second session, he was totally surprised to find that it was nearly ten—almost two hours later. He was even more startled at this, because, although he had reached the point where he could accept the loss of contact with any sense of time for an hour or so, he was sure that he would have some consciousness of a lapse of time that long.

He felt very relaxed and comfortable as he came out of the trance and thought that he could remember talking about everything up to Indian Head, even within the trance. He seemed vaguely to be aware of the doctor's voice, but there was no clear remembrance of this.

"Actually," Barney later said, "I did not have any recall as to the actual sessions under hypnosis. But I seemed to develop a tremendous recall apart from the sessions of hypnosis, as if suddenly, I could say, 'Betty, do yon know the color of the rug at the motel we stayed at before we got to Montreal? It was pale blue.' Things of that sort. And tying the dog to the radiator in the lavatory. I could remember things like that. And also, I remembered—consciously, that is—details of all the route numbers we had traveled. And after the second session, I recalled that we stopped at this quaint, farmhouse-type restaurant before Montreal.

And the picture that came to my mind was so vivid. It was very quaint and attractive, lovely. Large fireplace, the side of the entire wall was a fireplace. We had a delightful breakfast there on the trip, the kind you would feed lumberjacks. Large chunks of ham, three or four eggs, if you wanted them. The picture came back so sharply. In other words, the picture of the conscious part of the trip was sharpened, even though I had no idea what I had said about the missing segment.

"Then, after this second session, I began having dreams. I had peculiar dreams, where I began dreaming about UFO's for the first time in my life. And I read a book about a doctor in a concentration camp in Germany who was in great distress, and I began to picture him as Dr. Simon, and this made the book acutely distressing to me. Because somehow, Dr. Simon had become sort of a close friend. He had become more than a close friend. He had become someone I loved, and I didn't want any harm to come to."

CHAPTER SEVEN

With the second session over, Dr. Simon reviewed the case in the first real light that had been thrown on the amnesic period. The case was breaking down into two separate phases: the first encounter, which was described as happening at Indian Head, and the second encounter, which apparently took place in a wooded section of a road off Route 3, involving a roadblock, and the bizarre description of an abduction aboard a space ship.

The evidence revealed in the two sessions with Barney seemed to indicate that he had undergone a severe emotional upheaval with an experience with an unidentified object, either real or interpreted to be real. The second experience—the abduction—had much less support from established reports of the UFO phenomenon and had to be considered as far less probable or unreal. Much more data would have to be available to weigh the scales convincingly as far as this was concerned. At this stage of the treatment, it appeared that part or all of the first encounter could be real. The second encounter had no valid precedent and appeared to be unreal, consequently reflecting back on the first experience.

Before proceeding further with Barney, Dr. Simon decided to begin with Betty and probe her recall. The doctor was working with facts, data, and logical conjecture, which he would test and add new data to to confirm or reject as he went along. A physician must be skeptical but should have some working hypotheses to help evaluate the material revealed.

The doctor was not interested in the UFO aspect, per se, except as an integral part of the Hills' experience. His presumption as he prepared to continue with Betty Hill on the following week was that the first encounter could have happened; the second encounter was unlikely.

*   *   *

On her way in to her first session, Betty Hill found herself actually looking forward to the experience. She had sat through two long sessions waiting for Barney, with some discomfort. She could not imagine herself getting as emotional as the first confused noises she had overheard during his first session seemed to indicate, and which she still had not mentioned to him.

At Dr. Simon's office on March 7, 1962, the procedure was reversed. Barney was reinforced, and Betty remained in the office for the session to begin. She was not sure whether the doctor would put her in a trance or conduct a conscious interview.

She had with her in her pocketbook a copy of the paper she had written out describing her dreams in detail. Driving in with Barney, she asked if she should show them to the doctor, but Barney suggested that she wait until the doctor asked for them. Barney's feeling about Betty's dreams was always one of extreme discomfort. He didn't like to think about them—didn't approve of Betty's preoccupation with them—didn't believe they had any basis in reality. Although he had not directly told Betty, he didn't want Dr. Simon to be influenced by her dreams. Consequently, the detailed description of the dreams remained in Betty's pocketbook as she prepared for her session.

She distinctly remembers hearing the cue words, as they were spoken by the doctor at her first long session on March 7.

"When he said them," Betty recalls, "it was always with the feeling of complete surprise to me. It's like suddenly someone slaps you. He says the words, and whatever you're doing immediately stops. I was in the middle of putting a cigarette out and was conscious for a brief moment that I was trying to do this, and I couldn't do it. I actually think when you're going into a trance, you just don't immediately go. It's like going to sleep. Sort of like drifting. You slide into it. I think you really couldn't stop yourself if you tried."

Betty heard the words distinctly. But almost immediately, she thought, she heard the words from the doctor: "You may wake up, Betty." In between the phrases, for over an hour, Betty reexperienced in full detail the incident at Cannon Mountain. What she revealed would not be known to her for weeks later.

DOCTOR
(Her eyes close; her head nods.)

You are in a deep, deep sleep. Deep asleep. Fully relaxed and far asleep. Very comfortable, fully relaxed, deep asleep. Far asleep, deep, deep sleep.

(With the repeated reinforcement of the induction she has experienced over the weeks, this was all that was required to put her into the trance state.)

Now we're going to go back, back to your vacation in September of 1961 as you were coming from Niagara Falls to Montreal. You will remember what you did, and you will recall everything, all your experiences, all of your memories, all of your feelings, and you will give me all of this in full detail. Now you're coming from Niagara Falls to Montreal. You're on your way home from vacation. Now tell me all that you experienced, all that you felt. You and your husband.

BETTY
(Her voice is less monotonous compared to Barney's flat and vacant tone but she is in a deep trance, as he was.)

We're driving along, and the streets were wide, sun was shining. There were quite a few people in the streets. And I was looking at the houses and stores and windows . . .

(She speaks, however, with longer pauses, as if she waits for the scene to pass by her eyes before she relates it.)

We stopped at a gas station to get directions, and the attendant spoke French and couldn't understand us. So we went to another garage, and they told us how to get back into the center of Montreal. And I saw a mink coat in the window for $895. Then we decided we'd find a hotel, but then we didn't know if they'd allow Delsey to be in a hotel. So then we thought we'd look for a motel somewhere outside of Montreal. And we passed a place with a sign I thought said "potato fritters," and the woman in this little drive-in restaurant came out and started speaking in French. And I said I didn't understand French, and she kept saying she was sure I was French. But I'm not. And then I found out it wasn't potato fritters, it was potato chips. So we had the potato chips and coffee, and I can't remember if I had a hot dog or a hamburger, or one of each . . .

(Again, the struggle to remember minutiae, even if not significant. If she were instructed to, she could remember. Also, different details of the trip are selected for description by Betty than Barney chose to relate. She continues with her description of the basic story of the trip down through Canada to Colebrook and then on to Lancaster, her story paralleling Barney's account of this portion of the journey. Then:)

And we kept driving and looking around. The moon was bright, but not quite full, but very bright and large. And there was a star down below the moon, on the lower left-hand side of the moon. And then right after we left Lancaster I noticed that there was like a star, a bigger star up over this one. And it hadn't been there. And I showed Barney, and we kept watching it. It seemed to keep getting brighter and bigger looking. And we watched it for quite awhile. And I was puzzled by it. Also curious. And while I was watching it, Delsey was getting somewhat restless. And then we went by a mountain that obstructed the view. And when I got to where I could seee the star again, I thought it had moved . . .

(Again, Betty Hill rarely begins her sentences, in ordinary conversation, with and. Yet, like Barney, she persistently does so in trance.)

But I wasn't quite sure, so I kept watching it. And it seemed so it did move, and Delsey was restless. So I told Barney we should let Delsey out. And it would give us a chance to look at this star through the binoculars. We drive along, and we came to a parking space off the highway, one that had been built there. And I guess it was so people could drive off and look at the view. And there were woods all around. And there were a couple of trash barrels. And Barney said we should look out for bears. I got out of the car and put—let's see— yes, I got out of the car and put Delsey on her leash and started to walk her. And I noticed that the star was definitely moving, so I went back to the car and got out the binoculars. And Barney took Delsey, and I was looking through the binoculars at the object. And Barney was saying it was a satellite, but it wasn't. It was moving fast, but it went in front of the moon, and I saw it. I saw it travel across the whole face of the moon, and it was odd shaped. And it was flashing all different colored lights.

DOCTOR

How far away would you say it was?

136

It looked at the time it wasn't close to us. But I could see it outlined in front of the moon. And there were like searchlights rotating around it.

DOCTOR

Like those lights you see on police cars?

BETTY

No. You know what a searchlight looks like?

DOCTOR

Yes.

BETTY

And how it's sort of in a pencil line of light, and it swings around. They were like that.

DOCTOR

You could see those long beams?

BETTY

Of white—and they were different colors.

DOCTOR

Were they usual colors that you know, or were they—?

BETTY

Yes, they were bright colors. Like a bright orange light, almost a reddish beam. And there was like a blue, well, you said like a light on a police cruiser. You know, it was something like that because when the cruiser light turns around somehow, and it flashes. Even though they seem to come out into a ray thing, somehow. All these different kinds of lights seemed to be that same flash, flash, flash.

DOCTOR

There were colors other than red, amber and green?

(The doctor of course is referring to conventional lights used in this country on planes, vehicles and for traffic control.)

BETTY

Like a blue and like a flash. Flash, flash, flash. And I had never seen anything like it before. And it was moving quite fast. But I've never seen a satellite, but I've always thought of a satellite as traveling almost like a shooting star, maybe not quite as fast. But this wasn't traveling that fast. Well, when I saw it go in front of the moon, I was sort of fascinated, and I kept watching. But then I tried to get Barney to look, I wanted him to see it before it got away from the face of the moon. But he kept saying, "Oh, it's a satellite."

DOCTOR

Are you referring to Telstar or Echo—that sort of thing?

BETTY

Yes. And Barney said it was just a satellite, and he was over by the car, and by the time he got back it had gone from in front of the moon. But he did look at it, and then he looked at it for a few seconds and gave the binoculars back to me.

DOCTOR

You said it had an odd shape, did you?

BETTY

Yes.

DOCTOR

How would you describe this shape? Round? Shaped like anything you know? A plane?

BETTY

No. Not like a plane. All I could think of, like a cigar.

DOCTOR

Like a cigar?

BETTY

Yes. It was long, and there weren't any wings. And it was going sideways. You know, like a cigar. It was going from the left to the right. It was just like holding a cigar up in front of the moon, with all these lights flashing around it. So then Barney looked at it, and I took the binoculars and looked again and gave them back to him. And then I went over and put Delsey in the car and got in the car myself and shut the door. And then Barney came over and got in the car, and he said, "They've seen us, and they're coming this way." And I laughed and asked him if he had watched Twilight Zone recently on TV. And he didn't say anything.

DOCTOR

Why did you mention Twilight Zone?

BETTY

Because the idea was fantastic.

138

DOCTOR

Had there been anything like this on Twilight Zone?

BETTY

I don't know. I never see Twilight Zone. But I had heard people talk about this program, and I always was under the impression that it was a way-out type of thing. And so when he said that they had seen us, and that they were swinging around and coming in our direction, I thought his imagination was being overactive.

DOCTOR

Did he have binoculars at the time?

BETTY

I left him standing on the edge of this parking area, looking at this thing when I took Delsey, and she and I got in the car. And I sat down and waited for him to finish looking. And this is when he came back and said that it had turned around and was coming toward us.

DOCTOR

Did you look to see if it was doing that?

BETTY

Not at that moment. I thought this was sort of, I didn't know. Well, Barney kept saying that it was headed toward us. So I thought, well, I don't know what gave him this idea, but I was beginning to get a little curious why he felt this. So I picked up the binoculars, and at first I couldn't find it, couldn't find the object. But then I did see it. And I could see it was getting closer to us and was coming in. And it was still far, far away, and even when it was coming in, it still looked like a star. It was a solid-light type of thing. And then, when I would take the binoculars down and look at it, it was just like a star coming in closer.

(An echo of many more reports in NICAP and Air Force files.)

But then when I looked at it through the binoculars, it would, of course, appear to be much bigger. But it was flying in a very odd way. And this is what I was all excited about.

DOCTOR

What do you mean by odd way?

BETTY

Well, you know how an airplane flies along in a straight line? It wasn't

139

flying like that. It was turning, it was rotating. And it would go along in a straight line for a short, just a short distance, and then would tip over on its side, and go up.

DOCTOR

Well, let's see. It was shaped like a cigar, you say.

BETTY

Yes.

DOCTOR

Did it fly like it was a cigar going along? Like an arrow?

BETTY

This is the way it looked.

DOCTOR

When it tipped over, what did it do? How did it tip?

BETTY

Well, all right. You take a cigar and you lay it flat on the desk. Now you stand the cigar up on one end. Right straight up and down. This is what this did. And in the meanwhile, it gave the appearance of spinning all the time.

(Other reports of this nature indicate that the cigar shape, as in Barney's case, is an indication of a disc that is seen in profile.)

DOCTOR

Was it turning on the long axis?

BETTY

Yes. It would go along straight, and then it would suddenly go right up straight. And then it would flatten horizontally. And then it would drop down straight. This seemed to be the overall pattern. It wasn't done in an exactly precise way. It would jerk out. It would flatten out. So it was sort of, it wasn't smoothly done. And as they got closer, there seemed to be more of this jumping back and forth in the sky. And then it followed us for a long time. And Barney was driving, and I was watching this almost completely—and the way it was flying, I thought maybe it was the vibrations of the car that was causing it to look this way.

DOCTOR

You mean this jumping effect?

UFO as seen by Betty Hill in first encounter.
From sketch by Betty Hill.

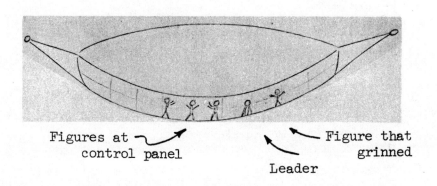

Figures at
control panel

Figure that
grinned

Leader

UFO as seen by Barney Hill showing figures,
"fins," and red lights. From sketch by Barney Hill.

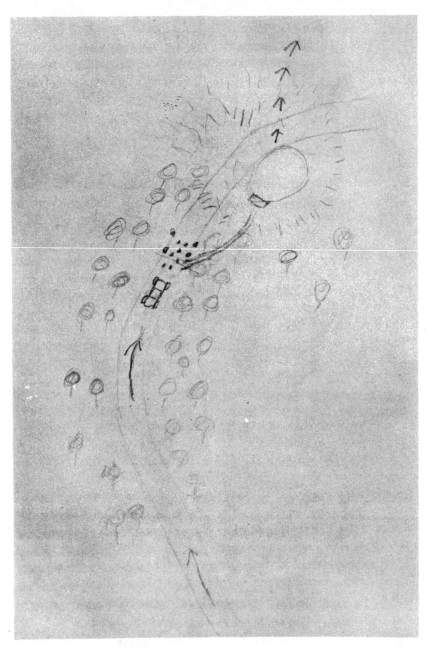

Sketch by Barney Hill, drawn after the therapy had released the repressed material, of his recollection of the actual site of the possible abduction. Dots represent his recollection of the "men in the road." Round object in clearing is his recollection of the approximate position of the object.

Barney Hill, under hypnosis, drew the
above sketch of the "leader" of the alleged
abductors. Later, while he was listening
to the tape recording of his own account
of the incident, he seemed to go into a
trance-like state, and drew the more finished sketch below. The eyes were elongated, he said, and the lips appeared to
have no muscles.

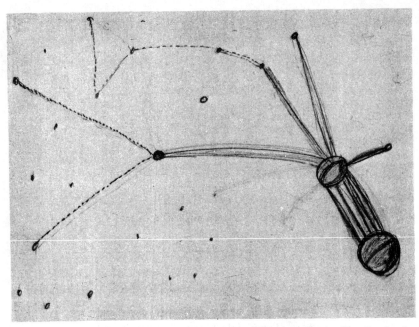

Under hypnosis, Betty Hill described a map she was shown "by the leader aboard the ship." Later, she sketched it. She said she was told that the heavy lines marked regular trade routes, and the broken lines recorded various space expeditions. The following year, the map seen below was published in the New York Times. (Note the caption.)

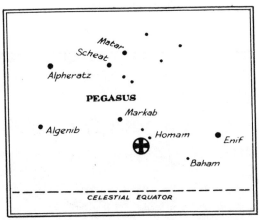

The New York Times   April 13, '65

FROM DEEP IN SPACE: Radio source called CTA-102 (cross), in direction of constellation Pegasus, may be sending intelligent radio emissions, Russian believes.

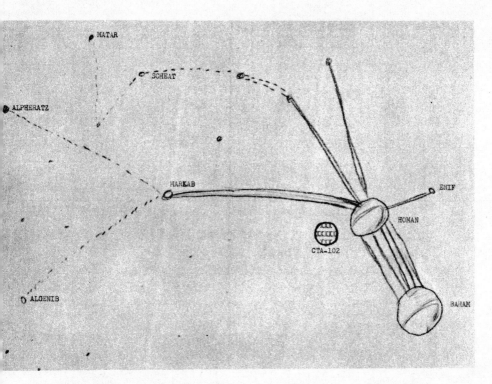

Mrs. Hill, struck by the similarity between the Times map and her sketch, **then added the corresponding names.**

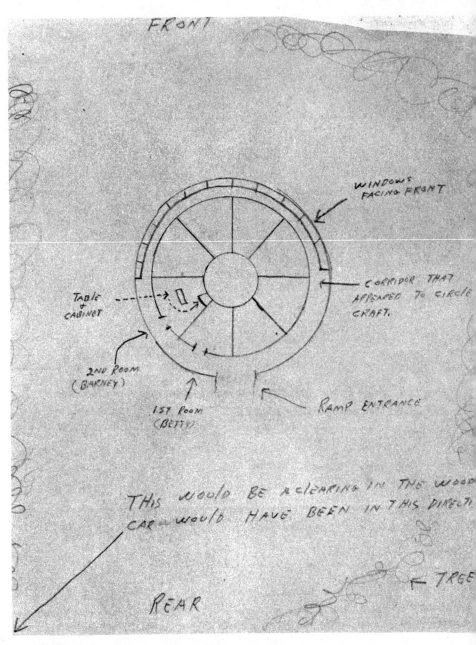

Sketch by Barney Hill, drawn for the writer four years after incident, in an attempt to reconstruct his impression of the craft. Hypnosis sessions penetrating the amnesic period tended to bring out more memories after the formal therapy was concluded.

DR. BENJAMIN SIMON

Barney and Betty Hill with their dachshund, Delsey,
who was with them on their interrupted journey

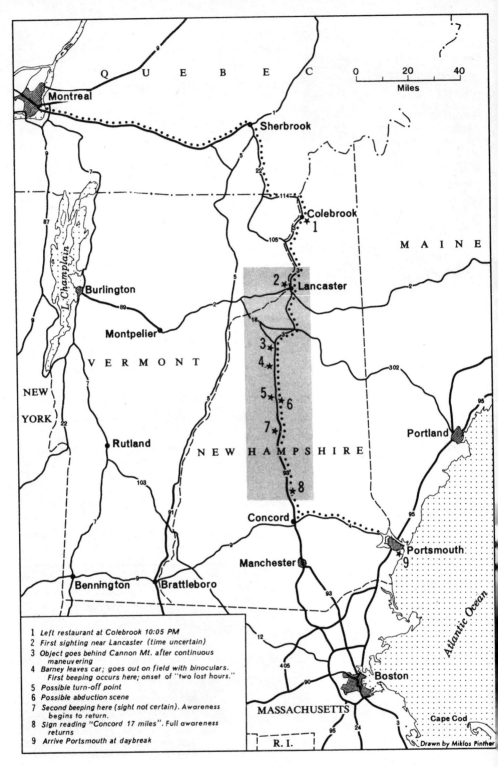

1. Left restaurant at Colebrook 10:05 PM
2. First sighting near Lancaster (time uncertain)
3. Object goes behind Cannon Mt. after continuous maneuvering
4. Barney leaves car; goes out on field with binoculars. First beeping occurs here; onset of "two lost hours."
5. Possible turn-off point
6. Possible abduction scene
7. Second beeping here (sight not certain). Awareness begins to return.
8. Sign reading "Concord 17 miles". Full awareness returns
9. Arrive Portsmouth at daybreak

Drawn by Miklos Pinther

Route taken by Barney and Betty Hill on the night of Sept. 19, 1961.

Yes. I thought maybe the vibrations of the car was giving the effect. And so, I was keeping asking Barney to stop the car and look at it. And he would stop and say he couldn't see it flying this way, while I could. And so then I would look at other objects, like a star, to see if it would give this appearance. And it wouldn't. I kept trying to figure out, I kept saying, "Nothing flies like this, so it's something I'm doing to make this idea that it's flying like this." Everything else I looked at was all right. It didn't jump around. It was just this one object. We kept starting and stopping and looking at it. And we would drive along. Now when we got by Cannon Mountain, this is where the tramway is . . .

DOCTOR

(He needs to make an adjustment of the tape recorder.)

All right, we'll stop there now. You will not hear anything further until I speak to you again. You will be perfectly at ease . . .

(He completes the adjustment.)

All right, Betty. Continue now where you left off.

(She continues at exactly that point.)

BETTY

. . . we came by the tramway at Cannon Mountain, and there's a lighted area on the top . . . I think the lights might have been from a restaurant. And as I was watching, the lights went out.

(There are many reports of electrical disturbances by UFO's, including lights, auto ignition, headlights, radio and television.)

I don't know if it went down in the valley between the two mountains, or if it turned its lights off. And this puzzled me, because I kept looking for it. And then I thought, well maybe they're going away, they aren't interested in us. But then we came out by Old Man of the Mountain, and there it was. But it looked almost as if it were bouncing along the top of the mountain, the ridge. And it would go down a little bit on the other side, and I would lose sight of it. And I kept wondering why they were following us. And I would figure that, I was wondering if they were as curious about me as I was about them.

DOCTOR

You speak of "they"?

149

I mean, well, I figured there must be somebody inside of the object, you know, someone directing its flight. And so, whoever was inside, this is "they." I was very curious, and I had the feeling that someone might be there, and they saw us. In a way, it was all very intriguing. And I didn't know what was going to happen, but I wasn't afraid. I was just curious. And I just had a feeling that something is going to happen, and I don't know what it is. And I hope I won't be too afraid when it does happen. And so we kept riding along, and we stopped at one place, there were too many trees, we lost sight of it there. When we got to the Flume, Barney drove in on the parking area on the right-hand side. And we stopped there and tried to really get a good look at it again. But there were too many trees there, too. But we would go along and there would be areas where we could get, it would be fairly clear. And then we went past the Flume, somewhere between the Flume and Indian Head, or it was just beyond the Flume, or just beyond Indian Head, there was a motel. It was like cabins, these small, neat-looking cabins, and the sign itself wasn't lighted, but there was one cottage on the end that had a light on. And there was a man standing in the door. And I saw this, and I thought, if I want to, I can get out of this whole situation right now. All we have to do is drive in here, and this object will go away. And that will be the end of it. I mean, this is our escape from it, if I want this. And I was thinking this, and I didn't say anything to Barney, I didn't say anything. All I could think of was, I don't know where we're going, but I'm ready for it. And Barney was sort of irritating me, because he wanted to, his whole attitude was that I was trying to wish something on him. I got the impression that he was trying to deny what was actually happening. That he didn't want to know that it was there, even though he would stop and look at it. He didn't have any realization of what was going on. Now it was fairly close, and I could see that it wasn't spinning, because I could see that there were lights on one side, and this gave it a blinking and twinkling effect. But then all of a sudden, it stopped doing this. And I got the idea that there were lights only on one side. And then all of a sudden, the object shot ahead of us and swung around in front of the car. Well, I was watching it when it did this. And it was on my side of the windshield, directly in front of me. And I looked at it through the binoculars, and I could see a double row of windows. And then, as I was watching it, I was thinking this side has the windows and the back of it must be dark. And this is why it twinkles. And while I'm sitting there, I'm amazed by all this. Then all

150

of a sudden on one side, on the left-hand side, a red light came out.
And then on the right-hand side, a light came out.

DOCTOR

You say left- and right-hand side?

BETTY

I was facing the object.

DOCTOR

You're looking through the windshield?

BETTY

I was looking through the windshield, right up at it.

DOCTOR

How far away would you say it was?

BETTY

Oh, I couldn't estimate. You couldn't see it too clearly without the
binoculars. I could see a band of light without them. And when I saw
the second red light, I kept telling Barney to stop. "Stop the car, Barney,
and look at it!" And he kept saying, "Oh, why it's nothing. It'll go
away." And I kept saying, "Barney! You've got to stop! Stop the car,
Barney, and look at it. It's amazing!" And he said, oh, he was going to
humor me then so he said, "Oh, all right. Give me the binoculars."
And he looked at it, and I kept saying, "Do you see it? Do you see it?"
And he said, "It's just a plane or something." And I kept saying, "OK,
it's a plane. Did you ever see a plane with two red lights? I thought
planes had one red and one green light." And he kept looking at it, and
then he gave the binoculars back to me, and I'd watch it. And then
he said he couldn't see very well. He opened the car door—no first, he
put down the window in his car door, and he tried to stick his head out
and look up over the roof of the car at it.

(Betty's voice has become increasingly animated now, but still
quite matter-of-fact.)

But the motor of the car was running, and he said, well, he got out. He
opened the car door and stepped out. He put one foot on the highway,
and one was inside the car. And he was standing with the car door open,
but he was leaning against the body of the car. He kept looking at it, and
then he didn't say anything. He just stepped outside. And he stepped

151

outside, and he kept going away from the car. And I thought, well now, this isn't a very bright place for us to have stopped the car, because we're right on the main highway. We're not on the right side or the left side. We're right directly in the middle. And there should be traffic on the highway. So I thought, well, while he's out getting a good look at this, I'll watch if any cars come in either direction, in case I have to get the car out from the middle of the street. So I'd look out the back window and out the front window. And it seems as though I sat there and sat there and waiting and waiting and Barney didn't come back. And I was sitting there waiting. And I'd look. It was dark there. There weren't any street lights or anything. I noticed when I looked out, he was quite a distance from the car, and he was still going away from the car.

(Now, for the first time, emotion begins to come into Betty's voice. Oddly enough, it occurs at just about the same time and place that Barney's intense emotional outburst occurred.)

So I leaned over the front seat, and I was saying, "Barney! Come back here!

(Now her voice breaks in emotion. She begins to sob as she speaks.)

Barney! You damn fool, get back here! Barney, come back!"

(She is reliving the incident now, calling directly to Barney, rather than describing it.)

If that damn fool doesn't come back, I'm going after him! "Barney! What's *wrong* with you?"

(Her profanity is more affectionate than condemnatory. All of their bickering is rather congenial.)

And I'm calling, "Barney! Barney! Barney. Get back here! What's wrong with you?"

(Now back to description, but still breathless.)

I started to slide . . . I was going to get out his side of the car because that door was open all the way. I started to slide across the seat, because I was going to go out and get him. Just as I started to slide, and I got the door most of the way open, he came to the car. He was running like mad down the street.

(A New Hampshire colloquialism for "road.")

152

And when I heard him coming, I sat up. I was lucky I did, afterwards. Because he threw the binoculars in the car, and they landed on the seat beside me. He was hysterical.

(And now she almost is.)

He . . . he . . . he . . . he . . . he was. I don't know if he was laughing or crying. But he was saying that they were going to capture us. We had to get the hell out of there. They were going to capture us. Because the car motor was running, he put the car into first, and he stepped on the gas. And we started to take off very rapidly. He kept saying to me, "Look out! Look out! You can see them. They're right overhead. They're right directly over our car. . . ."

And so, I did want to see them again and I was sort of afraid—but I wasn't that afraid. And so, we were moving, we were going quite fast then. And so I wound down, I turned down the window on my side of the car, and I tried to put by body out through the window and look out. And I kept looking and looking, and I couldn't see them. I couldn't see the light. I couldn't even see the sky. I couldn't see anything. And so I told Barney, "I don't think they're out there. I don't see anything. It's all black. I don't see them." So then I pulled my head in, and I wound up the window of the car. And I thought, well, maybe they're out the back, because I kept looking for the lights. And I looked out the back window, and I didn't see anything. And the, all of a sudden, there was this: Beep, Beep, Beep, Beep, Beep. And Barney said, "What's that? What's that? What's that noise?" I said, "I don't know." All I could think of, is some kind of electrical signal. You know—beep, beep, beep, beep-beep . . .

(Now she is rather matter-of-fact in her tone, analyzing what this might possibly be all about.)

I wondered, oh, darn. Why didn't I learn the Morse code, cause maybe this is the Morse code, and I don't know it. Then I thought, maybe it's electrical. Maybe it's a shock. So I put my hand on the metal of the car, and I kept feeling and feeling, and I didn't feel a shock, no kind of electrical shock. But the whole car was vibrating. You know, little vibrating. And I thought, well, that's funny. The—the—there was no—well, I don't know. There was a beeping, and there wasn't any electrical shock. What happened next?

(The sharpness of detail, of minutiae, leaves her, at the same point in time and location as with Barney. She continues to speak, but in puzzlement, as if she is probing, searching for a lost memory.)

We're riding along . . . and I kept waiting for Barney to tell me about what he saw on the highway. . . .

(She stops talking. Her groping at this point is unavailing.)

DOCTOR

(After waiting a considerable length of time.)

How long would you say he was away from you when he was on the highway? Actually, how long was it?

BETTY

Oh, it seemed a long time.

DOCTOR

Well, how long was it?

BETTY

I don't know. I would say, for some reason I don't know why, I would say four or five minutes.

DOCTOR

Four or five minutes.

BETTY

Yes. I don't remember looking at my watch, and it was dark anyway. And I heard the beeping sound.

DOCTOR

Did you see this object anymore?

BETTY

I kept trying to see it. Every once in a while, I would look out the window for it, but—my mind's a blank.

(Another pause. She is groping.)

But I can almost remember . . .

DOCTOR

Yes, you can.

BETTY

(She is obviously straining to remember.)

Right at this point, I can't get beyond that beeping.

(Nor could Barney, at this point.)

DOCTOR

You can. It's all right now. You can get beyond it.

(Now a very long pause. Betty is breathing heavily, but she makes no other sound.)

Yes, go on. It's all right.

(Now Betty begins to cry, in short, rapid sobs, as if she were trying to hold herself back.)

All right. You needn't be too upset.

BETTY

(Another long pause. Then she draws a sharp breath, as if she has made a forced resolution in her mind. She speaks very rapidly, breathlessly, as if she doesn't want to say this.)

We're driving along . . . I don't know where we are . . . I don't even know how we got here . . . Barney and I, we were driving, I don't know how long . . . I don't know how long. . . .

(The words come out between sharp, short sobs.)

And we haven't even been talking . . . I've just been sitting here . . . feeling that something is going to happen . . . and I'm not really too afraid . . . except right now I am . . . at the time I didn't feel afraid . . .

(She stops talking, then cries.)

DOCTOR

(After a long pause.)

Why are you crying if you're not afraid?

BETTY

I'm afraid now . . . but I wasn't . . . I don't . . . I wasn't . . . I wasn't afraid . . . I was afraid when I saw the men in the road . . .

DOCTOR

Men in the road?

BETTY

(Now she breaks out with an anguished cry.)

I've never been so afraid in my life before!

155

DOCTOR

(Very calmly.)

Tell me about the men in the road. It's all right now.

BETTY

(She begins to say something, but she is sobbing too much to get it out.)

DOCTOR

You're safe here. Tell me about the men in the road.

BETTY

(Her voice is trembling, her breath rapid.)

We're driving along . . . we're on a tarred road . . . and all of a sudden . . . without any warning or rhyme or reason or anything . . . Barney made a—he always—the brakes squealed, he stopped so suddenly . . . and made this sharp left-hand turn off the highway . . . and we went on to this narrow road . . . I was wondering what he was doing, to turn down here . . . He wasn't saying anything, and I wasn't either . . . so I figured, well, maybe we're lost . . . But so what, we'll come out somewhere . . .

(She is still having difficulty in speaking.)

And we're going along . . . and there was a sharp curve . . . there were trees . . . there were a lot of tall trees on my side . . . I don't know about Barney's side of the road . . .

(Again, the desire for complete accuracy in reporting.)

But—there were these men standing in the highway . . . and I wasn't too afraid when I saw them . . . they were standing there, and I thought, well, you know, they weren't so awful . . . there was, oh, I don't know . . . and they were just . . . I wasn't too afraid when I saw them. And they were just—I couldn't get a good look at them . . .

(She reflects a moment, then:)

But then I thought, well—they in a car? A car broken down? What are they doing here? And Barney of course had to stop. And then he stopped the car, and these men started to come up to the car. They separated. They came in two groups. And when they started to do

156

that, I got real scared. And the car motor died. The car stalled. And then they started to come toward us.

(A brief pause, then:)

And when they started to do that, I got real scared. And the car motor died, the car stalled. And when they started to come up to us, Barney tried to start the car. And you know how a motor of the car will just turn over, and it won't fire? He couldn't start the car . . . he couldn't start the car!

(She bursts into tears again. The last words are muffled.)

DOCTOR

He did what?

BETTY

He tried to start the car, and it won't start! And the men are coming toward us! And I thought, well, I can get away from them if I get the car door open, I can run in the woods and hide! And I'm thinking of that, and I just put my hand on the car door to open it, and the men come up, and they open it for me!

(She sobs profusely.)

And they open the car door . . . and this . . . this man . . . two men behind us . . . and . . . and . . .

(Her words are again muffled by her crying.)

DOCTOR

I didn't hear that.

BETTY

(Trying to get herself under control.)

Two men at the car door . . . and there's one . . . two . . . three men . . . and there's one . . . two more behind them . . . and one man puts his hand out . . .

(She stops again.)

DOCTOR

Go on.

BETTY

(A long pause of deep breathing.)

I—I don't know what happens . . .

DOCTOR

You can remember everything now. What do these men look like? Did you see their faces?

BETTY

No.

DOCTOR

How were they dressed?

BETTY

Alike. Somehow or other.

(More sobbing, a little more controlled.)

DOCTOR

Do they have a uniform, or ordinary clothes?

BETTY

More like a uniform.

DOCTOR

A uniform. Did it resemble any uniform you already know?

BETTY

I couldn't say.

(And she lapses into silence again.)

DOCTOR

(He waits a considerable length of time, then:)

All right, your memory is very sharp. You needn't be worried. You remember everything now. Tell me what happened.

(Another long pause.)

What are you thinking now?

BETTY

I'm thinking I'm asleep.

DOCTOR

You're asleep in the car?

BETTY

(This is the same point at which Barney became vague and diffuse . . . when he felt he was "floating about" . . . when he saw "the eyes.")

I'm thinking I'm asleep . . . I'm asleep, and I've got to wake up! I don't want to be asleep. I keep trying . . . I got to wake myself up . . . I try

. . . and I go back again . . . I keep trying . . . I keep trying to wake up . . .

(Long pause, then:)

Then I do! I open my eyes! And I'm walking through the woods . . . And I just open my eyes quick, and I shut them again . . .

(She begins sobbing intensely.)

But even though I'm asleep, I'm walking! And there's this man on this side, and a man on this side . . . and there's two men in front of me. And I look all around . . . and it's a path . . . and there's trees . . .

(More words come out, but the sobbing completely obscures them.)

And I look at these men . . . and I turn around . . . Barney's behind me . . .

(She stops short again.)

DOCTOR

Barney's behind you?

BETTY

There's a couple of men behind me, and then there's Barney. There's a man on each side of him. And my eyes are open . . . but Barney's still asleep. He's walking, and he's asleep . . .

(She is still sobbing, but then gets under control.)

And then I begin to get mad! And I say to myself, "Who the heck are these characters, and what do they think they're doing?" And I turn around, and I say, "Barney! Wake up! *Barney!* Why don't you wake up?" And he doesn't pay any attention. He keeps walking. And going a little bit further, and I turn around, and I say his name again, *"Barney!* Wake up!" And he still doesn't pay any attention. And then the man walking beside me here says, "Oh, is his name Barney?" And that's where I looked at this man, and I figured it's none of his business. So I didn't speak to him. Then we keep walking, and I try to wake Barney up again. I keep saying, "Barney, Barney, wake up!" And he doesn't, so the man asks me again, "Is Barney his name?" And I wouldn't answer him, so he says, he said, "Don't be afraid. You don't have any reason to be afraid. We're not going to harm you, but we just want to do some tests. When the tests are over with, we'll take you and Barney back and put you in your car. You'll be on your way back home in no time." I mean he was, he was sort of reassuring in a way, but I can't say I trust what he said. And I wasn't sure what was going to happen. And we kept walking and walking, and Barney was still asleep . . .

(Although she has her sobs under control, they are still punctuating all this.)

DOCTOR

You mean he was walking in his sleep?

BETTY

Yes, he was like sleep-walking.

DOCTOR

These men spoke good English?

BETTY

Only one spoke, the one who was on my left. Then he was more or less . . . he had an accent. He had sort of a foreign accent . . . but he was, you know, very businesslike. So then we kept walking, and we came to a clearing. And there was—I wish it were lighter so I could get a better picture of it—there was a ramp to the door. The object was on the ground . . .

(She pauses.)

DOCTOR

The object was on the ground?

BETTY

(Very matter-of-factly now.)

I think it was the same one I was watching in the sky. And there were trees and a path, and there was this clearing. And they're taking me up to the object. I don't want to go on it. I don't want . . . I don't know what's going to happen if I do. I don't want to go. Barney's no protection . . . he's sound asleep. And I don't want to go on it.

DOCTOR

He's sound asleep. What was he doing? Walking along, or was somebody supporting him?

BETTY

Yes. There's a man on each side. One has each arm, and they're sort of . . . well, he's sort of . . . his eyes are shut, and he doesn't hear any-

160

thing I say. But he's standing on his own two feet. But he's in a daze, and they're sort of directing him, helping him along. And he's quite a bit taller than the men.

DOCTOR

He's taller than the men?

BETTY

Yes. Yes, he's way above them. So when we get to the object, I don't want to go on. And so the man beside me says to go on. He's a little angry with me. He said, "Oh, go on. The longer you fool around out here, the longer it's going to take. You might as well go on and get it over with, and get back to your car. We haven't got much time, either." So he, and one of the others, each take my arm, and I get sort of a help-less feeling. There's not much I can do at this point, but to go on with them. I go up the ramp, I go inside, and there's a corridor to the left. We go up the corridor, and there's a room. And they stop to take me in the room.

(She is calmer now, much calmer.)

I'm standing in the doorway, and I turn around, and I'm waiting for them to bring Barney in. But they don't do this. They lead Barney right past the door where I'm standing. So I said, "What are you doing with Barney? Bring him in here where I am." And the man said, "No, we only have equipment enough in one room to do one person at a time. And if we took you both in the same room, it would take too long. So Bar-ney will be all right, they're going to take him into the next room. And then as soon as we get through testing the both of you, then you will go back to your car. You don't have to be afraid." And so I watched them take Barney into the next room. And I go into this room. And some of the men come in the room with this man who speaks English. They stay for a minute—I don't know who they are, I guess maybe they're the crew. But they only stay for a minute, and the man who speaks English is there, and another man comes in. I haven't seen him before. I think he's a doctor. And they came in the door . . .

(As with Barney, under hypnosis she tends to mix the past and present tenses.)

. . . and in one corner, there's a stool, a white—is it white? I don't know if it's white or chrome, but there's a stool, there's a stool, and they put me on it. I sit on the stool. And they—I have a dress, my blue dress on, and they push up the sleeve of my dress, and they look at my arm here. They both look at my arm, and then they turn my arm over and they look at it on here . . .

(She indicates a portion of her arm.)

. . . and they . . . they rub, they have a machine, I don't know what it is. They bring the machine over and they put it, I don't know what kind of machine, it's something like a microscope, only a microscope with a big lens. And they put—I don't know—they put, I had an idea they were taking a picture of my skin. And they both looked through this machine here, and here—

(She gestures.)

And then they were talking. I don't know what they were saying. I couldn't understand this part, what they were saying. And then they took something like a letter opener—only it wasn't—and they scraped my arm here . . .

(She indicates again.)

and there was like little—you know—how your skin gets dry and flaky sometimes, like little particles of skin? And they put—there was something like a piece of cellophane or plastic, or something like that, they scraped, and they put this that came off on this plastic.

(She has fully recovered her calmness now, is very matter-of-fact.)

And then he, the man who spoke English, they both spoke English here, the man who brought me on this contraption is the one who took this, he took this plastic, and he rolled it all up, and he put it in the top drawer. And then they put my head, there was like a dentist, not like a dentist, something like, you know, the brace of a dentist's chair. You have this thing that holds your head, I don't know, it seemed to pull out the back of the stool, somehow or other, and they put my head in that.

(Again the doctor has an adjustment to make. He stops her for a moment, then she continues right on.)

So I'm sitting on the stool, and there's a little bracket, my head is resting against this bracket. And the examiner opens my eyes, and looks in them with a light, and he opens my mouth, and he looks in my throat and my teeth and he looks in my ears, and he turned my head, and he looked in this ear. And then he takes like a—oh, a swab or a Q-tip I guess it is—

they use it on babies—and he cleans out, he puts it in my left ear, and he puts this on another piece of this material. And the leader takes it and rolls it all up and puts it in the top drawer, too.

(She stops a minute, as if to recall the picture more clearly.)

Oh, and then he feels my hair down by the back of my neck and all, and they take a couple of strands of my hair, and they pull it out, and he gives this to the leader, and he wraps that all up and puts that in the top drawer. Then he takes something maybe like scissors, I don't know what it is, and he cut, they cut a piece of it, and he gives that to him. And then he feels my neck, he starts feeling behind my ears, under my chin, and down my neck and in and through my shoulders, around my collarbone, and—

(Again, a pause to recollect.)

Oh—and then they take off my shoes, and they look at my feet, and they look at my hands, they look my hands all over. And he takes—the light is very bright so my eyes aren't always open. I'm still a little scared, too. I'm not particularly interested in looking at them. And so I try to keep my eyes shut. But no, I do open, not all the time, just to give myself a little relief. When I'm not looking at them, I shut my eyes. And he takes something and he goes underneath my fingernail, and then he, I don't know, probably manicure scissors or something, and he cut off a piece of my fingernail. And they look my feet all over, they keep—I don't think they do anything to them, they just feel my feet and my toes and all. And then the doctor, the examiner says he wants to do some tests, he wants to check my nervous system.

(Now she speaks with firmness.)

And I am thinking, I don't know how our nervous systems are, but I hope we never have nerve enough to go around kidnaping people right off the highways, as he has done! And, oh, he tells me to take off my dress, he tells me to take off my dress, and then before I even have a chance hardly to stand up to do it, the examiner—my dress has a zipper down the back? Yes, it has a zipper down the back. And the examiner unzips it, and so I slip my dress off. And I don't have my dress or shoes on. And there's next, over the stool and sort of in the middle of the room, there's a table, some kind of a table. It's not up very high, I'd say the height of the desk. So I lie down on the table, on my back, and he brings over this—oh, how can I describe it? They're like needles, a whole cluster of needles, and each needle has a wire going from it. I think it's something like a TV screen, you know. When the picture isn't on, you get all kinds of lines. Something like that. And so, he puts me down on the table, and they bring the needles over, and they don't stick them in me. No, not really like sticking a needle into a person, but they touch me with the needles. It doesn't hurt . . .

(At times, she pauses, as if waiting for the process to be completed.)

Except—where was it? Someplace. He just touches, and I feel just the needle touching, that's all. It doesn't hurt at all. But then he does it all up in the back of my ears, and in here somehow . . .

(She points to different parts of her head.)

and up here. Up in all different spots of my head. And then he probes more of my neck here and in through here somehow or other.

(She indicates her arms.)

And then down here . . . I don't know, then he puts it on my knee, and when he did, my leg jumped. And then on my foot, too. He did it around my ankle, somehow or other. And then they have me roll over on my stomach, and they touch all along my back. They touch with these needles, somehow or other. I don't know what they're doing, but they seem to be so happy about whatever they're doing. So then they roll me over on my back, and the examiner has a long needle in his hand. And I see the needle. And it's bigger than any needle that I've ever seen. And I ask him what he's going to do with it . . .

(She is beginning to get upset again.)

It won't hurt me. And I ask him what, and he said he just wants to put it in my navel, it's just a simple test.

(More rapid sobbing.)

And I tell him, no, it will hurt, don't do it, don't do it. And I'm crying, and I'm telling him, "It's hurting, it's hurting, take it out, take it out!" And the leader comes over and he puts his hand, rubs his hand in front of my eyes, and he says it will be all right. I won't feel it.

(She becomes calmer.)

And all the pain goes away. The pain goes away, but I'm still sore from where they put that needle. I don't know why they put that needle into my navel. Because I told them they shouldn't do it.

(Another pause.)

Did they make any sexual advances to you?

BETTY

No.

DOCTOR

They didn't?

BETTY

No. I asked the leader, I said, "Why did they, why did they put that needle in my navel?" And he said it was a pregnancy test. I said, "I don't know what they expected, but that was no pregnancy test here." And he didn't say any more.

DOCTOR

All right. We'll stop here now. You'll be relieved, relaxed and at ease. Perfectly at ease, comfortable and relaxed. When I wake you up, you will not remember anything that has transpired here. You will not remember anything that has transpired here until I tell you to recall it.

(He repeats the last phrase for emphasis.)

But it will not trouble you, and you will not be worried about it. You'll be comfortable and relaxed and at ease. No pains, no aches, no anxieties. You have no fear, no anxiety; you are comfortable and relaxed . . . You may wake now. . . .

(Betty opens her eyes slowly.)

BETTY

Am I all the way awake?

DOCTOR

You are awake completely. What happened?

BETTY

Waked—awake—waked up? Head feels fuzzy.

(She laughs lightly.)

DOCTOR

Feel all right now?

BETTY

Yes.

DOCTOR

That's good. We'll continue next time. A week from today. Same time.

(Betty is dismissed by the doctor.)

*   *   *

Betty woke up from her long session feeling drowsy, much as if she had been awakened from a normal night's sleep. She found herself looking around the office, a little startled, and was vaguely aware that she had been slightly upset.

"Somehow I had the feeling I had been crying," she recalls, "You've heard of people crying in their sleep, and the person wakes up, and they're sort of conscious that they've been crying in their sleep. I had this feeling. I really didn't have the feeling of actually awakening completely for about two days. I felt sort of in a daze, a shock, and it was difficult for me to concentrate. I felt that if I just closed my eyes, I would go right back to sleep again." In the car, Barney kept asking Betty about her reaction. She explained that she felt all right, but that she didn't feel up to talking about it. They spent Saturday night with some friends near Boston, but most of the time Betty felt exhausted and was not very good company.

However, she was more composed after a few days, and, as the doctor had suggested, calm and relaxation took over.

She did not know at the time, nor did Barney, that her recall was almost identical with the long report she had written about her dreams.

CHAPTER EIGHT

After Betty's first extensive session, Dr. Simon dictated in his notes:

This interview went on rather smoothly until the areas of fear in the latter part of the sighting of the flying object, when she began to show marked disturbances. Tears were running down her cheeks; she squirmed in her chair. The same occurred with very marked agitation during the procedure that appeared to be taking place in the strange object. During the apparent medical examination, tears were running down Mrs. Hill's cheeks, her nose was running. Although she accepted a Kleenex quite readily, it was felt best to stop at this point, even though she was still in the "operating room," because of the degree of agitation which ensued. Both were given appointments to return a week from today.

They did, on March 14, 1964. Just before the Hills came into the office for Betty's second session, Dr. Simon made a few preliminary remarks on the tape:

The Hills are expected at 8:00 this morning. And the examination of Mrs. Hill will be continued from the point at which it was stopped a week ago, just after the instrument had been removed from her navel for the "pregnancy test."

Before putting Betty into trance, however, the doctor chatted with her informally.

BETTY

I think I ought to tell you before we start that I had two nightmares since I was here last week.

DOCTOR

Would you say they were dreams or nightmares?

BETTY

I'd say they were nightmares.

DOCTOR

And the first one was when?

BETTY

On Tuesday night.

DOCTOR

The Tuesday after you saw me? What was it about?

BETTY

I can't remember what that one was about. I can remember water, a lake, I think, and a shoreline. But I can't remember any more about it.

DOCTOR

Make you think of anything? Any particular lake?

BETTY

No.

DOCTOR

What about the other dream then?

BETTY

The other one was that—I don't know where I was—there was a light, and it was bouncing all around. And I could see this light. It would bounce toward me and then away. And I felt as though I was in great danger from the light, and that it was going to touch me. It was going to shine on me, and I didn't want this to happen. And just as it was coming toward me, I woke up. I was trying to scream, I don't know if I did scream or not. But I woke myself up.

DOCTOR

Did Barney know about it?

BETTY

Well, it frightened me so much, I woke him up.

DOCTOR

You sleep in twin beds?

BETTY

No, double bed.

DOCTOR

You deliberately woke him up?

168

Yes.

DOCTOR

Apparently you must not have screamed, then.

BETTY

I don't think I did.

DOCTOR

Did this resemble anything—you remember your UFO experience—where you had this vehicle coming close to you. Was it anything like that, or was it different?

BETTY

This was like the light of a flashlight. This type of thing. And then it was bounding around, it was small.

DOCTOR

It was small. Not like a spotlight somewhere?

BETTY

It would seem like a spotlight.

DOCTOR

Like an operating-room light? Or something like that?

BETTY

Smaller than that.

DOCTOR

Anything like a light that some doctors would wear on a head mirror?

BETTY

I think it would be larger than that. I would say probably about six or eight inches in diameter.

DOCTOR

All right. Outside of that, everything has been all right? You haven't been worried or upset about our last session? Or don't you remember anything about it?

BETTY

I think I do.

DOCTOR

What do you think you remember?

BETTY

I remember crying, and I could remember, well, I think I remember sitting in the car and watching Barney out on the highway. And seeing men in the road.

DOCTOR

You saw men in the road? Can you envision them now?

BETTY

Yes.

DOCTOR

What do they look like?

BETTY

Not clear enough to make anything out.

DOCTOR

They look like ordinary American men?

BETTY

No. They're different somehow.

DOCTOR

Different in what way?

BETTY

I don't know.

DOCTOR

Was there a vehicle in the road? A car, motorcycle?

BETTY

No.

DOCTOR

Just men in the road? Dressed in any special sort of clothes? Uniforms, or some standard form of dress?

BETTY

I think they were all dressed alike, but I couldn't see, couldn't describe how they were dressed.

DOCTOR

Do you have any idea of why you were crying? You say you remember, you think you remember, crying?

BETTY

Why do I think I was crying? Because I was scared.

DOCTOR

What were you scared of?

BETTY

Because I knew something was going to happen, and I didn't know what it was.

DOCTOR

All right. Now we'll continue.

(The doctor gives the cue word; Betty's eyes close immediately.)

Deep, deep asleep, deep asleep, far asleep. You're fully relaxed, very, very deep asleep. Deeper and deeper asleep. Deeper and deeper, very, very, deep asleep. You're comfortable and relaxed. No fear, no anxiety, very deep asleep. We will go back to where we were a week ago, just where we left off in your experience. Just exactly where we left off. Where are you now?

BETTY

(In deep trance now.)

I'm on the table and the leader, they had hurt me by putting a needle in my navel. And the leader had run his hand in front of my eyes, and when he did this, all the pain . . . I didn't have any more pain. It went away. And I felt very relaxed, and I felt grateful to him because he stopped the pain.

DOCTOR

About this needle, is there anything attached to it? Like a wire or tube?

BETTY

Yes.

DOCTOR

What did it look like?

BETTY

It was a long needle. I would say it looked like a regular needle used for injections. Or maybe to take blood out. I don't know.

DOCTOR

Was there a syringe attached to it?

BETTY

There was something. And I don't know why they did it. It was some kind of test. And I didn't want them to do it. I said it would hurt, and the leader said it wouldn't. When his hand went over my eyes, the pain stopped.

DOCTOR

How far in did he stick the needle?

BETTY

Oh, it was a long needle. I don't know, I thought it—I didn't look, but I would say the needle was four inches long—six, maybe.

DOCTOR

Did you say something was attached to it. Like a wire or a tube?

BETTY

Like a tube. And they didn't leave it in very long. Just for a second.

DOCTOR

What kind of pain was it? Was it like the pain you get when you put a needle in your arm? I guess you have given blood, or something like that.

BETTY

No, it wasn't like that. It was—all I could think of was a knife.

DOCTOR

Like a knife.

BETTY

Because it was such, so much pain. I was—I think I was moaning and couldn't lie still.

DOCTOR

Was there a light there?

BETTY

The room was brightly lighted.

DOCTOR

Was there any kind of spotlight?

BETTY

Yes. There was a light behind my left shoulder. Like a spotlight.

DOCTOR

How big was it?

BETTY

Oh, it was like a desk light. I don't know. Six inches.

DOCTOR

All right. Go on.

Then, I was grateful to the leader for stopping the pain. And he seemed
to be very surprised. And so they said that was the end of the testing.
And the leader helped me sit up. He took hold of my arm, and I swung
around on the table.

DOCTOR

What sort of table was this? Was this an examining table? An operating
table? As in a doctor's office?

BETTY

Like a regular examining table. It wasn't like the examining tables that
some doctors—I don't know if all doctors have the same type of examining tables or not. This was more like a—it was a long table, but it wasn't
awfully long. I guess it was like a regular examining table. It was light,
well, I don't know. White or metal. It was metal, I know; it was hard.
It wasn't soft in any way. That type of thing. So the examiner was helping me. He helped me get off the table, and I swung around. And he
gave me my shoes, and I put those on and got down on the floor. And
my dress was there, and I put my dress on. And I was going to zip it up,
and he took hold of the zipper at the top and zipped it up. And then—
oh, I said, "I can go now. I can go back to the car." And he said,
"Barney isn't ready yet." And so then I begin to get worried, and I asked
him why it was taking so long with Barney. And he said that they were
doing a few more tests with him, but he'd be right along in a minute.
And, gee, there was a cabinet there, and the doctor—the examiner—he
had gone out of the room. There was just me and the leader there.

DOCTOR

So there was a doctor there, you say?

BETTY

The man who did the examining; he did the testing. And he left. So
there was just the leader and me. I felt, I was grateful to him because he
stopped my pain, and now I wasn't afraid at all. And so, I started talking with the leader. And I said to him that this had been quite an experience. It was unbelievable. That no one would ever, ever believe me.
And that most people didn't know he was alive. And that what I needed
was some proof that this had really happened. So he laughed, and he
said what kind of proof did I want? What would I like? And I said, well,
if he could give me something to take back with me then people would
believe it. And so he told me to look around, and maybe I could find

something I would like to take. And I did—and there wasn't much around—but on the cabinet there was a book, a fairly big book. So I put my hand on the book, and I said, "Could I have this?" And he told me to look in the book, and I did. It had pages, it had writing, but nothing like I had ever seen before. It looked almost like a—I don't know—it wasn't a dictionary—maybe a—it had the—the writing didn't go across, it went up and down.

DOCTOR

Did it look like any language that you know, or was it in English?

BETTY

No, it wasn't in English.

DOCTOR

Did it look like—what language do you know that goes up and down?

BETTY

I don't know it, but I can recognize it. I can't read it: Japanese.

DOCTOR

Japanese. Did this look like Japanese? This writing.

BETTY

No.

DOCTOR

Was it writing or printing?

BETTY

It was different. I don't know, because it was—I mean, I couldn't tell. Even though I have seen Japanese written, it had sharp lines, and they were, some were very thin and some were medium and some were very heavy. It had some dots. It had straight lines and curved lines. And the leader laughed and he asked me if I thought I could read it. And I told him no. I laughed too. I said no, but I wasn't taking it to read. But this was going to be my proof that this happened. That this—this was my proof. And so he said that I could have it. I could have the book if I wanted it. And I picked it up, and I was delighted. I mean this was, this was more than I had ever hoped for. And I'm standing there and I'm saying that I had never seen anything like the book and that I was very pleased that he had given it to me. And that maybe some way I could figure out in time how to read it. And so then I said, I asked him where he was from. Because I said that I knew he wasn't from the earth, and I wanted to know where he did come from. And he asked if I knew anything about the universe. And I told him no. I knew practically nothing. That when I was in graduate school we were taught that the sun was the center of the solar system, and there were nine planets. And then later, of course, we did make advances. And I told him about seeing, I think I met him at one time, Harlow Shapley; he wrote a book, too. And I had seen photographs that he had taken of millions and millions of stars in the universe. But that was about all I knew. So, he said that he wished I knew more about this, and I said I wish I did, too. And he went across the room to the head of the table and he did something, he opened up, it wasn't like a drawer, he sort of did something, and the metal of the wall, there was an opening. And he pulled out a map, and he asked me had I ever seen a map like this before. And I walked across the room and I leaned against the table. And I looked at it. And it was a map—it was an oblong map. It wasn't square. It was a lot wider than it was long. And there were all these dots on it. And they were scattered all over it. Some were little, just pin points. And others were as big as a nickel. And there were lines, there were on some of the dots, there were curved lines going from one dot to another. And there was one big circle, and it had a lot of lines coming out from it. A lot of lines going to another circle quite close, but not as big. And these were heavy lines. And I asked him what they meant. And he said that the heavy lines were trade routes. And then the other lines, the other lines, the solid lines were places they went occasionally. And he said the broken lines were expeditions . . .

So I asked him where was his home port, and he said, "Where were you on the map?" I looked and laughed and said, "I don't know." So he said, "If you don't know where you are, then there isn't any point of my telling where I am from." And he put the map—the map rolled up, and he put it back in the space in the wall and closed it. I felt very stupid because I did not know where the earth was on the map. I asked him would he open up the map again and show me where the earth was, and he again laughed. And I thought, well, I still have the book— it's a big book. I went back to the cabinet and put the book down and started to look through it again. All of a sudden, there's this noise in the hall. Some of the other men came in and with them is the examiner. They are quite excited, so I asked the leader what's the matter with them. Did something happen to Barney? It has something to do with Barney. The examiner has me open my mouth, and he starts checking my teeth. And they are tugging at them. I asked them what they are trying to do.

DOCTOR

What are they doing with them?

BETTY

They were tugging, pulling at them. They were very excited.

(She laughs.)

The examiner said that they could not figure it out—Barney's teeth came out, and mine didn't. I was really laughing, and said Barney had dentures, and I didn't, and that is why his teeth came out. So then they asked me, "What are dentures?" And I said people as they got older lost their teeth. They had to go to a dentist and have their teeth extracted, and they put in dentures. Or a person sometimes—Barney had to have dentures because he had a mouth injury. He had to have his teeth extracted. And the leader said, "Well, does this happen to many people?" He was—uh—he acted as if he didn't believe me. And I said, "Yes, it happens to almost everyone as they get older." And he said, "Well—older. What is older?" I said, "Old age." So he said, "What is old age?" And I said—"Well, it varies, but as a person gets older there are changes in him, particularly physically. He begins to sort of break down with age." So he said, "What is age? What did I mean by age?" And I said, "The life span—the length of time people lived." He said, "How long was this?" And I said, "Well, I think a life span is supposed to be about a hundred years at the most. People can die before that—most of them do—because of disease, accident, this type of thing. And I think the average length of time—I don't know—was sixty-five or seventy." So he said, "Sixty-five or seventy what? What did I mean?" I said, "Years." He said, "What is a year?" And I said I did not know exactly how it was figured out, but it had to do with how many days, and the days had so many hours, and the hours had so many minutes, and the minutes had so many seconds. And I thought that in the beginning time had—depended on the rotation of the earth and the position of the planets and the seasons and all. And I had my watch on, and I showed him from twelve to twelve could be from midnight to noon to midnight. I tried to explain, but he did not understand what I was saying. And I couldn't—I don't know—

DOCTOR

But he did understand English?

BETTY

Yes. So then he asked me, well what did we eat? And I said, we ate meat, potatoes, vegetables, milk. And so he asked me, "What are vege-

176

tables?" And I said that this is a broad term and could cover a great variety of certain kinds of foods we eat. But I couldn't just explain what vegetables are, there were too many. And he said was there one kind I liked. I said that I ate a great many, but my favorite is squash. So he said, "Tell me about squash." So I said that it was yellow, usually, in color. And he said, "What is yellow?" So I said, "Well, I will show you." And I started looking around the room, and I couldn't find anything yellow at all. And I wasn't wearing anything yellow. I told him I couldn't show him what the color was, but it was a bright color—something like—we consider sunlight yellow. And there was no sense talking about vegetables, because I couldn't explain what I meant. And —oh! I said, "I can't—I don't know how to do this. I can't tell you where the earth is on the map, I don't know. All these things you ask me—I am a very limited person, when trying to talk to you. But there are other people in this country who are not like me. They would be most happy to talk with him, and they could answer all his questions. And maybe if he could come back, all his questions would have answers. But if I did, I wouldn't know where to meet him." And he laughed, and said, "Don't worry, if we decide to come back, we will be able to find you all right. We always find those we want to." And I said, "Well, now what do you mean by that remark?" And he just laughed. And then Barney is coming. They are bringing Barney out. I hear the men out in the corridor. And I said, "Barney's coming." And he said, "Yes, you can go back to the car now." And I got the book, and Barney is coming up—and his eyes are still shut!

(She laughs again.)

He missed an awful lot. I wonder if they are making him keep his eyes closed. And so it is time to go back to the car, and the leader said, "Come on, we will walk back to the car with you." So I said, "All right, but I do wish I really knew if you were going to come back." And he said, "Well, we will see."

(She pauses a moment, then:)

And we are out in the corridor. Barney is behind me, with his eyes shut and a man on each side of him. And I am all ready to go down the ramp when some of the other men—not the leader—but some of the men are talking. I don't know what they are saying, but they are very excited. And then the leader comes over and takes my book. And I say—ohh— I'm furious.

(She is very intense, almost crying.)

177

And I said, "You promised that I could have the book." And he said, "I know it, but the others object." But I said, "This is my proof." And he said, "That is the whole point. They don't want you to know what has happened. They want you to forget all about it."

(Now she speaks as if talking to the leader.)

"I won't forget about it! You can take the book, but you can *never, never, never* make me forget! I'll remember it if it is the last thing I do." And he laughs, and says, "Maybe you will remember, I don't know. But I hope you don't. And it won't do you any good if you do, because Barney won't. Barney won't remember a single thing. And if you should remember anything at all, he is going to remember it differently from you. And all you are going to do is get each other so confused you will not know what to do. If you do remember, it would be better if you forgot it anyway."

(Again on the verge of crying.)

And I said, "Why? Are you trying to threaten me? Because you can't scare me, because I won't forget. I will remember it somehow." And then he said, "All right now, let's get back to the car." And I was standing there by the side of the ramp, and I'm not so mad now. They have taken Barney ahead, while we were talking. I said, "I do wish I could have some proof of this, because it is the most unbelievable thing that ever happened." We were walking, and the path—just a short distance—it doesn't seem as long as it did going in. Going in seemed awfully long. And he said, "I am going to leave you here. Why don't you stand by the side of the car and watch us leave?" So I said, "All right. I would like that. If we are not in danger from it." He said, "No, you will be far enough away from it." And he said he was sorry that I was badly frightened in the beginning. And I said, "Well, this has been a new experience, and I didn't know what was happening. But I certainly wasn't afraid now." It has been an amazing experience, and I don't know—maybe I would forget it. And I hoped that somehow we would meet again. Maybe he would come back, and there would be people who could answer his questions. And he said, well, he would try. And then they all turned around and started to go back. And I get up to the car, and Barney is inside. I open the car door, and I say, "Come on out and watch them leave." Barney is still in a fog, but his eyes are open, and he is acting more normally now. Delsey is sitting on the seat where I sit, so I felt Delsey, and she is trembling all over. I pick Delsey off the seat, and I'm patting her, and I say, "Don't be afraid, Delsey. There's nothing to be afraid of." I am leaning against the fender of the car, and Barney comes out and stands beside me. And we are going to watch them leave. Delsey won't look, she is still shaking. And it starts glowing—it is getting brighter and brighter.

DOCTOR

What is getting brighter?

BETTY

The object.

DOCTOR

This is the object you saw in the sky before?

BETTY

Yes. Only now it is a large ball, a big orange ball, and it is glowing, glowing, rolling just like a ball.

(Later, Barney and Betty were to recall this as what they felt was the huge moon that appeared to them to be on the ground.)

Now it does and goes down, and there is a dip, and then—zoom—it keeps going away farther and farther. And I say, well, Barney, there they go, and we are none the worse for the experience. Let's get in the car and head back to Portsmouth. And he goes around and gets in his side, and he is driving. I get in the other side. I put Delsey over in the back seat, on the floor, and pat her on the head and tell her she is a good dog. And Barney starts the car, and we start to ride. And I'm just so happy, and I said, "Well, Barney, now try to tell me that you don't believe in flying saucers." And Barney said, "Oh, don't be ridiculous!" And I think he is joking. But then all of a sudden we get this beep-beep-be—beep-beep on the trunk of the car again.

DOCTOR

This is the second time you are getting the beep?

BETTY

Yes. And I said, "Well, I guess that is their farewell. They are off, wherever they are going. And I don't know, it is just so fantastic I suppose we should forget all about it."

DOCTOR

What did you say to each other now?

BETTY

Well, when Barney said, "Don't be ridiculous," I don't know whether he is kidding me or not. So I don't say anything. And he says—so I know he is conscious of this—he said, "Look and see if you can see it around anymore." How can he look out and see something around, if he's going to deny its existence? So I do. I look around, and every once in a while, all the way home, I keep looking for it. And I keep wondering, have they gone? How far away have they gone? But I still have the feeling that they are very close. I keep looking for them. I look through the binoculars.

(Another long pause, then:)

Outside of Concord, north of Concord—we did not stop, but we slowed down very, very slowly and I was watching with the binoculars, and I didn't see them again. But I kept looking all the way home. We kept riding along, and I said, "We won't believe it—no one will. What the heck, let's forget about the whole thing. It is too fantastic. People will think we are crazy. I mean—just to talk about flying saucers, people will think—you know—way out." But this is so much more than seeing something go through the sky. I think I wanted to forget about it. I might as well. What could I do about it? But I wonder if they ever will come back. I go around looking for them. And I look out the window in the kitchen at home.

(Betty repeats the details about arriving home in daylight, unpacking, taking a tub and going to bed exhausted. Then:)

DOCTOR

Your memory is sharp now. Did you at some time tell Barney about your experience? About being in the vehicle?

BETTY

No.

DOCTOR

And he didn't speak to you about being in the vehicle?

BETTY

I can't remember any time he mentioned being inside of it.

DOCTOR

Well, go on.

180

BETTY

I'm puzzled now as to why we didn't talk about it.

(Months later, after the therapy was over, the Hills summarized their thoughts on this question by comparing it to their hypnosis sessions, where they had no memory whatever about what they said, until they were instructed to remember by the doctor.)

Because you would assume that we would. I don't understand it myself. We just said, well, it is an amazing experience, and that is all I said.

DOCTOR

You had two experiences, you say. One of having sighted this thing and seeing the recognizable people. The other experience of being in the vehicle. These were two different experiences.

BETTY

But to me, well, the first one was so small. Actually, all I did was to see it flying through the air and over the front of the car. And you know, I didn't get too much of a look at it. The other part was so overwhelming in comparison.

DOCTOR

Why would you want to keep it a secret?

BETTY

Because I wanted to please the leader, because he told me to forget about it.

DOCTOR

You wanted to please the leader?

BETTY

He told me to forget about it. This had been their decision.

DOCTOR

Why did you want to please this leader so much?

BETTY

I don't know.

DOCTOR

Then you might wonder why Barney didn't talk about it. Do you think he wanted to please the leader?

BETTY

Maybe. Because I am quite sure that he was—well, his eyes were closed. But I think he had some consciousness of it, of what was going on.

DOCTOR

What had they done to him?

BETTY

They had done something that made him keep his eyes shut. And they had to help him along, walking out to the object. And before we left, they were guiding him somewhat. But I think he was walking mostly under his own power.

(She pauses again.)

DOCTOR

Yes, go on.

BETTY

Maybe it was the fear of remembering it, too. It was something about the way he said it was better to forget it. Almost like a threat. And then I think maybe I wanted to forget it myself. I don't know—I was going to say I wanted to forget it myself, but that sounds like a rationalization. Because I really don't know if I wanted to forget. I just couldn't remember it. I can remember parts, but I couldn't remember other parts. It seems to be the part between the beepings.

(Again, after the therapy, in talking to the writer when their conscious minds were allowed to review all the data revealed on the recordings of the sessions, the Hills concluded that the original series of beepings seemed to put them in a trance-like state, which later became deeper on encountering the roadblock. The second series of beepings seemed to restore them to consciousness, although they recall remaining in a dazed condition most of the way home to Portsmouth.)

BETTY

It's very hard to understand. There seems to be the part between Indian Head and where we were stopped on the road. The part where I felt it should be forgotten.

DOCTOR

Why should it be forgotten?

182

BETTY

I don't know. But there was this beep in the beginning, and then I didn't remember anything. I remember somehow Barney turning off the main road, until we saw the men standing there in the road . . .

DOCTOR

How could you see? Did they have lights?

BETTY

I could see the shapes. I could see, you know, when you're driving at . . . along at night, and there's a group or something in the highway, and your headlights on, they show up. We couldn't get by. But I don't remember anything from then up to that time. I don't know how far we rode, or anything. Something must have happened in between in that period. Even if I was just looking at scenery.

DOCTOR

(Pursuing the dream possibility.)

Did you stop to sleep?

BETTY

To sleep? No, I don't think so. I mean I think I would know if we did. I don't have any knowledge of what happened until we saw the men in the road. And then all this happened. Yet we saw the men. Then there was the beeping again. I know I wanted to forget about it.

DOCTOR

When Barney took Delsey out of the car before all this, were you worried?

BETTY

I wasn't worried then. I was watching out for other cars coming along the road.

DOCTOR

Could you have gone to sleep in the car when Barney was out with the dog?

BETTY

No.

DOCTOR

What about when Barney walked away from you, and you stayed in the car?

183

BETTY

Oh, this was when the object was over us, when Barney was walking away from the car towards it . . .

DOCTOR

Did you go to sleep when he was out there?

BETTY

No.

DOCTOR

All right. Now, the next morning, you wished you had a Geiger counter. What happened then?

(Betty repeats in detail the long story of seeing the shiny spots on the car, calling the Pease Air Force Base, watching the compass needle react to the shiny spots, calling her sister. She recalls that when she waxed the car some time later, the spots did not disappear, but actually became shinier. She recounts how she wrote NICAP in Washington and her desire to find out everything she could about the subject of UFO's. At the conclusion of the story, the doctor closed her portion of the session and brings Barney in to check his experiences against some of the material Betty had given him.)

DOCTOR

(After he puts Barney in a trance. Betty, of course, has been dismissed at this point.)

Now Barney, I want to review with you a few points of your experience when you were apparently taken aboard this unidentified object. You are back now, you are comfortable and relaxed. But you are back— back when you were in the road. Tell me about these men.

BARNEY

(In his usual monotone. It is important to remember that neither Barney nor Betty is aware of either his own or the other's story.)

We're coming down the road, and they're waving to me . . .

DOCTOR

Waving to you?

184

BARNEY

Yes. Their hands were not up, but down. In a motion that indicated for me to stop.

(He later described it as a sideways, swinging motion.)

DOCTOR

Was there a vehicle there?

BARNEY

No, there was no vehicle.

DOCTOR

What light was there? Headlights?

BARNEY

It was just an orange light.

DOCTOR

An orange light.

BARNEY

And I could see this orange glow. And I started to put—to get out of my car, and put one foot on the ground. And two men were standing beside me, helping me out. And I felt very relaxed, yet very frightened.

DOCTOR

Did they identify themselves in any way?

BARNEY

No. They didn't say anything.

DOCTOR

Did they indicate what they wanted?

BARNEY

They didn't say anything. And I knew I was walking, or moving down the road from the position of where my car was parked. And I could see the ramp that I went up. And I closed my eyes.

DOCTOR

Where was this ramp going?

BARNEY

To a doorway. A doorway of a very, very funny shape. Like a doorway into a very strange looking craft. And I stepped inside. And I heard a voice, just like the voice I heard on the highway back at Indian Head, telling me that no harm would come to me. And I keep my eyes closed.

DOCTOR

You didn't actually hear it at that time?

BARNEY

That was what I couldn't understand.

DOCTOR

You thought the leader in the vehicle was talking to you?

BARNEY

Yes.

DOCTOR

That was the voice you thought you heard?

BARNEY

Yes.

DOCTOR

You didn't actually hear it, then?

BARNEY

That was what I couldn't understand.

DOCTOR

You think it was transmitted to you, or something?

BARNEY

Yes. I went down this corridor, just a few steps, and into another door.

DOCTOR

They were leading you?

BARNEY

They were holding me on both sides. And I went in. And I thought my foot stumbled over a bulkhead right at the base of the door.

DOCTOR

Was Betty around?

BARNEY

No. Betty wasn't with me. And I saw this table, and knew I would go over to it. I was carried . . . walked over to it. And I just knew I was to get on this table.

DOCTOR

What did this table look like? An operating table? examining table?

BARNEY

It looked like an operating table.

DOCTOR

An operating table. What is the difference between an operating table and an examining table?

BARNEY

Or an examining table. I don't know. I just knew that I could be supported fully on it. And it was very plain. Nothing elaborate. Just that I could lie on it. And my feet extended out from the bottom of it, overlapped it from the position I was lying in. And I felt my shoes being removed. And I could hear a humming sound that they seemed to be making. I was very afraid to open my eyes. I had been told not to open my eyes, and it would be over with quickly. And I could feel them examining me with their hands. . . . They looked at my back, and I could feel them touching my skin right down my back. As if they were counting my spinal column. And I felt something touch right at the base of my spine, like a finger pushing. A single finger.

DOCTOR

Did they speak at all to you?

BARNEY

I could only hear this low, humming sort of sound . . .

(He demonstrates it. It sounds like mmm-mm-mm-mm-mmm-mm.)

And then I was turned over, and again I was looked at. And my mouth was opened, and I could feel two fingers pulling it back. And then I heard as if some more men came in. And I could feel them rustling around on the left side of the table I was lying on. And something scratched very lightly, like a stick, against my left arm. And then these men left. And I was left with what I thought were three men. But the two who had brought me in and the other one who seemed to follow these two men—there were more than one person in the room. But only one man seemed to be moving around my body all the time. Then my shoes were put back on, and I stepped down. And I think I felt very good because I knew it was over. And again, I was led to the door where my feet kicked against this thing at the very bottom of the door, like a high door jamb. And I stepped over it and went back toward the ramp. And I went down and opened my eyes and kept walking. And I saw my car, and the lights were out. And it was sitting down the road and very dark.

And I couldn't understand. I had not turned off the lights. And I opened the door and felt for Delsey and got in. And I sat on the tire wrench, and I took it, removed it from the seat and put it on the floor. And Betty was coming down the road, and she came around and opened the door.

DOCTOR

Was she alone?

BARNEY

She was alone. And she was grinning. And I thought at that time she must have made a road stop in the woods. And she got into the car, and said, "Well, no one will believe this." Or I might have said it, because I said, "No, no one. This is so ridiculous. No one will believe it." And I was thinking what had happened and that we were sitting there, looking down the road, and I could see this glow get brighter and brighter. And we said, "Oh, my God, not again." And away it went. And then I put on the lights and started the car up and drove silently down the road. And I thought I must have driven twenty miles, and I came back to Route 3.

DOCTOR

What did you say to Betty?

BARNEY

Betty said to me, "Well, do you believe in flying saucers?" And I said, "Oh, Betty, don't be ridiculous."

DOCTOR

Did you tell her about your experience in this vehicle?

BARNEY

I had forgotten the experience.

(Both Betty and Barney maintained under the stiffest questioning that their memories for these experiences were immediately wiped out after they left the vehicle . . . until the hypnosis restored them.)

DOCTOR

You had forgotten.

BARNEY

Yes.

DOCTOR

Did she tell you about her experience?

188

BARNEY

No. She did not.

DOCTOR

Then neither of you spoke about your experiences in the vehicle?

BARNEY

No.

DOCTOR

*(He is fully aware that they have consciously claimed that they
had no memory of their joint experience, but he is continuing to
test under hypnosis.)*

Why not?

BARNEY

I didn't remember it.

DOCTOR

I see. This memory had just been wiped out? Do you think that she
had seen the vehicle?

BARNEY

I didn't know.

DOCTOR

And you don't know it today?

BARNEY

No.

DOCTOR

All right, then. We'll stop there.

*   *   *

Dr. Simon woke Barney from his trance, and the session was terminated for the day. Out of it had come the confirmation that Betty's
recall under hypnosis paralleled her dreams almost exactly. Dr. Simon
did not know at the time that Barney, because he was embarrassed about
Betty's dreams and wouldn't consider their basis in reality, had per-
suaded Betty not to talk out her dreams with the doctor until he asked
about them. Betty had agreed not to bring them up until she was asked,
in order not to unduly influence the doctor. He was to explore the dreams
later as the therapy progressed, along with other aspects of the puzzling
case that had to be reexamined.

First, there was the nature of the experience. What was real? What

189

was not? Barney might have certain anxieties on a trip away from home because of his racial sensitivity. Certain fears might be exaggerated under these conditions, making Barney excessively sensitive.

The question marks were obvious: How could two people describe similarly a complex phenomenon in detail, both in the conscious state and under deep hypnosis? How could they recount remarkably similar details of an abduction by humanoid intelligent beings which defied any encounter documented in history, when neither was aware of what the other had seen or reported under hypnosis to the doctor? Did this or did this not happen?

If a person were a believer that hypnosis is absolute, that the individual under hypnosis cannot produce anything but the truth, and if both the Hills were fully under hypnosis, then he would believe their story. The weight of authoritative evidence indicates that in hypnosis what the subject believes determines what is truth to him. Consequently, the truth of the Hill's experience was determined by the strength of their conviction. Where the likelihood of lying is slim, the possibility of reporting a fantasy, fully believed by the subject as true, was a possibility. The probability of two similar fantasies, reported by two different people is slight. What is the answer?

The story at this point could be assessed from two polar points of view: the Hills were lying or the experience was true. An outright lie on one hand and the truth on the other. But what about in between? One possibility: hallucinations. A person may have a temporary hallucination in a period of extreme fear.

In spectrum form, the possibilities at this stage might be considered as follows:

1. The incident was a complete lie.
Dr. Simon did not accept this possibility. He felt the Hills were sincere, credible people, telling what they believed to be the truth both consciously and in the trance state.

2. The incident was a dual hallucination.
The doctor also felt this was improbable. Throughout the sessions, there were no indications of this.

3. The incident was a dream or illusion.
This would be explored in detail as a possibility, that an actual experience had taken place on a sensitized background. A background existed on which could be imprinted illusions or fantasies, later to be reexperienced in dreams.

190

4. The incident was a reality—the abduction took place.

This type of experience had never been documented reliably with any convincing evidence. The doctor believed this to be too improbable, and much material was similar to dream material.

The conscious sighting of UFO's, in the light of reports from scientists, technicians, Air Force personnel, airline pilots, and radar men all over the world remained a distinct possibility, if not a probability. Further, the Hills' honesty seemed sure. They corroborated each other's story both consciously and under hypnosis.

By substantially ruling out lying and hallucinating, the doctor began to weigh the evidence of illusory elaboration, especially an examination of the dreams involved.

Betty did have dreams. Elaborate dreams. Dreams that were repeated in detail under hypnosis. The doctor had examined in Barney's session whether he, too, fell asleep on the road and dreamed the abduction. Barney was convinced that he did not fall asleep on the trip, and the doctor was willing to accept this.

After the first sessions with Barney, Dr. Simon began to assume that the illusions and fantasies were his—and that Betty had absorbed them from him. But in the following sessions, Betty, under hypnosis, confirmed Barney's experiences to a remarkably close degree. This might have been conscious collusion. But here were two people, neither aware of what he was saying, who were telling identical stories (which the Hills weren't permitted to know until later). If the story couldn't be accepted as truth, a rational alternative, given every kind of test, was needed. The doctor would be alert to absurdities and incongruities in finding an explanation that would either support or refute.

With the completion of Betty's second trance, it appeared that the reverse of the doctor's initial assumption might be true. If the total experience were not true, a dream of fantasy initiated by Betty might have been absorbed by Barney, who appeared to be more suggestible. Dr. Simon noted that the things Barney experienced in the abduction portion of the incident were in Betty's story. On the other hand, very little of Betty's abduction sequence was included in his story. His recall of being taken through the woods was vague compared to hers. The details of the examination aboard the craft were much more extensive in Betty's story than in his.

If this assumption were true, then the question of how Betty's dreams were absorbed by Barney would have to be carefully examined.

By the time of the next session on March 21, 1964, the following Saturday morning, Dr. Simon planned to work on the theory that somehow Barney had absorbed and been influenced by Betty's dreams, and that Betty's dreams had developed into convictions that seemed real to her. This possibility had been suggested by a friend.

As with Betty on the previous week, the doctor conversed with Barney before putting him into a trance. At the beginning of the conversation, Barney told the doctor that for the first time in his life he had dreamed about UFO's, on three different nights over the past week—on Sunday, Tuesday and Wednesday. The dream was a recurring one: Barney was standing on the ground looking at UFO's in the sky, and Betty was screaming about them.

The discussion continued for several minutes, with Barney reviewing how he had casually brought up the UFO story to Dr. Stephens, which in turn had led to the Hills' visit to Dr. Simon.

DOCTOR

(Barney is still fully conscious—has not yet been put into trance.)

Also—Betty had been troubled with dreams and nightmares.

BARNEY

Yes. She had been.

DOCTOR

Is that right?

BARNEY

Yes. That's correct.

DOCTOR

(He is going to press hard on the dream aspect now, both in conscious and trance parts of the session.)

And she told you about these things. She told you about these in ordinary conversation?

BARNEY

Yes.

DOCTOR

Did you ever witness any of her nightmares?

BARNEY

No, I had not.

DOCTOR

You were always asleep.

192

Yes.

DOCTOR

Now, you two sleep in a double bed?

BARNEY

Yes. We do.

DOCTOR

Does Betty talk in her sleep?

BARNEY

No. She doesn't.

DOCTOR

As far as you know, she doesn't.

BARNEY

I know she doesn't.

DOCTOR

She does not.

BARNEY

Or when I am awake sometimes, and she's asleep. I've never heard her.

DOCTOR

You've never heard her talk in her sleep.

BARNEY

No.

DOCTOR

Now—when she described these dreams, how much did she tell you about them? What did she tell you she had dreamed?

BARNEY

She would tell me that somehow she is wondering if there is a reference or relationship of her dreams to the missing time period up there in the White Mountains.

DOCTOR

This missing time period—it was pointed out by Mr. Hohman?

BARNEY

He thought it was interesting that the distance between Ashland and Indian Head, which is about thirty-five miles, he thought it was interesting that we just couldn't recall anything about that part of the journey. And I just couldn't seem to recall. And I thought I was just probably driving my car.

You hadn't been aware that the trip took an excessively long time?

BARNEY

No.

DOCTOR

Only when Mr. Hohman pointed it out did it seem to be the case?

BARNEY

Yes. He thought it was interesting when we said we heard these beeping sounds at Indian Head, and then we picked up the story by saying, "And then when we reached Ashland, we heard this beeping sound again." So he said, "Well, what happened in between the period of time, those thirty-five miles?" And I just couldn't seem to recall. Then I realized that I had been driving for a period of time with no knowledge of passing anything, or going down Route 3 in this section.

DOCTOR

Did you pass any cars? Meet any people?

BARNEY

No. We did not.

DOCTOR

So you were particularly impressed by this lapse of time?

BARNEY

No, I wasn't.

DOCTOR

And Betty wasn't. All right.

(The doctor now proceeds to put Barney in a trance, with the usual instructions.)

And now you recall fully all the experiences that we have talked about in this office. All of them—and all of your feelings. But they will not upset you any more. You will recall all of your feelings and all of your experiences. I want to go back and talk about the experiences you had being stopped in the road by some men in dark clothes. Now: from whom did you learn about this experience? You didn't really have it, did you?

BARNEY

(Now in full trance.)

I was hypnotized.

194

DOCTOR

You were hypnotized. By whom?

BARNEY

By Dr. Simon.

*(Barney disassociates the present Dr. Simon in a hypnotic relation-
ship from the Dr. Simon of a past session.)*

DOCTOR

Yes, that's true.

*(The doctor now begins to test the extent of Betty's influence over
Barney. He must be careful, though, of unduly influencing the subject, because of the high suggestibility hypnosis creates.)*

But somebody told you something else about it. Who was that?

BARNEY

Betty.

DOCTOR

And how did she tell you about it?

BARNEY

She said that she had a dream and that she had been taken aboard a
UFO. And that I was also in her dream and taken aboard.

DOCTOR

How did she tell you this?

BARNEY

Usually when someone was visiting. And I just told her it was a dream
and nothing to be alarmed about. She told me a great many of the details of the dreams. She would tell me that she had gone into the UFO
and talked to the people there on board. And she was told that she
would forget. And she told these people in the UFO that she would not
forget. And I told her they were only dreams and that I can't believe
that, whatever these things are. But she says no. That somehow she
feels there is a connection between these dreams and what happened.
Because she has never dreamed of UFO's before. And she would tell
me that they stuck something in her navel. And she was not telling this
to me, but I would be listening as she told this to Walter Webb, as she
told about the UFO sighting that we had had. And then I would hear
her dreams. But never did she tell me directly about her dreams.

*(Barney is now correcting himself from the statement that Betty
told him her dreams directly.)*

DOCTOR

But she did tell you something about them?

BARNEY

Only that they had come into the room with my teeth, and they were quite startled that my teeth would come out and hers would not.

DOCTOR

How about the other things you described to me, about what happened to you when they were examining you. Did she tell you about that?

(Again: Was Barney's recall only that which Betty had put into his mind?)

BARNEY

No. She never told me that. I was lying on the table, and I felt them examining me.

DOCTOR

Is this part of Betty's dream?

BARNEY

(Firmly.)

I am telling you what actually happened. At the time Betty was telling about her dream, I was very puzzled, because I never knew this happened. Now I have found out that it did.

DOCTOR

(More testing, more challenging.)

Now all this dream about being taken aboard—and all the details about it, this was all told to you by Betty, wasn't it?

BARNEY

No. Betty never told me. Only about my teeth.

DOCTOR

Only about your teeth.

DOCTOR

How do you know this happened?

BARNEY

I was hypnotized by Dr. Simon. He has made me go back to September 19, 1961, when I left Montreal, and I told what was happening to me each time he asked. And I talked to people I had never seen before.

196

And I knew that I had seen a UFO, and I came to Indian Head and had gotten out of my car and walked toward this UFO, and I could not believe it was there. And yet I could not make it go away.

(Now Barney becomes emotionally upset again.)

And I felt compelled to go closer—and I prayed to God to make me—
(He breaks down in sobs.)

DOCTOR

This won't trouble you now. Just take it easy.

BARNEY

(A little calmer now.)

And I prayed that I could get away and run back to the car. And I did. And the eyes kept following me back to my car. And I felt very, very upset. . . .

(The doctor lets him go on to recount the Indian Head part of the story again. There are no inconsistencies revealed; it is the same as he has always related it. Then Barney continues into the amnesic period.)

And I kept driving and driving. And I made a turn, and I never knew the reason—and—well—I made that turn. I turned to the left, and I found we were in a strange area where I had never been before. And I was very uncomfortable, and somehow the eyes were following me, telling me that I could be calm, that I would not be harmed, that I should relax. And I saw these men coming down toward me.

DOCTOR

Now what about these men on the road. Are you sure they were there?

BARNEY

(Very firmly.)

They were there. And I never knew this. I never knew this. Because I was hypnotized by Dr. Simon, and he told me I would relate this, and I related this . . .

DOCTOR

(Bluntly.)

Did you dream this?

BARNEY

No. I did not dream it.

DOCTOR

You mean these men actually stopped you?

BARNEY

Yes.

DOCTOR

All right. Go on from there.

BARNEY

And I started to get out of my car. And I felt myself supported by two men, and my eyes were closed ... .

DOCTOR

(It is obvious that Barney is going to stick to his previous story.)

Just a minute. Didn't Betty tell this to you while you were asleep?

(It is possible sometimes to give a strong hypnotic suggestion to a person when he is in certain stages of normal sleep.)

BARNEY

No. Betty never told me this.

DOCTOR

Didn't she have dreams of this and talk to you in her sleep?

BARNEY

She has never told me this. I have never heard her tell me this. Betty said that we were inside a UFO in her dreams. Not how we got there.

DOCTOR

Yes, but didn't she tell you that you were taken inside?

BARNEY

Yes, she did.

DOCTOR

Then she told you everything that was seen inside and about being stopped by these men?

BARNEY

No. She did not tell me about being stopped by the men. She did not have this in her dreams.

(He is correct in this.)

This is only when I was hypnotized . . .

DOCTOR

Only when you were hypnotized.

198

BARNEY

Yes. I saw this.

DOCTOR

How do you account for this? How do you account for this happening? Do you think it really happened?

BARNEY

It did happen. I don't know what to say. I don't want to remember it. I suppose I won't remember it.

DOCTOR

Who told you you won't remember it?

BARNEY

I was told in my mind that I would forget that it happened. It was imprinted on my mind.

DOCTOR

Imprinted on your mind? Who told you?

BARNEY

I thought it was the man I saw looking down at me, and I was looking back at him. And I thought it was him. And he told me that I should be calm and that I should not be afraid. And that no harm would come to me. And that I would be left alone to go on my way. And that I would forget everything, and I would never remember it again.

DOCTOR

How do you account for the fact that you know nothing about Betty's experience, yet she seems to know everything about yours?

BARNEY

I was not in the same room with her. I don't know where she is. I—somehow felt relaxed. I thought it would soon be over and that no harm would come to us.

DOCTOR

You said before you don't know what happened—but you also said that Betty told you a lot about what happened in her dream.

BARNEY

She told me about herself. I did not know about what happened to Betty on the highway, but I never believed her dreams.

DOCTOR

If you don't believe her dreams, why do you believe yours?

BARNEY

I never dreamed about UFO's until last Sunday . . . I had them on Sunday night and on Tuesday night and on Wednesday night. And this is the first time I have ever dreamed of UFO's.

DOCTOR

You told me some time ago that you felt disassociated when you saw this UFO. What did you mean by that?

BARNEY

I felt that I had never known what this feeling was like. And I felt disassociated. As if I had my body moving, and yet my thinking was separate from it. And I had never felt like this before in my life. And I felt disassociated. And I never experienced this feeling again unitl I was in your office. And you made a little doggie come into the room. And I got hypnotized, and it made it seem as if the little doggie was there.

(He is referring to the test the doctor made with him.)

DOCTOR

This was an hallucination then, was it?

BARNEY

That was an hallucination.

DOCTOR

Then how about this story of being kidnapped. Couldn't that have been an hallucination, too?

BARNEY

(The doctor cannot shake him.)

I wish I could think it was an hallucination.

DOCTOR

(Pressing hard.)

Why couldn't it have been?

BARNEY

I don't know.

DOCTOR

How about Mr. Webb suggesting to you that something must have happened with that time?

200

BARNEY

Mr. Webb didn't suggest that. Mr. Webb did not suggest that something happened to me.

(Again, the strict adherence to literal truth under hypnosis. It was Hohman who had made this suggestion.)

DOCTOR

Well, he pointed out that some of your time was not accounted for.

BARNEY

There was a period of time from Indian Head to Ashland, and I kept thinking that all I could remember was getting out on the highway at Indian Head. I could never remember except to run back to my car and drive away. And I did not know what I was doing from Indian Head to Ashland. Mr. Hohman suggested that some of my time was not accounted for.

DOCTOR

Did you feel "disassociated" about this part of the experience?

BARNEY

I did not feel disassociated. I just didn't think about it. I did not feel anything except I had to have driven, and that is all I felt.

DOCTOR

And you're sure this actually happened?

BARNEY

I feel very sure it happened.

DOCTOR

Did these men speak to you?

BARNEY

Only the one I thought was the leader.

DOCTOR

The one you thought was the leader in the space ship?

BARNEY

Yes.

DOCTOR

What kind of language did he use?

BARNEY

He did not speak by word. I was told what to do by his thoughts

201

making my thoughts understand. And I could hear him. And I could not understand in that I *could* understand him. And I was told that I would not be harmed.

DOCTOR

Was this some kind of mental telepathy?

BARNEY

I am not familiar with this term.

DOCTOR

Mental telepathy is being able to understand someone else's thoughts or having your thoughts understood by someone else.

BARNEY

I could understand his thoughts. His thoughts came to me, like I feel your thoughts—when you talk to me, that is. And I know you are there, and yet my eyes are closed. And you ask me questions. And I know you are there, but I don't know where. And this is how he told me that I would not be harmed. And that I would be let alone to go as soon as they had taken me to this room. And then I did not see him or hear his thoughts, telling me I would not remember any of this because I was not harmed, and I wanted to forget. And he helped me to forget by telling me that this is what I wanted to do. And I did not remember anymore.

DOCTOR

You told me that Betty tried to hypnotize you at one time.

BARNEY

When we were standing on the highway in the White Mountains, and we stopped the first time to get a better look at this light that was moving through the sky coming toward us, I could see this happening. And I said, "It's a plane." And Betty said, "Look how it is flying . . ."

(*Barney continues with the long detail of their first stop on Route 3, in which Betty tries to influence him that this is something strange, and not a plane. And how he felt strange about it, because there was no sound. But he indicates that he would not let Betty influence him unduly. His recall is again identical to his previous statements. When he mentions that he hoped to see some traffic, or a State Trooper, the doctor interjects with a question:*)

DOCTOR

You wanted to see some men in the road?

BARNEY

I didn't want to see these men.

DOCTOR

When no harm came to you—did you feel better?

BARNEY

I felt funny. And I could not remember. And yet I *knew* something had happened. And I was confused that I was off Route 3. I was driving back to Route 3, and I just could not understand why I went off it . . . And shortly after that, we heard the beep—beep—beep—beep. And I kept quiet after that.

DOCTOR

Didn't Betty hypnotize you?

BARNEY

No. Betty did not hypnotize me. I wanted to think she was wrong about the object to make me feel better. Because I kept seeing this object in the sky . . .

(Now he repeats again the details of his stop at Indian Head, indicating that he thought the object would have to be a helicopter to stay suspended in the air. Yet there was no sound, and he knew it wasn't a helicopter. Barney reaches the point in the description where he is going to run back to the car.)

And I ran back to the car. And yet I knew it wasn't there . . .

DOCTOR

You knew it wasn't there . . .

BARNEY

I knew it couldn't be real; to have something like these eyes in my head . . .

DOCTOR

In your head?

BARNEY

Yes. These eyes.

DOCTOR

This whole thing was in your head then?

BARNEY

No.

DOCTOR

Why couldn't it be?

BARNEY

I remember it just like I remembered everything up to when I stopped at Indian Head. I remember everything I did. Then I drove down the highway, and I went through North Woodstock and then made a left turn. And Betty was looking at me sort of puzzled. And yet she did not question what I was doing. And I could sense what she was thinking. And I said, "I know what I'm doing all right. I know we're on the right road."

DOCTOR

What do you think she was thinking? You said you sensed what she was thinking.

(Again, the possibility of Betty's beliefs transferred to Barney.)

BARNEY

I thought she was thinking that I had gone off the highway, and that . . .

DOCTOR

Do you often sense her thoughts?

BARNEY

Yes, we sometimes do this. We sometimes try to see if we can sense what the other is thinking. It's not too effective.

DOCTOR.

You've actually tried this? To see if you can sense each other's thoughts? You practice at it?

BARNEY

Well, when I was in Philadelphia, she would say that she would want me to call her. And she said that many times, she would lie there in her room, and say, "Call me, Barney." And then I would call her. Not that I thought that she had asked me to call. But I had already planned the call anyway. But she would say, "You must have read my thoughts, because I was lying here hoping you would call."

DOCTOR

Could she have planted all these thoughts about the UFO in your mind? You said that she wanted to hypnotize you.

BARNEY

I know Betty didn't hypnotize me. I wanted to think she had hypnotized me. I wanted to think that the object wasn't there. And that's why I said, "What are you doing, Betty? Trying to hypnotize me?" And since I kept saying it was a plane, I wanted her to say, "Yes, it's a plane." And then we'd drive on. But it kept following us, and I did not like that. I knew it was very peculiar that a plane would follow a car down the highway like that. And I hoped it was not there. And I did not want it to be there. And yet it kept staying and going down the highway with us . . .

(Again, with full detail Barney recounts what happened at Indian Head, indicating that he could not believe this thing possibly would be there, but it was, and that it seemed as if it were going to capture them.)

DOCTOR

How did you know that it was going to capture you?

BARNEY

I could see this thing coming very, very much closer. And I, too, was walking closer. And I saw like a—it was not like a ramp—but a low object coming down from the bottom of it. I could see this through the binoculars . . . I thought of a ladder, but I didn't really know what it was. Except that something was coming down from it. And the wings that slid out were not like the wings of a plane, but they were like a military bat-type of wing. It slid out.

DOCTOR

You mean the wing slid out from the fuselage?

BARNEY

It did not have a fuselage-type shape. And as the wings began sliding out, the red lights began moving away. And I noticed that they were an extension of these wings. And I was able to break away and run back to the car.

DOCTOR

What was the shape of this? If it wasn't a fuselage shape, what kind of shape was it?

BARNEY

It had more of an oval, pie-plate-type shape.

DOCTOR

Betty described it as cigar-shaped.

BARNEY

When it was soaring in the sky, it gave the appearance of a cigar, because I thought it was a passenger plane because of the longness of it. But then it was off in the distance. And only when it came close did I notice what I thought was a straight row of lights of a plane, turned out to be a curved type of series of lights.

DOCTOR

All right now. We'll stop there unless you have anything further, and this will not trouble you.

(For the first time now, the doctor is going to permit Barney to recall some of the things he has recounted under hypnosis—a major step in the therapy.)

And now—you will remember these experiences to the extent that they will not trouble you. You understand me? After I awake you, you may remember whatever doesn't trouble you about that. You will remember that they are not going to trouble you, they are not going to harm you, everything is past now, and gradually, gradually as we continue to see each other, you'll be remembering these things . . .

(It is important for the instructions to be absolutely clear because of the tendency of the subject to take things quite literally.)

But they will not cause you any nightmares, cause you any trouble, and you will know more and more about it as we go along. Is that clear?

BARNEY

Yes.

DOCTOR

You will have no fear, no anxiety; you will be comfortable and relaxed. And we will continue to talk about these things in this way. The same will be true for Betty. You will remember these things to the extent that you can remember *without being upset, without being bothered.* I will see you again a week from today. That all right?

BARNEY

Yes.

DOCTOR

All right. You may wake now.

(Barney wakes up on the command.)

How do you feel now?

BARNEY

I feel fine.

(A pause, then:)

Uh, I'm puzzled about something. I can remember being hypnotized. Usually when I come in here, I know I have been hypnotized, but I wouldn't remember. And I would look at my watch, and a couple of hours might have gone by. And I would think only about ten minutes had passed. And—and—uh—I can remember things that—about this today's session that I couldn't remember about any session that we had.

DOCTOR

What do you remember now?

BARNEY

About the UFO sighting that I was talking about and—uh—certain things puzzled me that I could not quite understand. Uh, I could never understand—I used to talk to Walter Webb when he would pay us a visit, and we would talk about our sighting, my sighting and Betty's sighting. And I would always talk and would come right up to the men in the craft turning to the panel. And I never could go further than that. But now I can almost see just what that fellow looked like that was looking down at me. And he was not frightening—not frightening in a— a—horrible sense, like a distorted, unhuman type of creature. He was more—the frightening part was the military precision of—as if a person who knew what to do, could do it, and was willing to carry it out. And when I said that he was going to capture me, uh, I used to remember that—but never could remember why I felt he was going to capture me.

DOCTOR

Well—why was he going to capture you?

BARNEY

I don't know why. Why was he going to capture me?

DOCTOR

Well, why did you think he was?

BARNEY

Well, now. I was forced out there. And I never could understand what caused me to walk out to that object when all my senses—uh—would not do a thing like that. And—it's very strange. Almost unbelievable.

DOCTOR

Well, now, some strange things from here on out will occur to you, as we go along. And you're going to become more and more conscious of what was going on in hypnosis than you have remembered. It won't trouble you, and you will remember it more and more as you get used to it and won't be thrown off guard.

BARNEY

Yes—uh—you know, Betty and I used to go to the White Mountains after this sighting, this would have been in 1962, occasionally in 1963. And we would drive around in these different back roads of the mountains. We could never seem to understand what we were doing off the main highway, because I just couldn't seem to understand why I felt I was on Route 3. And yet I wasn't sure I was on Route 3. But now I know that I turned off the highway.

DOCTOR

Now you remember, don't you, you and Betty talking about these things. About her dream?

BARNEY

Yes, yes. Betty would mention those.

DOCTOR

You know a lot more about her dreams than you remembered?

BARNEY

Well, no. Some of the things she told me about her dreams, where I was part of them, was my teeth being taken out. And I said, "Well—what was I doing?" And she said, "You weren't doing anything." Because she really didn't know, other than that.

DOCTOR

You didn't stop to rest any time on this trip, did you?
(The possibility is being explored of a dream along the road, while Barney was asleep.)

BARNEY

Yes. We stopped—oh, it was quite—I'd say approximately twenty miles out of Montreal.

DOCTOR

Yes, but I mean after the sighting.

208

BARNEY

No. We didn't stop at all.

DOCTOR

You didn't stop for a steak, or take a nap, or anything like that?

BARNEY

No. It was just a continuous drive down. And I felt in good spirits. I felt in high spirits. I was well-rested from the night before. And we spent a delightful day, and I knew I could drive from the White Mountains down to Portsmouth, so I didn't stop. I didn't feel too tired. But that's puzzling—because vaguely, I could remember a red glow in the highway, and I always thought someone was doing something like that—flagging me down.

DOCTOR

You mean like swinging a lantern?

BARNEY

No. No. Well—yes—if he had had a lantern in his hand.

DOCTOR

I see from somewhere else?

DOCTOR

Well, that would have given a red glow, wouldn't it?

BARNEY

No—the glow wasn't coming from an object in his hand.

BARNEY

The glow was just a large glow. I—I thought, oh, my God, it can't be in the daytime.

DOCTOR

You had a pretty large moon that night, didn't you?

BARNEY

Oh, I thought about the moon. But the thing was right there on the highway. I could never seem to understand. I have looked for that spot, and I looked for it. I said, "Now, how can the moon be on the highway in that kind of position?" And I could never seem to find any terrain up there that would fit what I sort of dimly remembered. This thing was sitting there was like—and I kept remembering this man flagging me down. And then I sort of don't remember. And now I remember.

209

All right, then we'll continue next Saturday. I'll talk to Betty for a while now.

BARNEY

All right.

* * *

Barney's part of the session had come to an end. For the first time, the things he had forgotten were beginning to come back into his conscious mind. Betty, too, would be permitted to recall those things that would not trouble her after her session on that same day.

But still the questions remained unanswered, and an ultimate solution to the puzzle seemed quite distant.

CHAPTER NINE

The session of March 21 continued, after the discussion with Barney, and Betty was brought back into the room. Betty went into the trance again quickly and easily, as usual. Again, the instructions were given to recall not only the details of what happened, but the feelings Betty experienced about these details.

DOCTOR

(Betty is now fully in trance.)

Now, I want to ask you about your experiences when you thought you were taken aboard this flying object. When you sighted this thing, Barney saw men in the object at the time of the sighting with his binoculars. Did you see any men?

BETTY

This is when he got out and walked toward it?
(She is referring to the Indian Head portion of the experience.)

DOCTOR

Yes. You never saw any men in this object?

BETTY

No. I didn't.

DOCTOR

He described them to you, did he?

BETTY

Yes.

DOCTOR

How did he describe them?

BETTY

He said they were wearing uniforms. He thought they were uniforms. And he said that their leader looked down at him and frightened him. And there was another man and it looked as if they were pulling levers in the wall in back of the leader.

DOCTOR

This wasn't later that he told you this? It was at that time, was it?

BETTY

No. Not at that moment.

DOCTOR

Was it at some time after you got home?

BETTY

It was after we got home.

DOCTOR

At the time, he didn't tell you anything about it?

BETTY

No. He didn't.

DOCTOR

Well, go on.

BETTY

He did say that they . . . I had the idea that there was someone, he must have seen someone, even though he didn't say so. Because he kept saying, "THEY are going to capture us."

DOCTOR

I see.

BETTY

He didn't say IT was going to.

DOCTOR

He was quite frightened, then?

BETTY

Yes.

DOCTOR

And you were frightened?

BETTY

No, I don't think so. Not at that time. I was more curious and interested. And I had the feeling of being sort of helpless. That something was going to happen, and I didn't have too much control over it. But I wasn't really afraid. I guess I was looking forward to it.

DOCTOR

You were looking forward to something happening?

BETTY

Yes.

DOCTOR

What sort of thing did you look forward to happening?

BETTY

I didn't know what was going to happen.

DOCTOR

A new experience?

BETTY

Uh-huh.

DOCTOR

Now, when you were supposedly on board, and you say he put this needle into your navel . . .

BETTY

Yes.

DOCTOR

Was there any blood?

BETTY

Not to my knowledge.

DOCTOR

Did you find anything after you were home to indicate something had been put into your navel?

BETTY

I don't remember looking.

DOCTOR

You didn't think of looking?

BETTY

No.

DOCTOR

So you wouldn't know. And now——there is no indication, I take it?

BETTY

I don't think so.

DOCTOR

When the leader was talking to you, he spoke in English, you said, and yet he seemed to be of foreign origin.

BETTY

Yes.

DOCTOR

And he didn't know a good many things.

BETTY

And he had an accent.

DOCTOR

And he had an accent. Are you familiar with the accent? German? French? Japanese? Some other?

BETTY

No, I don't know what kind it was. One of the men had a worse accent than the leader.

DOCTOR

Did you ask these people their names?

BETTY

No.

DOCTOR

Why not?

BETTY

I didn't think of it. They didn't ask me my name, either. But I kept saying Barney's name, so they knew this.

DOCTOR

And you and Barney did not talk about these experiences afterward?

BETTY

Right afterward?

DOCTOR

Well, at any time. You did say, I believe, that you didn't talk about it on the way home.

BETTY

No. We didn't.

DOCTOR

But you did tell it to him afterwards, did you?

BETTY

Well, when I had the dreams, I told him I was having nightmares, well not really nightmares, but strange dreams. But I didn't tell him about my dreams at that time. And then, when Mr. Hohman and Mr. Jackson came to the house, and we were trying to recall—I think it was Mr. Hohman asked us why the trip took so long to come home. And that's when I said that I remembered about the moon being on the ground.

DOCTOR

Is this that big yellow object, or light, you saw?

BETTY

Um-hmm. It was just like a big moon. And it was on the ground. I could see sort of right through the trees in front of us.

DOCTOR

Barney heard you describe all these things, I suppose?

BETTY

Well, when they said, "What took so long?" I said, "We didn't know what took so long." But then I started to think about the moon being on the ground. And I mentioned seeing it. And Barney said, "Yes. I saw it too." Then we thought that we should check and see, try to find out what time the moon set that night, to see if it were the moon, or what it was. And, when we were talking about this, I got quite upset —I don't know if I showed this or not—when this happened, I thought of my dreams. And I thought, well, maybe there was some basis to the dreams I'd been having. Maybe this is what took us so long.

DOCTOR

Now your dreams—

BETTY

Yes?

DOCTOR

Were they the things that happened in this experience you thought you had had? The dreams were of being placed aboard this vehicle?

BETTY

The dreams were something like it, but not. There were still a lot of differences.

(Betty goes on to recount the story of how she told her supervisor, who suggested that this might have happened, might have been the dream of an actual experience.)

215

(Referring to Betty's supervisor.)

She is the one who said this actually might have happened to you?

BETTY

Yes. She said this must have happened to you, because if it had not happened, then you wouldn't be acting this way. That I wouldn't have this concern about it. I'd say, "Well, it was a dream, and I should forget it." And then I began to feel that something had happened, I wasn't sure what it was. There was something more than what I could really, actually, truthfully say I could remember.

DOCTOR

Now—was she the only one you told your dreams to?

BETTY

No. I told my sister Janet.

DOCTOR

How about your upstairs neighbor?

BETTY

No.

DOCTOR

Did you tell anyone these dreams in Barney's presence?

BETTY

I think he must have heard me talk about them.

DOCTOR

So he really did know about your experiences, didn't he?

BETTY

He knew some of it. I think he must have heard me saying something to somebody.

DOCTOR

Didn't all these things that you feel happened—didn't they happen in your dreams? Couldn't this *all* have been in your dreams?

BETTY

No.

DOCTOR

Why do you feel sure of that?

BETTY

Because of the discrepancies.

216

Now tell me about the discrepancies that make it clear that it couldn't have been your dreams. Now—we know your supervisor told you it must have happened. Up until then, you couldn't believe it. Now after she told you that, you believed it happened. What were the discrepancies? You didn't know about the discrepancies because you couldn't remember about this experience, you told me.

BETTY

I knew what I had dreamed and that it was different. This was different.

DOCTOR

What makes the difference?

BETTY

There's so much more. And—

DOCTOR

Suppose that "so much more" had been parts of dreams that you couldn't remember? One doesn't always remember all of his dreams. Isn't that possible?

BETTY

I don't know.

DOCTOR

In other words, the dream that you can remember did not have everything that you were able to tell me. Is that right?

BETTY

That's true.

DOCTOR

But if you were able to tell me all of your dream, including the part of it you couldn't remember, would that fit in?

BETTY

No. Because some things were different.

DOCTOR

Some things were different.

BETTY

Yes.

DOCTOR

Well, could it be then that when you remembered the dream, some things were different? You just remembered differently because you were afraid to remember everything.

BETTY

You mean in my dreams, I would be afraid to remember?

DOCTOR

No. If you remember dreams, sometimes you forget parts of them. Because you're fearful. You know that, I think, from your own training as a social worker.

BETTY

Uh-huh.

DOCTOR

And yet there might be some parts of a dream that are misremembered, for the same reason. Is that possible?

BETTY

Well, I dreamed in my dreams I walked up steps. And here, I didn't walk up steps. I walked up a ramp.

DOCTOR

Is that a very significant difference, do you think?

BETTY

I don't know.

DOCTOR

The way you walked up?

BETTY

But the map—I could almost—in here . . .

(She is referring to her recall under hypnosis when she says "in here.")

in here, I could almost draw it. If I could draw, I could draw the map.

DOCTOR

You want to try to draw the map?

BETTY

I'm not good at drawing. I can't draw perspective.

DOCTOR

Well, if you remember some of this after you leave me, why don't you draw it, try to draw the map. Don't do it if you feel concern or anxious about it. But if you do, bring it in next time, all right?

BETTY

I'll try to.

218

DOCTOR

But don't feel as if you're compelled to do it.

(Sometimes a post-hypnotic suggestion can be very distressing. The doctor is guarding against this by leaving it up to Betty's volition.)

BETTY

Okay.

DOCTOR

Now—what other discrepancies. You mentioned the ramp and the stairs.

BETTY

There's always so much more. Here.

(Again, here *means under hypnosis.)*

DOCTOR

There's always so much more in what you've told me than there is in the dream. Is that right?

BETTY

Yes.

DOCTOR

It could be that all that extra that you remember could be the part of the dream that you didn't remember. Couldn't it?

BETTY

No. I don't think so.

(Like Barney, she is unshakeable.)

DOCTOR

Again—why don't you think so?

BETTY

Because—I know that you can dream, and not remember. But—

DOCTOR

How can you account in this experience for these men who seemd to speak our language and yet didn't know a lot of things about it. Like dentures. And aging. And things like that. And you felt they came from another world, I take it. Didn't you?

BETTY

Ummm—yes.

219

DOCTOR

Then how would they know all about this? How could it happen? Have you tried to explain all this to yourself?

BETTY

How could they speak English?

DOCTOR

Yes. How could this happen? That they could communicate with you in this way? And yet they were not of this world?

BETTY

Maybe they've been studying us.

DOCTOR

That would mean they would have to come here and know us, and everything else—wouldn't it?

BETTY

Umm, yes. And maybe they picked up some radio stations.

DOCTOR

But in a dream, this could all happen. Things don't have to be explained in a dream. Did you feel that they could communicate with you in any other way than words? Were they able to transfer thoughts?

BETTY

I don't know about thoughts.

DOCTOR

Do you believe that thoughts can be transferred?

BETTY

Yes. To a certain extent.

DOCTOR

Have you been able to transfer your thoughts to anyone, or receive someone else's thoughts?

BETTY

Barney and I are always saying the same thing at the same time. That type of thing.

DOCTOR

Well, do you communicate in any other ways? Could you have communicated all this to Barney through thought transference?

220

BETTY

(She laughs.)

No. I don't know as I could believe to that extent. Like, sometimes I used to have a teacher in college, and I would sit in the front row, and I might be bored. I would sit there, and I would think, "Scratch your face, you know, scratch your leg." And then wait to see how long it would take him to do it. You know—play around like this.

DOCTOR

Then you wanted to see how much power there was in thoughts?

BETTY

Yes.

DOCTOR

But you had no such communication between yourself and these strangers?

BETTY

(She pauses a long while, as if thinking this over.)

I don't know if I did hear them in English.

(Is she trying to please Dr. Simon by giving him the answer she thinks he wants? This is common in hypnosis.)

DOCTOR

Oh? You didn't hear them in English?

BETTY

I don't know.

DOCTOR

How do you think you heard them, then?

BETTY

I've been telling myself I heard them in English, with an accent. But I don't know.

DOCTOR

Well, did you hear them in any language? Or was it by thought transference?

BETTY

I knew what they were saying.

DOCTOR

You knew what they were saying—

BETTY

And they knew what I was saying—

DOCTOR

(As Betty begins to show signs of emotional strain.)

All right. This won't trouble you. You're all right.

(She is calm now.)

Well—do you think that was some form of thought transference?

BETTY

(Musingly.)

It could have been. But if it was, I knew what they were thinking.

DOCTOR

You knew what they were thinking. You rather liked this leader, didn't you?

BETTY

I was afraid of him at first.

DOCTOR

But afterwards?

BETTY

I—you know—began to feel that they weren't going to harm me.

DOCTOR

So it all works out that you're not harmed, and everything is all right.

BETTY

Yes.

DOCTOR

All right, now. After this, it will not be necessary for you to forget everything that goes on here. But you will remember only that part that you can remember without being upset and without being worried and bothered. Do you understand?

(Again, as with Barney, the important step of permitting Betty to slowly filter in to her consciousness the material she has revealed under hypnosis.)

BETTY

Yes.

DOCTOR

And it will not trouble you, any of it. As you go along, it will bother you

222

less and less. And you will be able to remember those things that you can remember without anxiety and without fear. You will be able to talk more and more about it in that way. But, in the meantime, you will not be troubled by any of the things that you do remember. And gradually, it will come back more and more clearly. And you will talk about it more and more. Is that clear?

DOCTOR

BETTY

Yes.

DOCTOR

You will have no fear, no anxiety. You'll be comfortable and relaxed, and we will continue to recall these things and discuss them together. You'll have no fear, no anxiety. I'll see you again a week from today. All right. Wake, Betty. You may wake.

(Betty wakes from her trance.)

How do you feel now?

BETTY

All right.

DOCTOR

Do you know more about what happened?

BETTY

Yes.

(The doctor reassures her that she'll be all right, and plans are made for the appointment the following week.)

After the Hills had left, the doctor dictated his brief summary:
There seem to be indications that a great deal of the experience was absorbed by Barney Hill from Betty, in spite of his insistence that this was his own. And there are definite indications that her dreams had been suggested as a reality by her supervisor. The implications are self-evident, and it is planned now to continue these interviews at a more conscious level. Both of them appear to have been remembering more now after the sessions.

CHAPTER TEN

By March 28, the following Saturday, the recall of what had been taking place in the sessions had increased progressively on the part of both Barney and Betty. Dr. Simon explored this aspect when the next session began. He spoke first with Betty before putting her in trance.

DOCTOR

Do you recall much of your experience now?

BETTY

Yes, I think so. I've also had a couple of nightmares again.

DOCTOR

Is that so?

BETTY

Yes. And Barney's been having nightmares all week. He seems to have the feeling right now, we were talking about this last night, trying to figure this out: Are they going to come back?

(The doctor reviews Betty's dreams in detail, comparing them with the recall of what she feels is the actual experience, as revealed under hypnosis. The session continues with Betty now in trance.)

DOCTOR

You seemed in some ways to anticipate, in spite of your anxiety, to look forward to these men coming back and taking you on some adventures. Is that the way you feel?

BETTY

Frankly, I wouldn't be surprised to see them.

DOCTOR

Would you like to see them?

BETTY

Not right now.

DOCTOR

Not right now. When?

BETTY

If I could get over being afraid. Right now I think I'd die of fright if I saw them again.

DOCTOR

All right. This will not trouble you. You will as during the past week be able to remember more and more as you lose your fright, fear, and you will not recall any more than you can tolerate and live with. You will be relaxed and comfortable and have no anxiety, and your memory will continue to improve for everything as you can remember without anxiety. You will be comfortable and relaxed, no pain, no anxiety. You may wake now. How do you feel?

BETTY

All right. Fine.

DOCTOR

Well, I'm going to see Barney, then I'm going to see the two of you together afterward.

BETTY

All right.

DOCTOR

Do you remember what happened?

BETTY

I think so, if I think about it.

DOCTOR

You don't feel like thinking right now?

BETTY

(Laughs)

I could think about it, maybe, in about five minutes.

*   *   *

To both Barney and Betty, now that the doctor was permitting their revelations under hypnosis to filter back to consciousness, the strange

226

experience became in their eyes a definite possibility, this in spite of Barney's previous stout resistance to the whole idea of UFO's and Betty's dreams.

To the doctor, much was unresolved, even though the Hills had resisted his challenges both in and out of hypnosis. By working with them consciously now, with only occasional periods of hypnosis as might be indicated, he hoped to achieve alleviation of their anxiety, which in spite of the mystery of the reality or nonreality of the abduction story, was the main purpose of the therapy.

It was after this session that Betty gave the written dreams to the doctor to read. Of significance was the fact that these, too, were identical in detail both to the dreams she had just described, as well as her recall of the amnesic period under hypnosis.

Barney's discussion on that morning of March 28 reflected what had been going on in his mind during the week since Dr. Simon had instructed him that he could recall some of the material revealed in the trance state.

DOCTOR

Well, how've you been, Barney?

BARNEY

Not bad, Doctor. Uh, very interesting. So many things I had to talk about all this week, and I was quite amazed, last week, particularly, it's interesting how I know these things I want to say, and then when I get here I am not reluctant to discuss them, but I seem not to be able to put them in proper words. What I'm trying to say is that I just can't seem to believe—well, I'm just flabbergasted, if this is any explanation of what I'm trying to say.

DOCTOR

Flabbergasted about what?

BARNEY

At what I remembered from our sessions last week.

DOCTOR

Uh-huh.

BARNEY

This business of seeing a UFO, an object, and personal contact with it seems to stretch my imagination as to the incredibility of the whole thing. Last Sunday, Betty and I were so concerned at this point that we made a trip up to Indian Head where we turned around and slowly drove back. And I said that what I shall do is whatever more or less my instincts direct me. Maybe I'm using the wrong term when I say *instinct,* these are the turns I will take. And we traveled just south of North Woodstock where I made, as if I had done this before, a sharp left turn onto Route 175.

DOCTOR

North Woodstock, you say?

BARNEY

Yes. And I made a left turn at Route 175 from Route 3. Well, it was during the daylight so things would look different in the day than they would at night, but we both were saying, gee, this looked just like something we'd seen before. We had, to our conscious knowledge, never been in that particular area of New Hampshire, and there was a sharp right turn which would have carried us in a large circular drive toward a town called Waterville. What happened is that as we traveled a short distance, oh maybe three miles, we suddenly ran into a barricade, a barrier which would have indicated snows in the area. And in backing out we saw a fellow in the area that lived there, and I asked him about getting through. And he said not until the next month can you get through there, that area it's snowed in. But to reach Waterville you could go and approach from another area, but it is a continuous road that circles around this, in this particular location. And, we are now determined to travel that road when the snows thaw, and it's negotiable. Now, these were some of the thoughts that went through my mind. Another thought that I thought of was that Betty will say, "You don't accept or you can't, or are unwilling to accept things." And my answer to her is that it is not a matter of really accepting, but that I'm so flabbergasted by the entire thing that I find it difficult to accept it. I told her I wanted to ask you, What are the elements, what are the chances of a person uh, hallucinating something? I want to know the answers to these things. There are peculiar things that happened with Betty and me that we had never discussed prior to coming here and being hypnotized by you.

DOCTOR

Such as, what?

BARNEY

One is that the door of this thing that we went into had a bulkhead—well, that may be the wrong thing to describe it—but at the door jamb there seemed to have been an obstruction. And I tripped going, and I tripped coming back. And I mentally had the picture of the type of doors on naval crafts, of naval crafts or ships at sea—the type of door that swings.

DOCTOR

Have you been in the military service?

BARNEY

In the Army, not in the Navy.

DOCTOR

World War II?

BARNEY

World War II. And Betty realized that. And there was something else, too.

DOCTOR

She realized what, that there was an obstruction?

BARNEY

Yes. And there's something else that disturbs us both. And this has disturbed me greatly. Many times I was tempted to call you, but that inner mechanism of mine that causes me to fight things out, I guess, prevented me from disturbing you if it could have been prevented, knowing you are busy. But Betty said that somehow now she cannot believe she communicated with these creatures, if there had been these creatures, by word of mouth. And I was always aware that somehow there was something peculiar, which is the absence of a mouth. And I had no doubts about getting out of my car, walking toward this large thing hovering in the sky and staring down at me. In my conscious mind I always knew that this is what had actually happened. But then I would become confused when I said it would talk to me, or rather it had communicated something to me, and that was very frightening to me, and I ran, and I saw this through binoculars, 7 x 50 binoculars. So that next question would have been by someone hearing this is: What did they look like?

DOCTOR

Do you always carry binoculars with you when you travel?

BARNEY

Always in my car. I just always carry binoculars because Betty and I love traveling on weekends.

DOCTOR

It is relatively uncommon for people who are just traveling. They usually carry cameras.

BARNEY

Well, we also have a camera. But we didn't own a camera at that time.

229

Well, go on.

So that, I always knew that I had looked up at something. I had seen figures looking down at me, in what I thought was a smile by our conventional method of smiling with the lips going up. It was more of a twinkling or a recognizing an eye as being a part of the smile. And I just can't remember any mouth.

Uh-huh.

I just can't recall any mouth. And in a faint way of hearing these things talking, which is very confusing to me, it was like a mumbling when they were, when it was not anything addressed or directed to me. It was a mumm, mumming type of a thing. Less than a mumm mumm, but more of a mmmmmm. And this is baffling to me, particularly when Betty said well, last week, she realized that she was *not* talking to them. There is something else I want to say before I forget to mention it. Betty mentioned to me that at the time that this sighting had taken place, I was working nights. And we did not sleep together; only on weekends because it was the type of situation that I would sleep in the day and she at night. And when she had told me these dreams of hers, to be polite I listened. Well, she was not really telling them to me, but telling them to others. And I would never offer any opinion, because I had my own private opinion about dreams, that they were dreams. Because I dream, and dreams don't have any particular significance other than that you dream of something that you have associated somewhere in your past or in your life or in your present, and this stimulates your mind to dream when you are asleep. And this is the way I put Betty's dreams. Not that I was a physical part of her dreams, but only a part of her dreams in her mental capacity to dream. And so I never put any great emphasis on her dreams, I had never dreamed consciously of a UFO in my life until here recently. And I wanted to ask, "Is it possible I could have dreamed of a UFO unconsciously and not have had—?" To clarify what I am saying, I have had many dreams over many periods of times of my life and in many instances I can't recall what I dreamed about. But I do know that it was along a certain particular line. If I had dreamed of being in Philadelphia, I would waken and forget the dream. But I would know that somehow the dream content was somewhere in Philadelphia, and I would not be totally unaware. But, I had never, to my knowledge, dreamed of a UFO until recently.

DOCTOR

By recently, you mean last week?

BARNEY

Sunday before last, which would have been a week ago last week.

DOCTOR

You dreamed that before you saw me last time.

BARNEY

Yes.

DOCTOR

You didn't tell me about that.

BARNEY

I did mention that to you, that I had dreamed of a UFO—

DOCTOR

Yes, oh, yes. You said you dreamed of a UFO, but you didn't have any details.

BARNEY

No details were associated with it.

DOCTOR

In other words, you feel that you dreamed of a UFO, but you couldn't remember the dream, is that it?

BARNEY

You mean in the past?

DOCTOR

No, at that time, in the way we were talking about. You asked me if one could dream, say, unconsciously.

BARNEY

Well, what I meant is: Could I after 1961 have dreamed of a UFO, and then under hypnosis my dream is coming out?

DOCTOR

Now, what you're talking of, what do you think it might have been?

BARNEY

Repeat that question?

You say, now your dream is coming out. To what part of the things that you recall are you referring?

BARNEY

Well, the only part of my dream that I had recently that made any sense was the structure and walking up to the object. It was just a distorted dream, but the physical structure of the craft itself fitted in with my conscious attitude of what a craft like this would look like. And, last night, I dreamed again of being on a UFO. And this could have been a result of Betty having drawn a picture, what she was attempting to do was to draw a picture of a map with, she calls it perspective, and I call it a map in dimension. But this is what she was attempting to do. And this is what could have stimulated me to a dream of this type. But I dreamed that I was on aboard this UFO, and I was questioning the people there, where did you come from? And they were telling me that they had come from a planet . . .

(Barney continues to describe his dream, in which he reflects his growing preoccupation with the possibility that something strange and weird happened in the interval: talking with intelligent humanoid beings, etc. As he concludes, the doctor speaks.)

DOCTOR

Now, you and Betty have been talking to each other about what's been going on, you've been remembering things?

BARNEY

Yes.

DOCTOR

So, she's now told you about her experience on the object.

BARNEY

Yes.

DOCTOR

And you've told her.

BARNEY

Yes.

DOCTOR

About being on board, being examined, and all those things?

BARNEY

Yesterday, at the breakfast table, we were talking about it. And, gee, I get chills. I get chills even now. Ugh.

DOCTOR

So it's something you don't want to remember too strongly now?

BARNEY

Well, I do remember what we were talking about. I was telling her I can see it so clearly. This much I had always realized: that somewhere, this is prior to coming here for hypnosis, that I had always realized that somehow there were someone stopping us. But I never could put any sense to it. So I dismissed it completely from my mind.

DOCTOR

Could someone have flagged you down? Just someone, anyone who might flag you down?

BARNEY

I would have—I'm quite sure I would have remembered.

DOCTOR

Well, you were pretty frightened at the time.

BARNEY

I would have remembered someone flagging me down. Particularly a group of men.

DOCTOR

Well, now, about this experience. How do you feel about it? You have a lot of doubts about it. You're asking me, could it have been a dream?

BARNEY

Yes, I'm asking these kinds of questions.

DOCTOR

What do you think, could it have been?

BARNEY

Well, now, in the truthful answer, trying now not to conceal my feelings of being ridiculed, I would say it was something that *happened*. But I—I—I put a protective coating on myself, because I don't want to be ridiculed.

DOCTOR

You and Betty appear to have had somewhat similar experiences, but also different. It seems to me that Betty knew about everything that happened to you, but you know nothing about what happened to her.

233

BARNEY

Well, Betty didn't know. All she knew about me is that I had gone into a room and then had come from this room. And that they had come running out of it.

DOCTOR

That you heard from Betty telling her dreams?

BARNEY

Yes, I have heard of these dreams.

DOCTOR

And all these things were found in her dreams, weren't they? These things that happened to her?

BARNEY

The things that happened to her?

DOCTOR

Yes, that she said happened in the object.

BARNEY

I would say there is a similarity.

DOCTOR

You heard all this?

BARNEY

I had heard all that. Yes. The difference is that though I had heard her dreams, and Betty would talk about them, I never would talk about the idea of having or believing I had been stopped on the highway. I knew I saw a large object. I knew this, but I didn't think much of it.

DOCTOR

Well, you were pretty well convinced of having sighted something. But you have some doubts in mind about the rest. Of whether it was reality, or dream, or what it was.

BARNEY

Well, it is because of my unfamiliarity with hypnosis, what it can do.

DOCTOR

Never mind about hypnosis. How do you feel? You have, you were expressing some doubts about it. You asked me, could this have been an hallucination and a dream?

234

Yes, talking to you as a professional man.

DOCTOR

Then, why would you and Betty have the same experience? If you could give me some possible explanation there?

BARNEY

Uh, these are the questions I'm asking. Could she have influenced me?

DOCTOR

Well, you were always afraid she would influence you, weren't you?

BARNEY

That's interesting, because I knew she *wasn't*.

DOCTOR

You accused her of trying to hypnotize you to make you believe something you didn't want to believe. I'd rather reserve diagnosis of that for a while. I want to go through more material yet.

BARNEY

Yes. Well, at the time I would like to say this: that when I was standing out there, I knew she *wasn't* influencing me. What I was thinking is that I would rather not talk about it. Okay, we see something, now let's get in our car and drive about our business. And this irritated me when she kept saying, "But look, it's right over there!" And even as I would slow down to take a peek, I would see this object out there. And this greatly irritated me. And so I said, "What are you trying to do? Make me see something that isn't there?" Knowing that it *was* there and not wanting it to be there. And I think this is a part of why I'm confused.

DOCTOR

Now, Betty had a nightmare or two before she saw me last time. She tells me she woke you up and told you about it. Do you remember that?

BARNEY

Yes, she did wake me up.

DOCTOR

She thought she had possibly screamed. But if she had, you would've heard. But she said then she woke you up and told you about it.

BARNEY

I didn't hear her. And then she said she had this dream.

235

DOCTOR

Did she tell you what it was?

BARNEY

That I'm trying to remember. Whether she told me what the dream was or not. Uh, it had something to do with being on the craft and that. She had discovered that she wasn't talking to these people.

DOCTOR

This she told you was a dream?

BARNEY

This is what she told me was her dream.

DOCTOR

It's not what she told me was a dream. She told me that there were two dreams, really. One of them was sort of like a moonbeam down on a lake, something like that, or over a body of water.

BARNEY

Yes, she told me about that.

DOCTOR

And then of a yellow object, this great lighted object taking off, which both of you have experienced.

BARNEY

Well, that, yes. If this was a dream that she had, it is only an extension of something I do know and did see. But eliminating the water from what I'm saying, is this large object sitting there, and then it started moving off and going very rapidly away. This, too, I always knew about before hypnosis. But much of this I wanted to forget very badly.

DOCTOR

Why were you so anxious to forget it? You've been worried this week, haven't you?

BARNEY

Well, I don't know whether I can say this is the typical, or rather this is more of the typical manifestations of the male who likes things solid and explainable. I don't know whether this would be my answer as to why I wanted to forget.

DOCTOR

Are you afraid of something?

BARNEY

Am I afraid of something?

DOCTOR

Yes.

BARNEY

Yes, this is something else I'm grateful you brought out. Because somehow I always had a fear, after this sighting, that a great disaster—now how I could explain this disaster? There was harm that could come to Betty and me by pursuing this.

DOCTOR

I see.

BARNEY

By even trying to investigate. See, I've always been the reluctant person.

DOCTOR

What sort of harm, from where would it come?

BARNEY

From a position that I best can describe it that a person would know if ever I had gone too far by revealing something.

DOCTOR

You mean then that you had a secret of somebody's that you were afraid of revealing? Or do you feel you had been told that—

BARNEY

To forget.

DOCTOR

You had been told to forget these men?

BARNEY

Yes.

DOCTOR

At least, this is the way you feel about it, whether it was a dream or reality.

BARNEY

Yes.

DOCTOR

And this is part of a dream.

BARNEY

I know it *wasn't* a dream.

DOCTOR

That you were told to forget by the men?

BARNEY

Yes. That this is something that can really serve no purpose, and you have to forget it, you will forget it, and it can only cause great harm that can be meted out to you if you do *not* forget.

DOCTOR

You say you were told this?

BARNEY

Yes. As if this is a conclusion to an event. That now it is over, you forget.

DOCTOR

In other words, it is a feeling about the event.

BARNEY

Yes.

DOCTOR

That you mustn't speak of it.

BARNEY

Yes.

DOCTOR

There is a danger in speaking of it.

BARNEY

Yes.

DOCTOR

And the danger is going to be, what? Any notion about that?

BARNEY

Well, there is a reluctance on my part to be abroad with Betty up in the mountains at night. Not during the day, or not necessarily in the mountains, but in any isolated area. It was as if when I was walking out to this craft, and now I'm going back prior to hypnosis, the same type of effect that was drawing me to it. Before I broke and ran back to the car. It was the same type of power as I tried to describe, a force that was causing me to continue to come closer to it, even when I wanted to run away.

DOCTOR

A fascination in spite of your fear?

Well, fascination was there. I was amazed.

All of this was a feeling in yourself. Wasn't it?

Being out there on the highway?

No, the feeling of power, and so on.

Yes, yes, this was very, very—

This was a feeling in yourself, wasn't it? As if it were being produced from something stronger than yourself.

It was being produced by something stronger than me, outside of me, that I wasn't creating this.

I see. This power.

* * *

As the discussion continued, Barney brought up the fact that the small circle of warts that had developed in an almost geometrically perfect circle around his groin some four months after the incident at Indian Head had become inflamed after his therapy with Dr. Simon had begun. As the conscious memory of what he had revealed under hypnosis came back to him, he became aware of the recollection that in the examination on the craft, a circular instrument had been placed at exactly the same point where the warts had not appeared. He wondered: Had these been caused by the examination and the instrument used? Barney was also intelligent enough to realize that the reverse could be true: The warts might be a psychosomatic symptom connected with the feelings experienced under hypnosis. And yet, Barney reasoned, they had initially appeared back in 1962, when he had no conscious memory of the events aboard the craft. Now, in 1964, during the sessions, they became inflamed.

Neither Dr. Simon nor the skin specialist Barney visited appeared to be concerned about the warts, which were easily removed by electrolysis. But to Barney, the gnawing thought remained that this could be evidence —if indeed there was anything to this totally incredible story.

DOCTOR

Well, do you have any other thoughts?

BARNEY

Well, I haven't been answered one way.

DOCTOR

How's that?

BARNEY

Well, I was thinking, when I speak of hypnosis and its effect and the possibility of dreams. Yet I know I *did not* dream this. I know this for a certainty. I think all I am trying to do is be reassured.

DOCTOR

To be reassured of what?

BARNEY

Uh, I *know* it happened. I talk to people, not that many people, but I'm thinking of those I have talked to about it. And I only feel that I have to face the possibility of this happening. I know, unfortunately, the person who is listening to me cannot know what I do know. That these things did happen to me, particularly when I was out there on the highway and walking toward the—the hovering craft there. I also knew that something very strange had happened immediately afterwards. Yet, when I talk to a person, it is almost as if I had been given an A on a report card, and I keep asking others to look at it and tell me is it really there.

DOCTOR

When did you first have that feeling that something else had happened besides sighting the object and everything connected with that?

BARNEY

Uh, surprisingly, when I first arrived home in Portsmouth the same day. I had this feeling of foreboding, something would happen. I'd say, "Betty, let us forget this thing. Let us forget even the portion of having seen the sighting from Lancaster all the way down to Indian Head. Because no good can come of it."

240

Yes, but when did you get the feeling that something else had happened? Aside from the feeling of foreboding.

BARNEY

I had that. I can only think that that was a private part of what I knew.

DOCTOR

Wasn't this after Mr. Hohman brought up the question of what happened?

BARNEY

That might have been when Betty believed that, when she became interested after her dream and talked with Mr. Hohman. But I felt there was more to this. And what caused me to do that, is that I was talking to Walter Webb. And I had gotten as far as being out on the highway. And I had gone right up to the point of looking at the object with my binoculars, and it's looking back at me. Then suddenly it was almost as if a fleeting revelation that something happened. And now I can't even remember, and was brought up to a standstill, and I couldn't go any further.

DOCTOR

That's when you were talking with Mr. Webb?

BARNEY

This is when I was talking with Walter Webb, yes. I found that there was something very strange about this whole thing. Now, I can go right up to this point. I can remember walking back, running back to the car, but just what I had done, but I didn't pursue this any further with Walter Webb, because I felt a tremendous pressure, a tremendous pressure to say, "Let's drop this thing, Betty." Now you have your report, Mr. Webb, let us forget it. This was the extent of that. I used to privately think about this. That Betty was in the car with me, we were together, when after she asked me, "What did you see? What did you see?" I only said, "It's going to capture us. . . ."

DOCTOR

You were afraid it was going to capture you.

BARNEY

Yes, I knew that.

DOCTOR

You knew that; what do you mean? You knew it was going to capture you?

BARNEY

Uh, yes, if this can be an explanation of something you know is about to happen. I knew if I had stayed out there on that highway—

DOCTOR

I see, if you had stayed there, you would have been captured?

BARNEY

Yes. So I could only go up to that part and never go any further. Betty and I didn't talk about it, it seemed so fantastic, something happening at that point, and we not talking about it.

DOCTOR

But Betty talked a lot about it to everybody else. She called her sister, she called—

BARNEY

Well, I was thinking of that night—from the time I returned to the car, we didn't talk about it. She just said, "Well, what did you see?" And I didn't answer her. Other than I said, "It's going to capture us." And then I didn't answer her, or I didn't pursue the conversation further. And the next thing, as I could always remember, is seeing this big object sitting in the road, and my first remark was, "Oh, my God, not again." And Betty was saying, "It's the moon." And I was saying, "Yes, it's the moon." And we both thought how peculiar that the moon was going away. And then I didn't say anything else, and she didn't say anything else about it while we drove toward Portsmouth.

DOCTOR

Had there been any peculiarities in the road, hillocks, valleys, or things where the moon might look as if it's on the ground? You sometimes see that.

BARNEY

That's what I wanted to think, yes. But the moon wouldn't be moving. What was so surprising was that we weren't moving.

DOCTOR

You weren't moving?

BARNEY

No.

What had stopped you?

BARNEY

Well, nothing had stopped me. I just wasn't driving ahead at the time. I thought afterwards that the reason I wasn't moving is apparently I had brought my car to a halt to negotiate some kind of a turn, or something or another. And this I accepted. And as we drove further on, Betty then remarked to me, "Well, now do you believe in flying saucers?" And I said, "Don't be ridiculous, Betty."

DOCTOR

Well, now what's the question you say I hadn't answered?

BARNEY

Uh, hypnosis and dreams, and am I hallucinating or giving an event of a dream, thinking it a part of reality. Yet, even as you could answer this question, I basically *know* what had *happened, happened*. And this is why I think the whole thing's ridiculous, to even ask the question.

DOCTOR

Well, as I've said before, I don't want to go into any great detail of the answer at this time. All these things can happen, let me say that. Anything can happen, when you come down to it.

BARNEY

Yes.

DOCTOR

But, I can reassure you that you have nothing to fear and everything is all right. But I want to reserve any more concrete answer for some time in the future.

BARNEY

Yes.

DOCTOR

As we develop this thing more and more into consciousness.

. BARNEY

Yes.

DOCTOR

And I'm going to continue to work with you now, both of you more and more in consciousness. As you continue to remember the things that

243

came out only under hypnosis, and you won't have to resort as much to hypnosis. And at the proper time I think then we will go into more of it.

BARNEY

I think the only explanation as to how we would go into such detail about this, is that for the last three years Betty and I have both been puzzled greatly by this discrepancy or failure on our part to talk about a situation in Indian Head and not resume our conversation until Ashland. And I think this is where we have rather been more attuned to remembering these two incidents, these two locations rather. Because we wrestled with this problem so many times as to just what could we have been doing, and we never were able to conclude anything.

DOCTOR

Well, we'll hope that you will open up more and more about that as to what you were doing as these things begin coming back, as there comes a point where there's no gain in constantly repeating a thing in the hypnosis until we can bring it into consciousness. We want it to get into consciousness to the extent that you can tolerate it, without any anxiety, and this will come.

*　　*　　*

The session continued with a discussion of how Webb, Hohman, and Jackson had been influential in encouraging the Hills to consider hypnosis as a means of relieving their growing concern about the incident. While Dr. Simon emphasized that the therapy would be involved primarily with their conscious thinking and feeling, he would still use hypnosis when it seemed necessary.

For the purpose of reinforcement, however, he put both the Hills into a trance and reemphasized that they would continue to remember various aspects of their experiences that were tolerable to them without their being upset.

He also indicated that in the near future, if the Hills were willing, they would be permitted to hear the playback of the recordings, so that complete experience—not just fragments—would be relived on a conscious level.

To Betty and Barney, the chance to hear recorded experiences marked a milestone in their treatment. They reacted with a combination of intense curiosity—and some apprehension.

244

CHAPTER ELEVEN

April 5, 1964, the day of the next session, found the Hills leaving Portsmouth at an earlier hour than usual. Prompting this was the possibility that they might be permitted to hear some of the playbacks of the tapes, the contents of which were, of course, a total mystery to both Barney and Betty.

The Hills usually left their house at 6:45 on the morning of their sessions; this day it was 6:15. Arriving in Boston early, they found a luncheonette a short distance from Bay State Road, taking time to have coffee and doughnuts and to talk about their feelings if the doctor should let them listen to the tapes. Barney found himself repeating the question to Betty, "Are you curious? I certainly am," while Betty would tone him down with the suggestion that they might not hear the tapes after all, and there was no sense in overanticipating the event.

In discussing this period of therapy two years later, Barney Hill is not exactly sure what he felt at the time. But he recalls to some extent that the fragments of the sessions that began to come through to his consciousness brought him to the point that he felt, in spite of his resistance to the idea, that an extremely unusual experience had taken place that night in the White Mountains—that he could consider the possibility that Betty's dreams might be more than dreams. Further, he recalls that what stood out most in his mind as he became aware of what had taken place in the hypnosis sessions was the sharpness of the image of the men in the road. He even speculated that this might not be a fantasy, but could conceivably be an actuality. "When I look back at the therapy at this stage," he said, "I found that, in contrast to my former skepticism and

245

resistance to the entire UFO idea, that what I thought was the moon was not the moon at all, but the object itself."

However, he recalled at that later date two years after the therapy that no major portion of the repressed material came through. There seemed to be only leaks or flashes of recall.

Betty remembers being extremely curious about what might come out of the playback, but she seems to think that she was less emotional and more pragmatic than Barney. She remembers that she finished both her coffee and doughnut.

Barney hardly touched either.

* * *

As the Hills left the luncheonette and started toward the office, Dr. Simon was dictating his customary brief preface to the session which was to follow:

Mr. and Mrs. Hill are expected at eight o'clock for a continuation. Mrs. Hill revealed in the last conscious interview, not under hypnosis, that she had been walking in the woods and had been asleep. This was not pursued, but will be followed up at this time.

The doctor was still not certain whether he would begin the playback of the tapes but would reserve judgment on that until further on in the session. The material was emotionally strong and would have to be offered in small doses, under careful observation of the reaction of both the Hills.

Dr. Simon took Betty into his office first, and they talked informally.

DOCTOR

Well, Betty, have you both been feeling all right?

BETTY

Yes.

DOCTOR

I want to ask you one thing. When I talked to you last time, and you weren't under hypnosis, I asked you what you remembered about the experience in a general way. And you said that you remembered about seeing the object come down. And that just before you were beeped, Barney asked you to look out, and you did. And you said something like, "I looked at it, and I kept thinking I didn't see it, because I was expecting to see the lights. And I didn't see the lights." You went on

246

to say that you saw the bottom of it, right over the car. And you couldn't see the bright lights or the stars. That you knew that this big, dark mass was moving right over the top of the car.

BETTY

Yes. That's right.

DOCTOR

And I asked you if it was going away, and you said it was directly over the car.

BETTY

Yes.

DOCTOR

Then I asked how about the period of time you couldn't account for. Did you remember any of that? Did Mr. Hohman point it out? You remembered that. Then I asked you what happened. And you said something about going around the corner on a side road. And the men in the road. Do you remember that?

BETTY

Yes.

DOCTOR

Then after that, you said you could remember being asleep. And walking in the woods and going on a ship. What about this sleep? You had never mentioned about being asleep.

BETTY

Well, I seem to remember that when the men who were in the road came up to the side of the car, I went to sleep.

DOCTOR

When they came up to the side of the car, you went to sleep?

BETTY

Yes.

DOCTOR

Yes, and then what?

BETTY

And then I don't know what happened during this period of time. But it seems as though I was asleep and that I was really forcing myself to wake up.

DOCTOR

I see. Now—is it possible that you actually had fallen asleep while Barney was in the road?

BETTY

No. No, I don't think so.

DOCTOR

Well, under what circumstances would you be asleep then?

BETTY

Well, in thinking about this, I would assume that they did something that would make me not conscious of what was going on.

DOCTOR

But you never mentioned at any time before, either in or out of hypnosis, anything about being asleep. You don't think it's possible that while you were in the car, you were tired enough so that you might have fallen asleep?

BETTY

No, I didn't fall asleep in the car. No.

DOCTOR

Then it was a feeling that you were asleep, rather than any knowledge of it, is that it?

BETTY

Yes.

DOCTOR

That you must have been asleep?

BETTY

Yes.

248

DOCTOR

Well, how could that be? You mean that the men had put you to sleep and then taken you through all this procedure?

BETTY

They must have. Because when I saw them coming toward the car, my impulse was to open the car door and to get out and to run and hide in the woods to get away from them.

DOCTOR

But you didn't.

BETTY

No.

DOCTOR

And everything that followed after that you think might have been after you were put to sleep?

BETTY

Yes.

DOCTOR

Is that right?

(Betty nods.)

Do you remember anything else now? Anything that you feel you want to talk about before I get into the more general discussion with both you and Barney?

BETTY

There is one thing that puzzles me.

DOCTOR

What is that?

BETTY

This happened after all this was all over, and we were on the way home. I suppose this has nothing to do with anything, but after all, this had happened. We were driving home, we were looking for some place that was open, so we could see people and get a cup of coffee. And we drove, we were driving along, and we saw a diner. The lights were on in the interior, and we assumed it was open. So we drove into the yard and found that it was closed. And I always felt that if I could find this diner, it might be a clue to what actually happened.

DOCTOR

Yes.

BETTY

And I still haven't been able to find that diner.

DOCTOR

So there is a possibility later on that you might locate it, is that right?

BETTY

Yes. I'm still looking for it.

(She laughs.)

DOCTOR

All right. I think I'll talk to Barney for just a minute, then I think I'll talk to you together about the overall picture and what we might plan to do.

BETTY

All right.

(The doctor dismisses Betty and summons Barney to the office.)

DOCTOR

(To Barney.)

Anything special that you should like to discuss?

BARNEY

(He gives the doctor a sketch of what he recalls to be the abduction area.)

This is something that I drew. I don't know if it makes much sense, but this is the way the road looked. The arrow points up in the corner there. At the top is the direction this so-called moon had taken off.

DOCTOR

When did you draw this?

BARNEY

When I returned home last Saturday.

DOCTOR

Good. I'll keep this. Now, in my talk with Betty last time, she said something about she could remember the men in the road, walking in the woods, and going on a ship—and something about being asleep. Did you have any feeling of being asleep at any time?

BARNEY

Of being asleep? No, I did not. Or is this under hypnosis, or what?

DOCTOR

It doesn't matter which way.

BARNEY

Well, prior to hypnosis, I had no knowledge at all about this missing period.

DOCTOR

No, I mean as part of your experience there, you had no feeling of being asleep, or of being put to sleep, or of anything like that?

BARNEY

No. I have no recall of that.

DOCTOR

You were just dazed, I take it. Well, I think now we want to talk to the two of you together a bit and see where we go from there.

BARNEY

Very good.

(Betty is called back into the office to join Barney and the doctor.)

(To both Barney and Betty.)

I think we've gone far enough in the situation now, and while we haven't got every point clarified nor every detail clarified, it would take a pretty good deal of extensive repetition to do it. But much might come out if we proceed now on the general plan I have in mind. I want to go over everything in great detail. And of course I want to keep you from having any unnecessary amount of anxiety. What I'd like to do is to get this into consciousness and discuss it freely. Now there are two things involved. I mean each of you have had a common experience, and you have had separate experiences. I can take you each individually, and then together, or just take you two together. How do you feel about it?

BARNEY

I think that we can work together, don't you, Betty?

(Betty agrees.)

DOCTOR

So you can get a complete sharing of this thing and see it from each other's side. All right. Number two: I can talk about it, and give you the experiences. Or we can take a certain amount of risk in terms of your anxiety by going over all this together and playing it back.

BARNEY

Yes.

BETTY

Playing it back?

DOCTOR

Yes.

BETTY

(Emphatically.)

Play it back.

DOCTOR

There is quite a bit of it, and it's going to need quite a few sessions. But

252

I think it's probably the better way, and I think that I would rather not discuss the realities and fantasies until you've really gotten all the material that I have, of which you are unconsciously aware but consciously are not. Now, do you want to do it that way?

BARNEY

I think that would be good.

DOCTOR

And at any time, let's discuss. You are willing that we play back the tapes involving each of you together?

(Barney and Betty both agree.)

All right. Then we'll do that. Now if this thing gets hard to bear—and some of it isn't going to be easy to take—I want to know it. Let me know right away, and I can always help ease you.

BARNEY

Right.

DOCTOR

What we had better do is listen and then at the end of say ten or fifteen minutes, or whatever we want for discussion, we'll stop for a moment. If you feel we should have more discussion, we'll be able to stop the tape and talk freely at any time while playing this. Is that satisfactory?

(Barney and Betty both agree again.)

           *   *   *

Dr. Simon pushed the button of the recorder, and the first session, the tape containing Barney's recall of the trip through Montreal and down through New Hampshire, began.

When the tapes started, a strange thing happened. In his general reinforcement of the hypnosis with the Hills, the doctor had taken the precaution to make sure that no other person than he could put them into hypnosis by using the cue words.

When Barney's tape began, the induction procedure was the first material that came out over the speaker. Barney, glancing in Betty's direction, was startled to see her sink back in her chair. As Barney was finishing the discussion with Dr. Simon, he hadn't listened to the first part of the tape; Betty had. She remembers going under, while she was still aware of what was happening. She tried to stamp her foot to alert Barney and the doctor that she was slipping into a trance, but she couldn't move it. After waking Betty, Dr. Simon reinforced both so they would not respond to any cue words unless *he* gave them face to face. They continued.

"When I first began hearing my voice under hypnosis," Barney later describes it, "I was lifted out of my seat. I couldn't believe it. I knew it was my voice, but it was difficult for me to really understand that this was me, saying that this has actually happened. It was as if I had been asleep and had talked in my sleep. I just couldn't believe it. I wasn't too concerned about the first part of the tapes—coming down through Canada, and the first part of our leg through upper New Hampshire. I had remembered practically all this detail consciously. But as the tapes moved along toward Indian Head, I didn't know what was going to happen. I could feel my ulcer. I mean I could feel my stomach churning, my muscles tighten. I just didn't know what to expect. I know I sat on the edge of my chair, shifting my position frequently.

"The tone of my voice was interesting, because it didn't sound a bit like me. And also, the way I slurred my words."

Betty's reaction was similar: "I thought he sounded as though he were asleep. But then, I began to get scared. I said to myself, 'Oh, good lord— I'd just as soon go home and not hear them!' And then I began to wonder. Everything was building up to the part that I had heard all the way out in the waiting room, when I heard Barney's outcries. I was anticipating that and wondering what my reaction would be."

Slowly, the tape approached the portion involving Indian Head. "I knew I was getting to the point in which I had no complete memory," Barney continues in describing his reaction at a later date. "I felt quite secure being with the doctor in his office, and I had complete confidence in him. I knew that if the going got too rough, he could take me out of it. Then I was suddenly startled. When I put the binoculars up to my eyes, I couldn't believe I had reacted that way. And the eyes. The eyes that seemed to come toward me. Then I heard myself saying that the eyes seemed to be burning into my senses, like an indelible imprint. And I began, in the doctor's offices, to feel the pieces unfolding. I was beginning to remember. Suddenly the lost pieces began coming together. Even while listening to the tapes, I felt this. I suddenly realized how I had broken my binocular straps. And I remembered that for days after Indian Head, I had an intense soreness in the back of my neck. Listening to the tapes, this came back to me sharply—the violent thrust of my arms breaking the binocular strap. All of this was unfolding—not just on the tapes, but beginning to unfold in my mind, my conscious mind.

"I did not feel too much shock there in the doctor's office, perhaps because he had fortified me by posthypnotic suggestion that I would be able to tolerate this in relative comfort. But I noticed that Dr. Simon kept watching us very closely as he was playing the tapes. He was apparently conscious of any pressure being built up in us. And he would stop the machine, and talk with us several times.

"Every once in a while, I would look over at Betty. And she has a way of looking at me and being reassuring. It's sort of a look that she can give, almost to say 'I'm in love with you, Barney.' And I felt this reassurance. And it helped.

"I think you can say the best description was that I was numb, as I listened. Information was flooding back into my mind, but my emotions were numb. I continued to feel that if it became too distressing, the doctor would be able to control it.

"And then, as the tapes went deeper and deeper into the part I had never remembered, there was the feeling as if heavy chains were lifted off my shoulders. I felt that I need no longer suffer the anxieties of wondering what happened.

"I felt mainly that I was actually reliving the experience. It was a bright clear morning as we listened to the tapes. The sun was filling the doctor's office, but as the tape was played, it was as if a pall had descended, and I was sitting there out on that mountain road at night. I could actually *see* what I described as the Cheshire cat. This growing, one-beam eye, staring at me, or rather not staring at me, but being a part of me. I could turn my eyes, and I did while sitting in the doctor's office there listening. I blinked my eyes and shut the lids as if to get this from my mind. I was certain now, on listening to the tapes, that I had never really understood before. Suddenly, lo and behold, I could actually describe things beyond Indian Head. There are many emotions and reactions that occur within a fleeting second, so that I was running a gamut of these emotions and reactions. And I think this is why it never became too distressing for me to listen to the tapes. I could hardly wait to talk to Betty alone about it. I wanted to tell her my thoughts, my feelings. To tell her that this was just too much to digest at one time. I had to observe and study this more. It would take time to get used to it— listening to that person who was representing me on the tapes. I kept saying to myself, 'Is that *me* on the tapes saying this?' And then the word *incredible* kept coming up in my mind. It was just incredible, completely unbelievable that this was me.

"And I think I really felt in two minds about it. Maybe one reason I wanted to talk to Betty in the car was that it camouflaged my real meaning—I wanted to be rid of listening to the tapes so that I could quickly go back and join my full conscious mind, and forget it.

"At the part of the tapes where my voice said that I was just 'floating about,' I then knew that I wasn't really floating about. I was being half-dragged to the ship. I could actually feel the suspension—rather of being suspended with the arms holding me. And what was so curious is that I could feel the pressure of the arms. When I talk about this, I feel chills about the whole thing, the pressure of the arms, of these small men holding me and dragging me along.

"And then I thought of my shoes—the tops of them being scraped, literally scraped, that I noticed the day after Indian Head. How else would the *tops* of the shoes be scraped? And I was able to realize that these men made me forget what happened. They told me to. They told me to forget, and I wanted to forget. And I think this is why it wasn't too difficult for me to put this whole thing out of my mind for so long. I knew, I felt, I was almost sure as I listened to the tapes that this was no fantasy or dream. It was a matter of little doubt to me. It seemed without any doubt that this 'man' *could* communicate with me, and he did. I also know that I wasn't anxious to communicate with him. I was listening to this—being reassured by him that no harm was going to come to me, but I didn't accept it. I also took out a pencil and sketched from memory what the man might have looked like. I never had seen the sketch I drew under hypnosis at this point. They were fairly similar.

"And if we had heard no other session on tape beyond this, I would have had all this in my mind. I began to anticipate what was going to come out on the tapes the second session. I would have all this on my mind. I would have been highly confused as to why it was there, but it would have been there."

Betty, in recalling her further reactions as they listened to the tapes for the first time said: "When the tapes came to the part where Barney was standing there on the highway, I felt very sorry for him. I had sort of a feeling of being somewhat devastated. That—why had we bothered, now that we had gone so far? What was the reason to find out about the whole thing? Let's forget hypnosis ever happened. Maybe we would have been better off just to leave things as they were. Maybe it was better just to wonder. And suddenly I became aware that all through this, I had never really stopped to think of what Barney's experiences were. His having separate experiences alone. And listening to Barney's voice made me relive the incident too. It was just like being right back out there on the highway."

*   *   *

With frequent stops, the first tape was completed. Both Barney and Betty were somewhat stunned.

In the elevator going down, they were alone for the first time, with a measurable recall of the incident now thoroughly in their minds.

The first thing that Betty could say was in reference to Dr. Simon. "I certainly," Betty laughed, "hope that Dr. Simon isn't really a spaceman!"

And again Barney said, with the same whimsy, "Don't be ridiculous!"

Driving back to New Hampshire, Barney found himself rubbing the back of his neck, where back in 1961 the burning sensation from the leather strap of the binoculars seemed to have inexplicably appeared and disappeared.

His overall reaction to the tapes he summed up succinctly: "I felt so overwhelmed and relieved. Now parts of my life that had been missing were added to it again. Parts of my life were being put back together."

CHAPTER TWELVE

In summarizing the session of the first playback of the tapes, Dr. Simon dictated:

> The first interview with Mr. Hill was now played back to Mr. and Mrs. Hill together and carried to the point of the sighting and the outburst of extreme anxiety that Mr. Hill had. He showed considerable distress at this, but seemed to manage it quite well. And as it proceeded, he took out a piece of paper and began to draw. In this drawing, he sketched out again a head, with some very staring eyes, of almond shape, but not slanted. At the end of this, he seemed to be very well composed and wished to be assured of its fantasy nature. Both wish to continue in this fashion, and a date was set a week from today to continue the playback of the hypnotic sessions. It is of interest when the playback was begun and the cue word was used, Mrs. Hill went into a trance. Both were then intentionally put into another trance and were told that they would not respond to the cue word when they heard it on the playback, but only when it came directly from me.

During the week that followed, Barney tried to analyze the incident from the point of view that it might have been a fantasy, but so many details came flooding back as a result of hearing the recording that he found himself seriously doubting this theory. Both he and Betty were vacillating constantly, at one moment feeling that perhaps this could be a dream—at others becoming convinced of the reality of it.

The playback of the recordings stimulated release into the Hills' consciousness of further details, some which had not been expressed during the hypnotic sessions. This release of new material is a product of the "working through" process in psychotherapy, either with or without hypnosis.

Later, at his home in Portsmouth, Barney found himself remembering how he opened his eyes fleetingly on entering the craft. "I remember I had passed the outer door where my feet scraped against the bulkhead," he recalled some time later, "and I got a good look at the three men who were standing by the door of what would have been the room where they examined me. I saw them just as I was about to enter this. So that I could see the curved contour of the corridor just fleetingly. And I was quite upset about that, because they were talking to each other. Yet I was also being understood and was understanding someone else who was continuing to tell me that we were not going to be harmed.

"The interior of the craft was filled with this bluish light—and by that I mean a fluorescent kind of light, which didn't cast any shadows. The men had rather odd-shaped heads, with a large cranium, diminishing in size as it got toward the chin. And the eyes continued around to the sides of their heads, so that it appeared that they could see several degrees beyond the lateral extent of our vision. This was startling to me. And something that I remembered, after listening to the tapes, is the mouth itself. I could not describe the mouth before, and I drew the picture without including the mouth. But it was much like when you draw one horizontal line with a short perpendicular line on each end. This horizontal line would represent the lips without the muscle that we have. And it would part slightly as they made this mumumumming sound. The texture of the skin, as I remember it from this quick glance, was grayish, almost metallic looking. I didn't notice any hair—or headgear for that matter. Also, I didn't notice any proboscis, there just seemed to be two slits that represented the nostrils.

"Betty and I went to hear a lecture one time by Dr. Carleton S. Coon of the Department of Anthropology at Harvard, and he showed a slide of a group of people who lived around the Magellan Straits. We both had quite a reaction when we saw it, because this group of Indians, who lived in an extremely cold atmosphere high in the mountains where there was little oxygen, bore a considerably close resemblance to what I'm trying to describe. And the professor was telling us how this group of people had, in the course of many generations, shown considerable physiological changes to adapt to the climate. They had Oriental sort of eyes, but the eye socket gave an appearance of being much larger than what it was, because nature had developed a roll of fat around the eye and also around the mouth. So it looked as if the mouth had almost no opening and as if they had practically no nose. They were quite similar, in a general way, to the men I'm trying to describe.

"When I was in the corridor, I was surprised that the leader didn't follow me into the room. But again—the eyes seemed to follow me. It was as if I knew the leader was elsewhere, but his effectiveness was there with me. Wherever he was, he was still able to convey messages to me, such as recognizing when I would become more fearful or needed calming down. I know how ridiculous this sounds, but it's the only way I can describe it. He was able to do this. There was another person in the room with me beside the three men at the door. And he was the one who scraped my arms and did the examining, checking my spinal column and that sort of thing.

"I only got a very brief glance at the room, through the door. It was very barren, and the only furniture I could see was this table. The walls were smooth and barren, just this plain bluish-white color. No pictures or ornaments. The room was pie shaped, but as if the point of the pie had been cut off. I couldn't see any windows. The ceiling and floor and walls all seemed to be made of the same material, but I didn't notice what the texture was. Also, I didn't notice where the light source was.

"The main thing I was impressed by was the table that I was to lie on, because it was so much shorter than anything that would ordinarily hold a human being. So that when I got on the table, my legs dangled over the end. And I thought this was peculiar.

"I was escorted, sort of dragged I guess, both in and out of the ship. There was a slight difference in temperature, so that I knew I was in an interior as they took me over the bulkhead or whatever it was. I didn't notice any odor particularly. And I could breathe all right inside. There wasn't any struggle for breath. And as I was escorted out, I was still being held, and I could feel the night air rush toward me. There was a difference between being inside there and outside, and I could feel it.

"I bumped my feet again on this bulkhead on the way out, and I could feel myself being taken down the ramp. Then I found myself walking on rough ground, and I still thought that the people who had taken me out were still with me. But I opened my eyes, and I was standing there alone. And I thought, 'Oh, that's interesting.' And suddenly, I forgot what had happened completely. I had absolutely no memory of it. I thought, 'Oh, I must have walked into the woods to take a break in the trip. That's what must have happened. I'll go to the car,' and it was sitting there on the road, and I walked up to it. I was curious why the motor was off, and the lights were off. I wouldn't usually do this just to jump out of the car for a rest stop. And I sat down on the front seat on top of the tire wrench. I thought, 'That's interesting. What's this doing here?' And I pulled it from under me and placed it in the well between the door and the seat itself.

261

"Then I heard Delsey whimpering. I thought, 'Oh, Delsey—you're under the seat. I thought Betty was taking you for a walk.' I was sort of foggy—my mind was unclear. But I took Delsey out of the car after I had started up the motor and put the headlights on. Then Betty started walking out of the woods, and I thought, 'Well, that's what I'm doing. I'm sitting here waiting for Betty.'

"She came down the road from an angle, as if from the woods on the other side of the road. So to me it seemed that I had obviously stopped on Betty's request. And she almost casually said, 'Come on out, let's watch it leave.'

"Then I thought, 'That's ridiculous. Watch *what* leave?' But I thought I'd humor her, I'll get out. And then I saw the moon—I immediately thought of it as the moon, and then we both were amazed, because the moon was moving. I was sure it was the moon setting. But I was curious about it, because it just didn't seem to be a normal moon. Then everything seemed to go blank again, this fog, this haziness set in until I saw the sign: Concord—17 miles. I do remember vaguely wondering how this enormous disc, that had been very orange in color, could change so quickly to a brilliant, silvery color."

During this week Betty thought often about her reaction to Barney's description on the tapes. "It seemed as if I were reliving everything again," she recalls. "When he was out on the highway, there, just before the beeping sound, I could recall how I flew across the front seat and yelled for him to come back. A lot of other detail kept coming back to me, so vividly."

As the other sessions of the playback continued, the recall of both Barney and Betty accelerated, filling in more detail, with many half-remembered fragments falling into place. They became more acclimated to hearing their own somnambulistic voices but still found it hard to believe that these were their own stories.

To Betty, the moment the men came up to the door of the car at the time of the roadblock, she now felt that she had gone into a hypnotic trance of the same type she experienced in the sessions in the doctor's office. She felt as if both she and Barney had in some way been mesmerized by the beeping sounds to a quasi-hypnotic state, which deepened at the point where she began to open the car door to run into the woods and hide. At the moment that one of the men in the road opened the car door for her, he put his hand out, and she felt as if her consciousness were slipping away, just as she had so many times during the sessions. She noted that both she and Barney on the tapes had to struggle to remember at identical points, first at Indian Head and shortly after at the roadblock. To Barney, the sensation was one of floating. To her, there was the long period of haziness after the series of beeps, then a feeling of falling into a trance-like state that she forced herself to come out of by sheer will power.

"Hearing my portion of the experience on the tapes," she recalls, "I could feel the struggle I was making to get myself to wake up again after the men seemed to put me into a trance. I could remember shaking my head and feeling as though I were trying to climb out of a well. I was really struggling. I could remember saying to myself, 'I've got to wake up, I've got to wake up.' And each time I would say this, I would force myself a little more awake.

"When they took me out of the car, I wasn't very cooperative. When we got to the ramp, I think I probably braced my feet against it. Then I remember either this voice or this thought—whatever it was—saying to me that I wasn't going to be harmed. I did see the exterior of this craft as they were walking me up to it. I got the impression that it was sitting in some kind of depressed area in the ground. There was something underneath it, a gully or something, and I didn't know if the object itself was sitting there or if there was some kind of support. But there was this kind of rim that went around the craft. And I don't know why, but I had the idea that this rim was movable, that it would spin around the perimeter, maybe. Like a huge gyroscope of some kind. I don't know for sure, and this is just my impression.

"Well, the ramp took us up on this rim, and I guess they took us just a couple of steps along the rim to this door. In the part we entered, there was a curved corridor that appeared to go around the craft on the inside. I don't know where it stopped or ended. The entrances to the rooms were on the inner side of the corridor. And I kept looking for windows, but I couldn't see any. I got the impression that the craft was metallic, entirely metallic, and there was a light coming through the doorway, like that of a light coming out of a front door at night, sort of the quality of a fluorescent light.

"Then they started to take me into this room. And I wasn't going. I stopped and told them to bring Barney in, too. Because they were walking Barney past me. And they kept right on going with him. That's when they told me not to worry, he'd be all right.

"I got the impression that the leader and the examiner were different from the crew members. But this is hard to say, because I really didn't want to look at the men. It seemed to me that these two were taller, but maybe that's because I wanted to make them taller. I was sort of scared of the crew members, and I had the feeling that the leader and the examiner were keeping them back, away from us. I could see them out in the corridor, and they seemed to be going back and forth from Barney's room to mine.

"In a sense, they looked like mongoloids, because I was comparing them with a case I had been working with, a specific mongoloid child—this sort of round face and broad forehead, along with a certain type of coarseness. The surface of their skin seemed to be a bluish gray, but probably whiter than that. Their eyes moved, and they had pupils. Somehow, I had the feeling they were more like cats' eyes. And I couldn't remember any buttons or zippers—but then I really didn't want to remember.

"The room was triangular, with the point cut off. Barney and I both agree on that. The table was sort of in the middle, but down near the cut-off part. It was far enough out so that anyone could walk around it. Over beside it was a white stool and different kinds of equipment, gadgets, all over the wall. When they looked at my arm, they took this thing out of the wall, and then sort of put it back in. Then on the wall where the entrance was, there were these storage cabinets, built in. Thinking back, I think everything seemed to look as if it were made of metal or plastic, but there was a white tone to everything. The surface of the table was hard and smooth and cold.

"When they talked among themselves, they made a noise that had no meaning to me at all. And I had this impression that the leader seemed to look differently from the others, but again I might have been distorting on this. Their bodies seemed to be a little out of proportion, with a bigger chest cavity, broader chest. Now, if I remember correctly, I first insisted that they were talking to me in English, with an accent. Then Dr. Simon and I spent a lot of time on this, and I think my final conclusion is that while they weren't speaking English, I could understand what was being said to me as if it *were* in English. But whether it was English or not English, verbal or nonverbal, I understood clearly what they were trying to get across. This was when they were communicating with me. As I mentioned, when they talked among themselves, they were entirely impossible to understand."

The Hills were unable to agree on this point. Barney's recollection is: "It was much like being put into hypnosis by Dr. Simon. I knew this leader was there, yet I felt there was a complete separation of his words and his presence. Only that what was there was a part of my knowledge. I did not hear an actual voice. But in my mind, I knew what he was saying. It wasn't as if he were talking to me with my eyes open, and he was sitting across the room from me. It was more as if the words were there, a part of me, and he was outside the actual creation of the words themselves."

One reason why Betty felt that the communication might have been verbal is that she thinks that she spoke verbally to them. Both the Hills were aware of many inconsistencies of their recall, and these were constantly coming up in the exploration of the incident with the doctor. Among these was the impression Betty got that the humanoid beings seemed to have no concept of time. Barney pointed out, and Betty agreed, that it was a paradox for the leader to say "Wait a minute" when he had asked her what *time* was.

"When we were going out of the room with this book," Betty recalls, "the leader definitely said 'Wait a minute,' whether this was out loud or not, I don't know. I had been in a discussion with him about old age, too, trying to explain what a hundred years was, that sort of thing. And I found it hard to explain. I think we got into this discussion when he asked about Barney's false teeth. They were puzzled why Barney's teeth were able to be removed and mine were not. Then I said that people often have dentures when they get older. He asked me, 'What's older?' And I said, 'Old age.' This is when we also went into a discussion of diet, what do you eat? There was no way of getting across to them what I was trying to say, like meat, potatoes, vegetables, and so on. When I tried to tell them about squash, I said it was yellow, and that's when he said, 'What's yellow?' "

Barney feels Betty made a mistake in this, both from the point of view of time concepts and vocalizing the communication. "I still question whether Betty actually conversed with these people," he says. "It was communication, but it was nonverbal. Several things Betty has said have caused me to question it. The slip of whether this was time,* yet she said they didn't understand time as we understand it. I feel Betty has created other distortions in her mind. She referred to the so-called leader and examiner as different from the others, and I believe they were all basically the same."

Betty replies to this by saying, "When I was being taken aboard this thing in the beginning, I knew they indicated to me that if we cooperated and didn't waste too much time, they would take us back to the car and let us go on our way. But I don't know if the word *time* was used or not."

*   *   *

---

*Betty recalls that the "leader" said, "Wait a minute." Both Barney and Betty saw at once the strange paradox of his saying this and then asking what a year and other time elements were.

Inconsistencies and paradoxes like these were examined as the playback sessions continued over the next several weeks. The bizarre and unusual qualities of the case continued to be puzzling and challenging.

Primarily, the sessions were a long, detailed review, with the information on the tapes stimulating further recall and comment from both Barney and Betty. Other aspects, both in and out of the mainstream of the therapy were brought to light and considered. Barney's ulcers flared up at the beginning of the playback sessions, but gradually subsided again. With Walter Webb, the Hills retraced the route of the journey, filling in further details, and were convinced that they had found the exact spot of the roadblock on a side road two or three miles east of Route 3.

Both Barney and Betty were overwhelmed by the massive detail that came out on the recordings, much of it entirely unknown to them consciously. "I never had any idea of the extent of this material coming out on the tapes. I never realized how much of this I was trying to put out of my mind. The tapes seemed utterly incredible," Barney commented.

Barney still wanted to deny that this ever happened. "I was thinking I was ready to stop the entire seeking of the recall of the incident," Barney told the doctor in one of the sessions after they had listened to a long portion of the playback. "Betty asked me why. And I thought because I cannot explain what came out under hypnosis, and I hate to think I'm nuts. I also noted last week while listening to the playback of Betty, I wanted to close my eyes very much. It became almost an obsession. That's why I got up and moved over and looked out the window."

By May 30, nearly two months after the playbacks of the tapes began, Barney felt a definite relief from his tensions. "I haven't felt as tense this week as I have in previous weeks," Barney told the doctor. "Haven't had to take any medication for the ulcer at all."

On June 6, the doctor utilized hypnosis for some further exploration with Betty.

DOCTOR

(He completes the induction of Betty into a trance.)

. . . you are now in a deep sleep, deep, deep, sleep. I want you to think back to the time you told me you were asleep. Think back on that . . .

(He is referring to the moment of the roadblock.)

Were you asleep?

266

                         BETTY

No.

                         DOCTOR

Why did you think you were asleep?

                         BETTY

           (Again the literal answer above to the first question.)

I had been asleep.

                         DOCTOR

You had been asleep?

                         BETTY

When I was in the car. The men put me to sleep.

                         DOCTOR

The men put you to sleep.

                         BETTY

Somehow.

                         DOCTOR

How did he get to the car?

                         BETTY

I opened the door. I was going to get out and run.

                         DOCTOR

Why?

                         BETTY

Because I was afraid.

                         DOCTOR

Where was Barney?

                         BETTY

In the car.

                                                        267

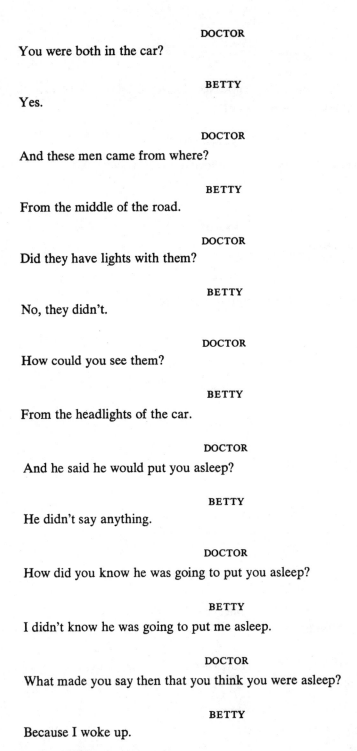

DOCTOR

You were both in the car?

BETTY

Yes.

DOCTOR

And these men came from where?

BETTY

From the middle of the road.

DOCTOR

Did they have lights with them?

BETTY

No, they didn't.

DOCTOR

How could you see them?

BETTY

From the headlights of the car.

DOCTOR

And he said he would put you asleep?

BETTY

He didn't say anything.

DOCTOR

How did you know he was going to put you asleep?

BETTY

I didn't know he was going to put me asleep.

DOCTOR

What made you say then that you think you were asleep?

BETTY

Because I woke up.

DOCTOR

You woke up where?

BETTY

When I was walking.

DOCTOR

Do you think they put you asleep?

BETTY

Yes.

DOCTOR

How?

BETTY

They did something. I couldn't remember. The man put his hand out. I was sitting in the seat. I was turning. I had the door open. And then I turned and I was going to run, because I was afraid. Then, when I opened the door, the man opened it wider. There were three men. And the one nearest me, nearest the handle of the door—I was going to get out—and he put his hand up. And then I didn't know anything.

(She later compared this to the experience of undergoing hypnosis.)

DOCTOR

Until when?

BETTY

Until I was walking. I made myself come awake.

DOCTOR

Now, you said they examined your skin. Was it something like a microscope?

BETTY

Yes.

DOCTOR

Why do you think they were examining your skin? Were they interested in the color of it?

(The interracial implications here are obvious.)

269

BETTY

I don't think so. I think they were interested in the structure of my skin.

DOCTOR

What about the structure?

BETTY

Well, they kept looking at it, and I guessed that from the way they reacted. I mean they all, you know, the examiner and the leader, they took one look, and then the other one would look. They looked two or three different times.

DOCTOR

Why this unusual interest in your skin? Do you have any thoughts about it?

BETTY

No. I don't.

DOCTOR

Do you think it might be because your skin and Barney's were of a different color?

BETTY

I don't know, but I think they were interested because their skin and mine were different.

DOCTOR

In what way was it different?

BETTY

In color.

DOCTOR

What was the color of their skin? Were they different—these men who were examining you?

BETTY

The leader and the examiner were more alike.

270

DOCTOR

In what way?

BETTY

They looked taller than the crew members.

DOCTOR

That's all?

BETTY

They were taller and their skin was of a different color.

DOCTOR

Well, what was the difference in the color? What was the color of the crew members' skin?

BETTY

Uh—

DOCTOR

Why do you have so much trouble telling me the difference?

BETTY

Because I keep thinking that the crew members are Oriental, Asiatic. Only they were not as—they're short.

DOCTOR

And the leader is not short?

BETTY

He's more, the leader and the examiner are taller. They're about as tall as I am.

DOCTOR

You mean the crew members are much shorter than you?

BETTY

The crew members were shorter.

DOCTOR

How much shorter?

BETTY

I'd say they were not—uh—five feet. I think the leader is about as tall as I am.

DOCTOR

Were you afraid of these people?

BETTY

I wasn't afraid of the leader. I was at first, but I wasn't afterwards.

(The doctor then asks Betty about her general background, her early days, her family influence, and her experience with an interracial marriage. Under hypnosis she reveals a better-than-average adjustment to the problems of the mixed marriage and the fact that she is unable to have children because of an operation. The doctor then goes on to explore Betty's general reactions the night of the incident.)

DOCTOR

You don't always express your fears so readily, do you? During these experiences with the flying object, you weren't afraid at first, and then you realized later how afraid you'd been?

BETTY

Well, I think maybe I'm the type of person if any emergency occurs, everybody else might be going to pieces, and I go to work until it's all over with. And then after it's all over, I have sort of a delayed reaction. But this is the type of person I am. When I saw that object out in the sky there, though, I don't think I had too much fear about it.

DOCTOR

When you had all these experiences with your dreams—why would you have dreamed all these things? The dreams were the same as the experiences that you felt you had.

BETTY

I figured that in my dreams, I remembered what actually happened.

*   *   *

This final session in which hypnosis was employed seemed to sum up the dilemma that had carried through the entire six months that the therapy took place in. Was the experience dream or reality? Where did the truth lie? Who could certify what the truth was? How were all the puzzling inconsistencies to be resolved—regardless of which solution to the question was assumed?

In a sense, among the principals, there were three points of view. Dr. Simon felt that from the available evidence from all sources, and our present knowledge of mental functioning, he could accept the probability that the Hills had had an experience with an unusual aerial phenomenon, a sighting that stimulated an intense emotional experience in both of them. While anything is conceivable, he felt that the abduction was improbable. Betty felt that the hypnosis had demonstrated marked evidence that her dreams were a reflection and remembrance of reality. Barney vacillated between these points of view, although his ultimate conclusion was that he could not distinguish between other known reality and the sequence of events that finally came out under hypnosis. In other words, once the amnesia was overcome, he could sense no difference between what he remembered consciously and what he re-called under hypnosis: The entire journey had been a complete, uninterrupted continuum, including the abduction sequence.

In the last three sessions, up through the final one on June 27, 1964, the three points of view frequently came out in the discussions. A healthy sign was that both Betty and Barney were less anxious after the recordings were played back.

"When we got to the end of the tapes," Barney recalled later, "I had an overwhelming sense of relief, a feeling of unburdening. Betty and I became more amiable than ever. My blood pressure condition eased up, as well as my ulcers."

Betty agreed. Even though the mystery was by no means completely solved, her anxiety lessened because she had done all she could to probe into the unprecedented story of their encounter. Her dreams grew less disturbed.

By June everyone recognized that there would be no full conclusion, either to the therapy or the incident which played so big a part in it. Both the doctor and the Hills regretted that it would be impractical to continue into deeper therapy over the long period of time that would be necessary. Summer had arrived, the long round trip would be more taxing than ever. It was a good stopping place, at least for a time. More important was the Hills' awareness that they were feeling much better—and less disturbed, even though everything had not been completely resolved.

As a scientist, the doctor tested a varying series of hypotheses as they developed and changed, testing against what phenomenon presented itself and what knowledge he could use to integrate it. At the place where the therapy was discontinued, the situation could rest with the minimum of danger. Short of acceptance of the whole experience as reality, which contradictory evidence prevented the doctor from doing, his best alternative lay in the dream hypothesis. "Anything beyond that," the doctor commented later, "would seem to stretch the limits of credulity too far. But I'm not absolutely convinced. I had to come to my conclusion. If you can call it a conclusion. It never really was one. Therapeutically, we had reached a good place to stop under the practical conditions existing, and the Hills' basic improvement. It was acceptable in my judgment to leave it not fully answered. I knew that we would be remaining in contact, and that perhaps time would bring a more complete answer."

In considering the theory that Betty's intense dreams were transferred to Barney, to become part of his reality, Barney stated his feelings to the doctor in one of the later sessions in this way:

"Doctor, if I can draw an analogy, let's say that yesterday morning I drove down from Portsmouth to Boston to work. And if somehow, I had been told that this had *not* happened to me, I'd be a bit curious. Particularly if this was said several months later, I would say, 'I'm not quite sure I drove that day,' but I'd get a calendar and check it. Then if this person kept insisting that I didn't drive there, in the face of my knowing that I did, I would have to terminate the conversation and leave it at that. I'd reach the point where I'd say to myself, 'I cannot convince this person, and he cannot convince me. There's no issue. I can drop it.' "

As the sessions drew to a close, the question of illusion or reality dominated the discussions. The doctor pointed out that he was not going to say it was either—that he and the Hills together would both have to grope for the truth, but that ultimately the acceptance or non-acceptance of the occurrence would have to rest with them.

In attempting to analyze his thoughts, Barney told the doctor, "Prior to coming to your office, I had, and still do have, complete acceptance of the fact that I had driven down to Indian Head, and the object was there, and these things did take place. I also am well aware that at Ashland we received a series of beeps. These things are not a matter of the dream world or of fantasy. I am also well aware of my attitudes

274

after arriving back in Portsmouth, which is to say, this is such a ridiculous thing. We can never tell anyone about it. Yet, so many months have passed that they have finally become years, two or three years. It is still an annoying issue with us. Now we come to hypnosis, where the technique allegedly will take us back and bring us through this period of apparent amnesia. And I can only say, 'Well, why would amnesia have existed to begin with? Why would there be this period between Indian Head and Ashland?' "

In reply, the doctor said, "Well, actually you have a partial explanation for the reason for amnesia. Psychological amnesia exists for the purpose of repressing or wiping out intolerable emotional experiences."

"So the intolerable emotional experience," Barney said, "has been the experience at Indian Head?"

"I have been going over this," the doctor replied, "and kind of separating this into two experiences. One is the experience of the sighting. I feel I have not been able to obtain out of hypnosis, data that will wipe that out. That, I'm willing to leave. The sighting itself. But the abduction, if we'll separate these two, by which I mean the experience of being taken aboard and examined, is another matter. I'm separating that out. No, you might say the whole sighting was a frightening experience. Therefore, why didn't the amnesia wipe out both? Why isn't there an amnesia for the whole thing? You remember that you were consciously, almost from the beginning, trying to have an amnesia. That is, you said, 'We won't talk about this.' You were producing amnesia in various ways. And then there came the amnesia for the other experience.

"Now, the question evolves here: Is this an amnesia in the sense of wiping out of a real experience, or an amnesia related to the wiping out of a fantasy—an intensely painful fantasy?"

The doctor indicated that he hoped there would be more light thrown on this in the closing sessions. Barney was puzzled that his reaction at Indian Head had been out of character with previous emergency experiences. He related one incident that he and Betty and two friends had encountered on a lonely highway in New Hampshire, in which two teenagers had followed their car, harassing them for nearly thirty miles before they found a state trooper, who apprehended the youths. All during this harrowing experience, Barney had remained cool and had planned to force the car off the highway and confront them himself if he had not found the police officer. "I'm only mentioning this," he told the doctor, "to illustrate the point that this is the way I usually function in the time of a crisis."

"The fact that you face these things with a clear-cut, definite plan," the doctor said, "even one that could cost you your life, is good—but what else would you do? Either, as they say, scream and go blind, or do something. And in the situation where there is no other alternative, you do well.

"Your anxiety," the doctor continued, "increased more powerfully as you were relieved of this whole UFO business, very much as the rate of psychiatric breakdowns in the First Marine Division, which took Guadalcanal. Their breakdowns increased very markedly not while they were taking the island from the Japanese, but when they were relieved by the Army. One may then afford the luxury of permitting one's anxieties to take over—to be sick. When action is necessary, action takes place.

"The rules that operate for the conscious mind won't operate for the unconscious. In the unconscious mind, consistency means nothing. Past and present don't exist. Everything is now. The past is now; the present is now; the future is now. Opposites exist together without any incongruity whatsoever. Things *are* and *are not* all at the same time. This, of course, is a fragment of the structure of dreams, too. I'd say that shortly, we can get this thing pretty well crystallized. Then I'm going to leave it in your hands as to how far you want to take the discussion. I think you must understand that I have kept focused on this experience. You can both see now that this experience cannot be seen as an isolated thing. I've kept it isolated to the greatest extent possible. This is part of the continuum of your lives. It's a stop in the roadway, and there's a great deal of material here we will not get to, which is strongly involved. Your whole past history—this is one reason why I wanted to have this session with Betty. I wanted to get into a little bit more of her life. Now any type of reasonable exploration for either or both of you would take a tremendous amount of time. And I don't know if you would want to go on to that extent. So I've been keeping ourselves focused on the best possible illumination of this whole experience. And so I would say that within a short time, we could probably bring this to a close.

"From there on, you yourself will see what might or might not be gained in continuing, depending on how acceptable the explanations. The hypnosis is not going to give us the absolutely final answers, as you can now see. It is subject to the same rules as the rest of the unconscious of a human being. But I think it's giving us enough with the mark of authority behind it, to the extent that you can have authority in anything. So that your capacity for reason, your reality-testing apparatus itself, can fill it out enough. So far as I have planned, a couple of sessions or so will be it. You may want to go one other session or two, but I'll have to leave that in your hands.

"Now, you are very active in your community work, Barney. Your energies are going into that, and I have the feeling that you're going into it better."

Barney agreed. He reported that his anxieties had been considerably reduced and his physical symptoms vastly improved; "I think this is a remarkable change, in just a brief period," he said. Betty also agreed.

* * *

During the closing sessions, both Barney and Betty were relieved that they had done everything possible to remove their anxieties about the experience. They felt that some kind of permanent record should be established in the event that future happenings should confirm what they both now were willing to consider as possible: the reality of the experience.

"I suppose I should say," was the way Barney put it to the doctor, "that what I've been thinking is that this is such an incredible thing—I don't know how it can ever be proven through any definite techniques —it isn't like mathematics, where you can use a definite equation to either prove or disprove it. What I was wondering is, What do you think of the idea that these tapes that we have accumulated over the months be placed in some secure place so that in the event of our deaths, or yours, and if, say, twenty or thirty years from now it's established that this experience is true and did happen, we would then have the tapes so at least we could protect ourselves from being considered eccentrics? You see, twenty or thirty years from now, we'll be sixty or seventy, and it's quite possible that some people will look on us as if we were really a bit eccentric."

The doctor agreed that the tapes would be preserved, and Barney added with a smile, "But you know, I just can't conceive of playing these tapes for anyone, and I can't help feeling, now that we're almost through, I become quite apprehensive thinking about what might have happened if we had foolishly permitted an unqualified person to hypnotize us, with the emotional impact that did come out, just what damage might have been done."

"You went pretty much on the brink of danger," the doctor said. "You can see what your reactions were in this thing. What the emotions of a human being can be when they are unleashed. Betty, with her calmness and all, still had plenty of emotion working through. This is the unconscious of the human being. And it's an area where the human protects himself by—repressions. And he wants to be very careful indeed about releasing repression. People think about repression as bad. Actually, repression is an essential of our mental lives. If we didn't repress a great percentage of our feelings, we would be chaotic human beings."

*　　　*　　　*

Six full months of sessions were over.

The Hills, puzzled but relieved, drove back to Portsmouth with the confused vacant feeling that comes at the end of a long, arduous job, a feeling that they would miss the doctor, the sessions, and the search for the solution to a mystery that still remained unsolved.

Dr. Simon, in his office some weeks later, opened his mail to find a letter from the organization that provided hospital and medical coverage for the Hills. At the Hills' request, Dr. Simon had submitted a brief summary of the Hills' treatment, indicating that they had suffered severe anxiety reactions after an experience with a UFO. Not surprisingly, the medical director of the organization wrote to Dr. Simon that he found it hard to accept a claim based on the diagnosis of a "UFO experience."

Dr. Simon replied in part:

"I can hardly quarrel with your unwillingness in your letter of August 4 to accept a diagnosis of 'emotional disturbance created by an experience with an Unidentified Flying Object' with respect to the claim of Mr. and Mrs. Hill. This was not made as a diagnosis, but as a statement of the circumstances under which these two people had come to me for treatment—and with the expectation that you would send me forms for a medical statement. I have always had such when there have been insurance claims but Mr. Hill said I must only write to your office, without being able to tell me what information I would have to give you.

"Mr. and Mrs. Hill were referred to me in December, 1963. During the course of previous treatment of Mr. Hill, it was discovered that this had followed an experience in September, 1961, when Mr. and Mrs. Hill had witnessed an unidentified flying object at night while returning from their vacation.

"This was a harrowing experience for both of them and led to a very considerable anxiety for some time to come. Mr. Hill began to suffer from insomnia, apprehension and persistent anxiety. Mrs. Hill suffered from repeated nightmares, apprehension and anxiety. More recently, Mr. Hill has had symptoms of duodenal ulcer. Mr. Hill was under treatment for some time before it became apparent (during the treatment) that this experience with the unidentified flying object had played an important part; in fact, the story of this encounter came out during Mr. Hill's treatment.

"Eventually, there was brought to light the fact that both Mr. and Mrs. Hill were suffering from amnesia for a part of that night's events in September, 1961. Ultimately, both Mr. and Mrs. Hill were referred to me. Hypnosis was the obvious method, and I undertook the treatment of both of them. Treatment involved induction of a deep hypnotic state in each, and for this purpose it was necessary to carry them to the state of somnambulism.

"Treatment was accompanied by violent emotional abreaction in both patients. Because of this, treatment had to be delicately controlled and introduction into consciousness only as anxiety permitted. A tape recorder was used to record the unconscious material, and then to assist in its ultimate review and integration into consciousness. During the treatment, Mr. Hill had severe symptoms of ulcer which abated as the treatment progressed. Anxiety abated in both Mr. and Mrs. Hill. . .

"On their discharge from treatment, both were considered as recovered . . ."

"I hope that this information is adequate, and I will be glad to answer any further questions."

The insurance claim was settled promptly, probably for the first time involving a UFO case.

The therapy was at a safe and practical resting place at which the doctor felt it best to stop, even though many questions were unanswered. The relief from anxiety was significant, and sustained. There could be more discomfort for the Hills in pursuing the experience further than in letting it remain at the present state. Further, the doctor encouraged the Hills in their desire to keep in contact with him, as they continued "working through" on their own, a normal, continuing process after formal therapy is concluded.

The treatment had begun with the opening up of an amnesia, an amnesia that produced many problems of its own.

"I began," the doctor commented to the author two years after the sessions were over, "by utilizing hypnosis to get the story separately from each of the Hills. The major part of the amnesia appeared to encompass an incredible experience on the part of both of the Hills. This was not only significant, but the two people shared both the experiences, and were amnesic for these same experiences. Persistent investigation produced more problems than solutions. I had started with the thought that Barney was somewhat more suggestible than Betty, and that the story had derived from him. The story was quite improbable in the basis of any existing scientific data, but on the other hand it appeared as the case went on that the Hills were not lying, and I felt convinced of that. After getting Betty's story and noting that her dreams were identical to her recall under hypnosis, the idea occurred to me that my original assumption might be wrong: that much of Barney's recall was contained in Betty's description, though little of Betty's recall was included in Barney's story. My assumption then was that Barney had absorbed Betty's dream story. On that basis I went on more intensively to examine this possibility with Barney and to probe Betty's story further.

"I was ultimately left with the conclusion that the most tenable explanation that the series of dreams experienced by Mrs. Hill, as the aftermath of some type of experience with an Unidentified Flying Object or some similar phenomenon, assumed the quality of a fantasied experience.

"But the whole thing could not be settled in an absolute sense. The case could be safely left as it stood, especially in view of their improvement. We would remain in contact, and time might eventually bring out a more complete picture."

*   *   *

In a brief follow-up session in the spring of 1966, the doctor had a chance to check the impact of the sighting some five years after the incident at Indian Head and two years after the sessions had terminated. Barney went quickly into the trance as usual. Dr. Simon asked him some general review questions, to which he responded objectively and accurately. In the latter part of the session, the doctor reviewed Barney's feelings again, in considerable detail:

DOCTOR

What is your feeling now about the experience? Were you abducted—or weren't you?

BARNEY

(His voice, as usual, is flat and expressionless.)

I feel I was abducted.

DOCTOR

Were you abducted. Not "how do you feel." *Were* you abducted?

BARNEY

Yes. I don't want to believe I was abducted.

DOCTOR

But you are convinced you were?

280

I say "I feel" because this makes it comfortable for me to accept something I don't want to accept, that has happened.

DOCTOR

What would make it comfortable?

BARNEY

For me to say "I feel."

DOCTOR

Do you mean it would be worse to say: "I actually *was* abducted"?

BARNEY

It is not worse.

DOCTOR

You're more comfortable the other way?

BARNEY

I'm more comfortable the other way.

DOCTOR

Why are you uncomfortable about it?

BARNEY

Because it is such a weird story. If anyone else told me that this had happened to them, I would not believe them. And I hate, very badly, to be accused of something that I didn't do, when I know I didn't do it. Or if I am not believed about something I did, and I know I have done it.

DOCTOR

Well—suppose you had just absorbed Betty's dreams.

BARNEY

I would like that.

DOCTOR

You'd like that. Could that be true?

BARNEY

No.

Why not?

BARNEY

Because—

(He quite suddenly becomes extremely tense and emotional, almost as much as during the first session when he recalled being drawn toward the object in the field at Indian Head.)

I—I didn't like them putting their hands on me!

(His breathing becomes fast and excited.)

DOCTOR

All right. Take it easy. You don't have to be upset.

BARNEY

(Begins to sob heavily.)

I didn't like them putting their hands on me! I don't like them touching me!

DOCTOR

All right. All right. They're not touching you now. They're not touching you at all. We'll let that go. You can relax.

(The doctor begins bringing him back out of the trance, with full reassurance. Barney's sobbing subsides. The review session—two years after the regular sessions—comes to an end.)

CHAPTER THIRTEEN

With the active treatment discontinued, Barney and Betty Hill settled down to their routine life, managing to put the incident at Indian Head into the background and to concentrate on their absorbing interest in community life, the activities of their Universalist-Unitarian-Church, and civil rights work. Betty Hill's schedule as a social worker for the state of New Hampshire was both demanding and rewarding; Barney's work for the post office department became more smooth and efficient now that he had been transferred to Portsmouth and was no longer working nights. His activities on the Board of Directors of the United States Civil Rights Commission, the NAACP, and the Anti-Poverty Program kept him inordinately active and occupied in his spare time. The overwhelming sense of relief and unburdening from the sessions strengthened his work, helped him to function better.

The experience of both the incident and the therapy, even if in the background, were of course far from forgotten. The Hills discussed these events both with close friends and family, hoping that more information on the elusive subject of UFO's would come to the foreground to illuminate their own experiences and to ease the feeling that they might be regarded as eccentrics. They would correspond at intervals with Hohman and Jackson and occasionally visit with Walter Webb at the Hayden Planetarium in Boston, or he would visit them in their home.

They assiduously avoided any publicity about their experiences, and by confining their discussions on the subject to their close circle of friends, they avoided any such problems. They were relieved to discover, in fact, that they could talk about it without any emotional disturbance now, and as long as this was done in private, they found it helpful.

They had almost forgotten that back in September 1962, they had been invited to tell their experience informally to a UFO study group in Quincy, Massachusetts, some months before they had begun their therapy with Dr. Simon. They had been unaware that at that meeting a tape recording had been made of their talk, which described in detail the experience and Betty's dreams resulting from the sighting. They were also unaware that this discussion later provided the basic information for the reporter who detailed the partial story in the series of articles in the Boston newspaper, appearing in the fall of 1965. Neither the Hills nor Dr. Simon had provided any direct information for this.

The Hills were both depressed and frustrated by the articles. They had turned down a request for an interview by the reporter and made it clear to him that they were not interested in putting their experience on public display. Dr. Simon, of course, had refused to discuss the subject with the reporter.

On reading the articles, Barney Hill's immediate reaction was that if he were reading this story about someone else, he would refuse point blank to believe it. Both he and Betty felt that a fragmented story like this would do nothing but place them in a position where they looked ridiculous. The story was too complex to be told superficially; there were too many cross-currents, too many involved factors that had to be taken into account. The Hills sought legal advice, but discovered that as long as the story was treated as a one-shot newspaper account and was not libelous, they could do nothing unless the story was carried beyond that.

When the Universalist-Unitarian Church in Dover, New Hampshire, extended an invitation to the Hills to speak at a Sunday evening meeting shortly after the newspaper articles had run, the Hills decided that in the talk they would try to correct the sensationalism of the news story and to convince the public that the articles were not anything to be sought or desired. The Hills would not discuss the hypnosis or therapy at all. Before the meeting, they were dinner guests of Admiral Herbert Knowles, USN Retired, one of the leading ex-military officers who was attempting to penetrate the UFO mystery in the face of the confused reports coming from the Pentagon. Here, some of the nervousness the Hills were experiencing about the idea of the meeting was overcome.

One interesting aspect of the Dover meeting was that the co-speaker of the evening was a Public Information Officer of the Pease Air Force Base. Although his talk was noncommittal, he was by no means deprecatory either of the Hills and their story or of the flood of UFO reports that had been building up all through 1965 in that area. The meeting was held on November 8 of that year, and hundreds of people were turned away from the church, in spite of a raw and chilly rain.

The turnout for the meeting and the reaction to it indicated to the Hills that the subject of UFO's was of extreme public interest, and possibly of historical importance in the light of increasingly competent reports of sightings throughout the world. The impact on their own lives was profound and far-reaching. While further reflection on their own part brought them to the conclusion that their experience with the abduction might possibly be real, they were acutely aware of how its strangeness could not be accepted by others easily, any more than they themselves could uncritically accept their own stories as revealed to them on the recordings of their therapy sessions.

The Hills' ultimate conclusion was, after considerable reflection, that a book should be written that would tell the story in complete detail, leaving it up to the reader to decide on its importance on the basis of the facts revealed.

"Philosophically, it has given me a broader appreciation of the universe," Barney Hill sums up his feelings. "After the incident happened, Betty and I would many times visit the Hayden Planetarium, listening to the lectures. The more we learned, the more fascinating the universe became to us. We bought books on the stars and planets, and our outlook broadened considerably. I became more open-minded about the possibility of life on other planets or in solar systems that might have planets.

"I tried to speculate on our own experience as to possibilities other than an extraterrestrial craft. I had to reach the conclusion that this theory was as valid as any other. At one time, I gave a great deal of thought to the possibility that this object might have been an advanced foreign reconnaissance craft, but I didn't get too far in my own mind with this. I can't believe that other human beings would be so interested in Betty and me, that they would have conducted the type of physical examination they gave us if they had been human. They could have used their own people for that kind of examination.

"While Betty and I don't at all like the idea of being considered eccentric, we still are not too concerned about the opinions of other people about us. If we were outer-directed people, our lives would have been changed a lot more than they now have been. I might be trying to convince people by saying, 'Look—believe me, this happened.' But I'm not too interested in trying to convince anyone against his own judgment. As far as talking to someone who is interested in listening,

I'm glad to do this, and they don't have to agree with me. I realize this case, until further proof comes along, will be controversial, and I accept that. I'm convinced now—against my own former beliefs—that we had an experience that is going to be extremely difficult to be believed. The only thing I can say is I have a strong feeling that this experience might have happened; you form your own opinion. If you want to believe it, you can. If you don't, that's fine too. But respect the fact that I've given this long thought, in the face of my own resistance to the idea, and I've had to come to the conclusion that there is a distinct likelihood that all this might have happened. I would much prefer it if I could be absolutely sure that none of this took place. But I can't fall back on that, much as I'd like to. I simply say that it cannot be ruled out that this happened, as it came out to me when I heard my own voice on the recordings.

"The period before the amnesia hit us both is a matter of full reality to me, and to Betty too. But just before the amnesia hit, I felt sure I saw persons of some kind aboard the craft. At that time, Betty did not. I felt this odd form of communication at that time; Betty didn't. This makes it a little difficult for me to accept the transference of Betty's dreams as an explanation—although the problem with this whole story is that *any* explanation of it seems as difficult as another to accept.

"When Betty was telling her dreams to Walter Webb or to friends, I resisted the whole idea of her telling them, because they seemed so absurd to me. Now—after listening to the recordings, I'm not so sure. When I heard my own voice describing what had happened, it seemed to me, at least, that there was no difference between what I was saying and what might have actually happened. Right or wrong, the whole story seemed to come together—both amnesia and pre-amnesia—as one stream of continuity.

"One thing I'm sure of is that I don't have that fear, that apprehension any more that I had after the experience at Indian Head. This was a vague thing, that fear, that I never had in my life before. And I'm glad that the therapy seemed to relieve me of it completely now.

"I guess this about adds up my convictions about the story. They are still only my convictions, and anyone is free to disagree with them. The main thing I can say is that they were not arrived at easily, and only after a lot of painful and costly self-examination."

"I think the most important thing to me," Betty Hill summarizes her feelings, "is that I've taken a broader look at the world. Where are we going from here? And to look ahead at the future, you've got to know the past. I've become very interested in anything that has to do with theories or ideas about man's past. We thought man was fairly recent on the earth, but now we're finding that he's been around quite a few, maybe millions of years more than we thought. I keep wondering about what caused us to suddenly begin so much progress. In the last forty years, we seem to have broken through more barriers than it has taken us all through history. We seem to be really just on the threshold of a new science and will move ahead even more rapidly than ever, if man doesn't destroy himself first.

"I was brought up to believe in what I suppose is called the scientific method: You don't believe in anything unless it can be dissected or put in a box. I don't believe in ghost stories. Before this experience, my attitude was that anybody who believed in anything I don't understand, anyone who seemed too far-out, I considered sort of a kook. Now I think I have more tolerance toward new ideas, even if I can't accept them myself.

"When Dr. Simon first suggested the idea that maybe it could be possible that I had converted the dreams about the amnesia period into a false reality, I thought, 'Well, this is wonderful.' I was perfectly willing to go along with it. In fact, I wanted to believe this, because this whole experience isn't easy to live with. I mean, it's really a tremendous pressure on a person. And so after the session in which the dream theory was presented, I came home and I said, 'This is wonderful.' I could compare it with thinking that I had a bad experience, like an auto accident, and then somebody says, 'Forget it, it's only a dream.' You know—you're greatly relieved. You can deny the whole thing ever happened. And so I went through a stage like that. Every time I'd think of it, I'd say, 'It's just a dream, so forget it.' I could get rid of the whole thing. This will be the end of it.

"And so every night when I went to bed, I'd say to myself, 'It's only a dream.' And I was able to do this for about two weeks, I guess, after the therapy was over. Then all of a sudden one morning, I woke up with the thought, 'Whom do I think I'm trying to kid?' Zoom—it was back again. And I haven't been successful in telling myself it was a dream ever since."

Both of the Hills are aware that others will interpret some of the dream content in various ways. "This is to be expected," Barney Hill says. "And I'm far from an expert. In my case, no dreams were involved in relation to the experience until well after the therapy sessions began. My recall of the incident is not related to dreams or dream symbols. It's related to the strong feeling that what I recalled under hypnosis could be one distinct possibility of having happened. This is a lot more than I could admit for several years. I like to consider myself a realist, and I would be less than one if I tried to interpret what went on in the amnesic period as only being in the nature of dreams or dream symbols."

In her studies in sociology and psychology, Betty Hill is well aware of the varied interpretations of dreams, but she points out that even the theorists of dream structure disagree among themselves. "What interests me is that the incidents in my dreams and the incidents of the story that came out under hypnosis were almost identical. I don't feel that in this case the interpretations of dream symbols can help determine whether our experience was real or not, and this is the part of the circumstance that is most important to us now—now that our anxieties are relieved."

* * *

If the experience of the Hills at Indian Head was a totally isolated incident, it would still be important and worthy of further scientific study, even if only to clarify it.

But it is far from isolated. Reliable reports from competent observers of increased UFO sightings—many of them reported as structured crafts similar to the Hills' description—have been building up constantly since the early spring of 1965, with police, military, technical and scientific observations prominent among them. The change of attitude toward the subject by scientists from skepticism to one of interested inquiry has been noted from the beginning of 1966 on. It is no longer fashionable to be skeptical. Some scientists have argued that if the phenomenon is purely psychological, then the story should be considered even more startling than if it were an indication of extraterrestrial visitors.

At a quiet scientific meeting in June of 1966, Dr. J. Allen Hynek, Chairman of the Department of Astronomy of Northwestern University, made a cautious talk to a regional meeting of the Optical Society of America on UFO's that had far-reaching implications as far as the scientific attitude toward the phenomenon was concerned. He lost no time in getting to the core of the speech.

"Unidentified flying objects demand serious and immediate scientific attention," he said. "I say this at the start so that you are not misled by the kooks, the nuts, and the gullible who have made this subject so difficult to explore rationally. UFO's are a real puzzle. The myth is *not* put to rest. And the scientific fraternity must now take cognizance of them. We can no longer dismiss the subject."

In addition to his astronomy post, Dr. Hynek was in charge of the optical satellite tracking program of the Smithsonian Astrophysical Observatory in Cambridge, Massachusetts, and scientific director of the U.S. Air Force balloon astronomy project *Stargazer*. For eighteen years, he has been scientific consultant to the Air Force on UFO's and has screened over ten thousand cases in their files, investigating many of them personally.

In the talk to the scientists, engineers and technicians of the Optical Society, he went on to say: "1 thought the whole thing would go up in smoke, like eating goldfish or seeing how many people could be jammed into a phone booth. But the phenomenon has stayed with us—and more than that—there are far more persons of status and competence who are reporting these UFO's in extremely articulate form. To those who don't know the background—which you're not likely to get from the press—these conclusions of mine might seem very strange. But I have given them long thought."

Dr. Hynek further revealed that a leading scientist of a top-ranking university had reviewed some of his data on UFO's, and berated him soundly for not coming out boldly with a statement that the objects *had* to be extraterrestrial. "How can you *not* accept this as a fact?" the scientist asked him. Dr. Hynek reminded his colleague that he was in a lonely position among other scientists.

"After eighteen years as a skeptic," Dr. Hynek said in the speech, "I have finally been bowed down by the sheer weight of *competent* evidence. As far back as 1953, I recommended that the subject be given definite scientific study, but I have never before made a categorical proposal. This program will include recommendations for: (1) An immediate study in depth by university teams; (2) a pattern analysis by computer of existing data; (3) the establishment of a UFO Research Center staffed by competent scientists. When a phenomenon has the potential capacity of a possible scientific breakthrough, we are neglecting our responsibilities by not at least exploring every facet. Ridicule is no longer appropriate."

*   *   *

In the light of the overall accelerated activity in UFO reports, the experience of Betty and Barney Hill indicates the necessity of further scientific study in an attempt to solve the mystery.

There are many unanswered questions precipitated by the case as it unfolded both consciously and under therapy. The Hills' story has come to public attention with their extreme reluctance, five years after the event, and only because of a leak that resulted in a series of local newspaper articles. The Hills sought no publicity and were successful in holding back the story for several years before it became public under their protests. Their views on the experience are the result of a long and painful period of intelligent examination and study, both in and out of therapy. Their approach to the subject has been rational and cautious.

The greatest mystery about the experience is that *any* assumption on the basis of the material revealed is hard to conceive or understand. An abduction by humanoid intelligent beings from another planet in a space craft has always belonged to science fiction. To concoct a science fiction story of this magnitude would require an inconceivable skill and collaborative capacity. It is as hard for the Hills to accept the possibility that the abduction took place as it is for any intelligent person. In fact the attitude of the Hills is: We did not expect or look for the sighting to take place. Barney resisted and persistently tried to deny its existence. We did not know what happened in the missing two hours and thirty-five miles of distance until we heard voices coming out on the tape recordings. What came out on the recordings was as difficult for us to believe as for anybody else. We only know that after the pieces began coming back together, our general feelings and convictions grew on us that these experiences seemed to be reality—as real as our other recollections of any valid, factual memories.

The assumption that Betty's dreams were absorbed by Barney to create his recollection of the abduction sequence is also hard to conceive or understand. If Betty's dream had been the sole source of information about the humanoid beings, what about Barney's glimpse of persons aboard the craft, recalled in full consciousness, just before the beeping sound occurred? What about other portions of the apparent abduction that Barney recalled and Betty did not? How could the couple concoct the enormous amount of detail, strikingly similar, and stick to it so consistently?

From the long and intensive exploration of the case, however, certain nearly irrefutable points emerge:

1. A sighting of some sort took place.

The two major alternatives to this point are substantially refuted:

1. To concoct the elaborate stories, matched in detail, a month after the sighting, and again more than two years later, would have required an inconceivable precision of planning, memory, and prevision of an imponderable future. Judgments from many sources as well as from two psychiatrists attested to the Hills' probity and integrity.

2. No evidence was ever brought out that either of the Hills had at any time experienced psychotic hallucinations.

Any theory (including the dream hypothesis) which excludes these alternatives is predicated on a sighting of some object or phenomenon.

2. The object sighted appears to have been a craft.

As perceived by the Hills, the craft was similar to many previously and since reported by others who have sighted unidentified flying objects.

3. The sighting caused a severe emotional reaction.

Much of the direct emotional response was repressed and suppressed, attaining conscious expression in diffuse anxiety, dreams of nightmarish quality, and physical symptoms—until released and discharged during treatment. Some of the inner emotional experiences came to consciousness only under hypnosis.

4. The anxiety and apprehension engendered by Barney Hill's racial sensitivity served to intensify the emotional response to the sighting.

Throughout the entire trip from Montreal to the "sighting," Barney Hill suffered from increasing apprehension and fear of hostile reactions to his race, though none materialized. This oppressive feeling could sensitize him to any unusual or strange experience and intensify his reactions to such an experience.

5. The Hills had no ulterior motive to create such a story. They had confined their experience to a small group of people for four years.

The Hills had kept their story restricted to a few intimates, and to interested scientists and investigators. Treatment was sought for their emotional disturbances, and they decided to release their story only after it had been publicized without their permission five years after the incident.

6. The case was investigated by several technical and scientific persons who support the possibility of the reality of the experience.

The investigations by Hohman, Jackson, and Webb, based on their experience with other cases, supported the possibility that the Hills' case could be a valid experience justifying scientific attention.

7. There is a measurable amount of direct physical circumstantial evidence to support the validity of the experience.

No explanation has been found for the shiny bright spots on the trunk of the car which caused the compass to oscillate nor for the failure of the Hills' watches to run after the sighting experience. Barney Hill's broken binocular strap and sore neck could attest to his extreme agitation.

8. Under hypnosis by a qualified psychiatrist, both the Hills told almost identical stories of what had taken place during their period of amnesia.

A dual identical psychosis (folie à deux) is substantially excluded by the absence of other characteristics of this rare psychosis, nor was there any other evidence of psychosis. A joint fabrication is also substantially excluded. The two remaining possibilities would appear to be:

1. A totally real and true experience.

2. An experience which had been so affected by the accompanying emotional state as to produce some perceptive and illusory misinterpretations—as embodied in the dream hypothesis.

*   *   *

There are no final answers. Where one question existed before, several others have come up to take its place. But if it can even momentarily be speculated that the event is true, the far-reaching implications concerning the history of the world are obvious.

Such an event would demand a reexamination of religion, politics, science and even literature. International relations would have to be thoroughly reexamined. An urgent need for a study and extensive scientific report on the subject would be quickly indicated, both national and world-wide. There is, in fact, evidence already extant that the United Nations is seriously considering a major scientific world-wide study of the subject.

Neither Barney nor Betty Hill had any thought that they might be involved in such an event when they left the little restaurant at Colebrook, New Hampshire, at 10:05 P. M. on the night of September 19, 1961. They are not crusading to convert nonbelievers or skeptics into the acceptance of the phenomenon, although they are hopeful that some new evidence might come along to clarify without question the strange circumstances of their experience. They are content now to let whatever facts that have come out of their story speak for themselves.

But as Tennyson has said: "Maybe wildest dreams are but the needful preludes of the truth."

EPILOG TO NEW EDITION

September, 1979

The publication of this book in 1966 drew considerable attention in the press, and among the public on the subject of UFO's, and the possibility of inter-planetary travel. Since that time, the subject has exploded with major unexplained sightings in almost every country in the world, including Russia. In fact, I recently received a letter from a Russian writer asking if I would send him a copy of this book in his exploration of the subject in his country.

After sending him the book, I received the following note from him:

Dear Mr. Fuller:

With many thanks I acknowledge the receipt of your book. Yes, UFO activity is observed in the USSR since the autumn of 1977 (even my son and wife saw this January two separate sightings).

Sorry, no conclusions! I'll send you, however, article soon to appear and another one.

Best wishes,

V. I. Sanarow
POB 16
630071, Novosibirsk-71
USSR

I have not received the articles as yet, but other reports from Russia indicate serious interest there in UFO's. Meanwhile, in America, recent surveys are showing that there is more interest than ever. In 1977, a national Gallup poll was taken with rather startling results. According to Gallup, ninety-four per cent of the adult population has at least heard or read about UFO's. Nearly half the adult population believes there is intelligent life on other planets. Over half of the population indicate that they believe "flying saucers" or UFO's are real, and not merely figments of the imagination. But most important, eleven per cent of the adults, representing nearly fifteen million individuals, have seen a UFO themselves. These figures are almost double the results of a Gallup poll taken in 1966, the year *The Interrupted Journey* first appeared.

By 1973, a new large wave of sightings hit the United States, characterized by many reports of humanoid contacts, far greater than in previous years. Many were consistent with the Barney and Betty Hill experience, but none have had the deep background medical attention that the Hills experienced. What distinguishes the Hill case is that two people were involved, whose stories coincided exactly under the most rigorous psychological investigation over a stretch of seven months of treatment.

Probably the most important scientist investigating the subject remains Dr. J. Allen Hynek, former Chairman of the Department of Astronomy at Northwestern University, and official Scientific Consultant to the United States Air Force for over twenty years. An avowed skeptic, as we have already seen, his long perusal of the Air Force files and his personal investigation of many UFO sightings brought him to the conclusion UFO's represent an unknown but very real phenomenon that takes us to the edge of reality, and that demands the most serious scientific attention.

I met Dr. Hynek shortly after this book was published, back in 1966. We met for a strange reason. The late U Thant, then Secretary General of the United Nations, had read the story of Barney and Betty Hill in *Look* magazine. He noticed that their story showed many similarities to those that had been reported from many member nations of the UN. Curious to learn more, he arranged for Dr. Hynek and me to meet with him at his UN office in New York.

As an astronomer and former Air Force consultant on UFO's, Dr. Hynek could fill the Secretary General in on the technical aspect. As a journalist, he questioned me on the human reaction to the strange phenomenon.

Dr. Hynek and I arranged to meet in the lobby of the United Nations, and chatted informally while we waited to be called up to U Thant's office on the top floor. We were both glad that the Secretary General had shown an interest in the subject because we now shared the conviction that intelligent research on UFO's was imperative in the face of the fast-accumulating evidence. Hynek's conviction had grown very slowly.

The Air Force was being swamped with inexplicable reports from every part of the country, and Hynek screened them with a caustic eye at the Wright-Patterson Air Force base in Dayton, Ohio. He carried out this assignment while he continued his own work as then-professor of astronomy and director of the McMillin Observatory at Ohio State University.

Hynek was able to knock down over four-fifths of the cases reported as being inaccurate or illusory sightings. But the residue bothered him. He referred to himself as the "resident skeptic" for the Air Force for many years. By the time the large wave of sightings hit in 1966, Hynek was becoming more convinced that the responsible sightings by pilots, ground control personnel, police, and responsible citizens could no longer be ignored. He still tried to explain the unexplainable, however, and in the widely-publicized Michigan sightings, he indicated that one possible explanation for this particular event might be attributed to swamp gas.

Although he had only suggested this as a weak alternate, the press seized on it as a blanket explanation for the entire phenomenon. Hynek wrote me in 1966, stating; "You will note my insistence that the swamp sightings do *not* constitute a blanket explanation for the UFO phenomenon. I'm afraid this point was missed."

We were ushered into U Thant's office on a bright June Saturday morning. The Secretary General greeted us cordially, and we were glad to be the only visitors there at the time. He told us that so many sightings had been coming into the UN that his interest was growing.

Our conversation centered first on the psychological reaction of the populace to the possible visit of aliens from another star system. I was able to tell him that in my general survey and interviews on the situation that while those who had observed the objects at close range were naturally apprehensive at first, their curiosity soon overcame their fear. Hynek agreed with this, indicating that the concern of government officials about mass hysteria developing was generally unfounded. In fact, the reluctance of officials to discuss the subject was a major block in establishing intelligent scientific study of the subject.

After interviewing several dozen Air Force officers from high to low rank, my own conviction is that there is no conspiracy in hiding the facts; there is only the problem that the Air Force *knows* that UFO's exist, are unable to explain them, and therefore doesn't want to admit its own ignorance. In other words, it's a public relations problem, and the Air Force doesn't want to dim its own image. As a result, the official stance, in contrast to the private opinions of many high-ranking officers, has been to try to brush the reports of the millions of sightings under the rug and look the other way.

In discussing the case of Barney and Betty Hill with Hynek, I found him impressed by the professional stature of Dr. Simon and the massive detail revealed under the Hills' regression. Hynek asked me if it might be possible to question the Hills under hypnosis so that he could learn even more details, in line with the other reports that he had been screening. I told him that I'd be glad to inquire about the possibility, since I knew that the Hills were extremely anxious to learn more about their own case, and would probably welcome a responsible scientific inquiry.

I was right. Both the Hills and Dr. Simon agreed. A meeting was set up at Dr. Simon's home in Arlington, just outside of Boston, in which both the Hills would be inducted into a trance state by the doctor so that Professor Hynek could query them on their encounter. What was especially interesting was that this would be the first time that both Barney and Betty would be regressed together. All the other sessions had been conducted separately, and all but the *Look* session as part of the therapy—not as an inquiry into the validity of the UFO experience.

I met Hynek at the Boston airport, and we both drove out to Arlington with considerable anticipation for an illuminating evening. One thing we both were interested in exploring was whether or not the recall of the encounter would stay consistent, and how Barney and Betty would interact in a dual state of regression. Even Dr. Simon was not sure about this, although the Hills were both so conditioned to his instructions under hypnosis there was no problem of control.

Hynek and I agreed that we would not attempt to ask the doctor to run through the entire story sequence. All of us were familiar with the overall picture. What we planned to do was to select certain points that might reveal more details concerning the experience, without any particular chronology. Since the induction of the trance state would allow Dr. Simon to shift the focus at will, and since he could, by a given signal, suspend the consciousness of either one of the Hills at any given time, we could explore those portions of the experience that might throw the most light on the UFO aspect.

The Hills were as receptive as we were to the experiment. Their interest in the whole subject of UFO's had naturally grown to the point where they were dedicated to finding out more. Barney still remained pragmatic and puzzled. In spite of hearing his own voice re-live the circumstances of the encounter, he still found it hard to believe. Betty was more receptive. She was now convinced of the reality of the abduction, and that the hours of their tapes she listened to, opened up the missing two hours in her life, and had joined her repressed memories with her conscious memories.

As the session began, we arranged the furniture so that Dr. Simon, Professor Hynek and I sat facing the Hills. Barney was in a comfortable chair on Betty's right. The microphone for the tape recorder was placed halfway between the two groups. The induction into the trance was swift and sure, and within moments Barney and Betty were settled back in their chairs, eyes closed, completely relaxed.

At the completion of his instructions for the trance, Dr. Simon said:

"In this session, Dr. Hynek may talk to you. And Mr. Fuller may talk to you. And you will both carry out their instructions as if they were mine. You will carry out all the instructions and answer all the questions that may be asked of you by any one of the three of us."

I was feeling the same sort of tension I felt when Barney had responded to the *Look* magazine session. I was also particularly interested in whether a duolog between Barney and Betty would take place in their trance state. Professor Hynek began the questioning first:

HYNEK

Barney, you will remember everything clearly, and I want you to tell me what is happening. You have just heard the beep-beep-beep. I want you to tell me what it sounded like, and then each of you just re-live those moments when you first heard the beeping sounds as you were driving down the road . . .

(At this point, Barney began stirring uneasily in his chair. There were signs of distress. Dr. Simon immediately cut in:)

DR. SIMON

You will not be upset, Barney. You will not have any anxiety, or upset feelings. Just tell us what is happening, without having any emotional disturbance.

BETTY

(Her voice shows some stress, but she remains quite still in her chair.)

I don't see anything!

(She now begins to breathe very heavily.)

I don't see anything!

(She is apparently referring to the time when she looked out the window of the car and the large object was blocking the view of the sky.)

BARNEY

(He is also breathing heavily.)

Betty, it's out there.

BETTY

(Very tense.)

Oh, God!

297

BARNEY

This is crazy.

BETTY

I don't see it. I don't see it. I don't see anything.

BARNEY

Where am I?

(His voice is very frightened.)

Ohhhhh. Oh, I don't believe it. There are men in the road. I don't want to go over. It can't be there. It's the moon. It's the moon.

(Barney is apparently trying to rationalize the appearance of the object as it rests on the ground.)

DR. HYNEK

Go on, Barney. You remember everything clearly. Everything is clear.

BARNEY

I gotta get out.

DR. SIMON

This won't bother you now. But you can tell about it. Same for you, Betty. It won't bother you, but you can tell about it.

BARNEY

I am coming down the road into the woods. There is an orange glow. There's something there. Ohhhhhhhh—if I only had a gun. What do they want? Those crazy eyes are with me. They're with me. Go up a ramp. I'd love to lash out, but I can't, I'd love to strike out, but I can't!

(Now Barney appeals directly to Dr. Simon, a common occurrence in regression when the re-lived experience becomes painful.)

Dr. Simon, give me my emotions back! I've got to strike out, I've got to strike out!

DR. SIMON

You have as much emotion as you need. Just keep right on telling us.

BARNEY

I can't, though.

DR. SIMON

(Calmly.)

You can't do anything, of course. So just go on and tell us about it.

298

BARNEY

(Apparently quite surprised.)

There's a difference in the temperature. There's a corridor. I don't know where Betty is.

DR. SIMON

Where are you now?

BARNEY

My feet just bumped. I'm in a corridor. I don't want to go. I don't know where Betty is. The eyes are telling me to be calm. If I'm not harmed, I will not strike out. But I will strike out if I'm harmed in any way!

(Now his tone changes sharply, to one of fear again.)

I'm numb. I'm numb!

(Loud and sharp.)

I don't have any feeling in my fingers!

DR. SIMON

Okay. Okay. It's okay now.

BARNEY

My legs are numb!

DR. SIMON

It's all right now, Barney.

BARNEY

I'm on a table.

DR. SIMON

Stop there. You're on the table, but you're quiet. And you're relaxed. You can just rest now. Until I say: "Listen, Barney," you won't hear anything for a little while.

(Now Simon addresses Betty.)

Betty, what's going on?

BETTY

We're riding, and Barney's putting on the brakes and they squeal. But he turns to the left very sharply.

(This apparently refers to the turn off Route 3 to a back road.)

And I don't know why he's doing this. We're going to be lost in the woods. The car is stopping. Barney tries to start it. It won't start. There's some men coming up to the car. There's something about the first man.

HYNEK

Where is Barney now, Betty?

BETTY

(*Her voice is low and sleepy.*)

Barney is still in the car.

HYNEK

And then what happens?

BETTY

There is one man ahead of the others coming up. And he's got something in his hand. I don't know what it is. I think they're men—but they're not men!

DR. SIMON

Have you seen anyone like this?

(*Suddenly Barney, who has been leaning back in his chair with closed eyes, begins stirring and squirming.*)

Stop, Betty. Stop for a moment. I don't want you to hear anything I say for a moment.

(*Now he addresses Barney.*)

Barney?

BARNEY

(*Yelling loudly.*)

Betty!

(*Barney suddenly leaps out of his chair and drops his knees to the floor.*)

DR. SIMON

(*Commanding.*)

Barney! Barney! It's all gone. It's all gone. You go to sleep now. It's all stopped. It's all stopped. No more until I tell you to. Do you hear me, Barney? All right. Deep asleep, deep asleep. You're completely relaxed, and it's all stopped for now.

(Turns to Betty, as he helps Barney back in his chair.)

Betty—you can hear me now. Go on.

(Dr. Simon's instructions have the effect of turning Barney and Betty on and off like a tape recorder, a necessary step to keep the session under control and to keep the line of inquiry moving.)

BETTY

(Somnambulistic.)

I'm going to open the car door and run out and hide in the woods. They opened the door . . .

(Her voice drifts off as if she is asleep.)

DR. SIMON

Then what did you do?

(Betty remains silent.)

What did you do, Betty?

BETTY

I went to sleep.

DR. SIMON

Where?

BETTY

In the car. I think.

DR. SIMON

Yes. Go ahead.

BETTY

I don't want to be asleep.

DR. SIMON

What happened while you were asleep?

BETTY

(She is alternating between past and present tense, a common response in regression.)

I tried to wake myself up. I don't want to be asleep.

DR. SIMON

Did the man make you go to sleep?

BETTY

Somehow. I don't want to be asleep.

HYNEK

Then what, Betty?

BETTY

I'm trying to wake up.

DR. SIMON

Did you wake up, Betty?

BETTY

Yes. I try to wake up. I keep trying and trying and trying. I walk in a path in the woods. There's a man behind me, and men—I don't know where I am. I am sleep-walking, and there is a man on each side of me to hold me up.

DR. SIMON

Is this after you woke up, or while you were asleep?

BETTY

I was awake. And I keep saying, Barney, Barney, wake up!

(At this point, Barney begins stirring from his relaxed position in the chair. In order to give him instructions to relax again, it is necessary for Dr. Simon to suspend Betty's present line of regression.)

DR. SIMON

Stop a minute, Betty. When I touch your head, you will not hear anything more from anybody, until I touch it again.

(The doctor leans over and touches her head, with the same kind of tape-recorder sort of shut off. She remains silent, eyes closed as he turns to Barney.)

Barney—you can hear me now. You are deep asleep. Fully relaxed. You are comfortable now—nothing is troubling you. When I touch your head, you will not hear anybody else until I touch you again.

(He reaches over and touches Barney's head, then does the same to Betty.)

Now, Betty, you can begin again. How far did you walk? How long did it take? Was it a short or long walk?

302

BETTY

(Still in a very sleepy tone.)

A fairly long walk, I think. I don't know how long I was walking before I woke up.

DR. HYNEK

Were your eyes quite open when you were walking?

BETTY

When I woke up, my eyes were open.

DR. HYNEK

Where were the men taking you?

BETTY

In a path in the woods. Toward the craft.

DR. HYNEK

Did the craft look anything like a helicopter?

BETTY

No.

DR. HYNEK

Did you ever see anything that resembled it?

BETTY

No.

DR. HYNEK

What color was it?

BETTY

It was—it was a metal. It was shiny.

DR. HYNEK

Was the moon shining down on it?

BETTY

It was quite a moonlit night. I could see that it was on the ground. There was like a rim around the edge.

DR. HYNEK

Was it resting on legs, or was it flat on the ground?

BETTY

The rim was a little bit above the ground. And there was a ramp that came down. If it was on legs, the legs were in a hole.

DR. SIMON

Keep right on, Betty.

BETTY

I don't think that it was on legs. I didn't see any.

HYNEK

How big was it, Betty? Was it as big as a Cadillac?

BETTY

It was—big.

DR. SIMON

Compare it with something you know, Betty. In size.

BETTY

I'm trying to think.

HYNEK

How about a railroad car. Was it bigger than a railroad car?

BETTY

I can't picture the size of a railroad car. I would say that if it landed out here on the street, it would go from the front of the house, beyond the garage. (A distance of some 60 to 80 feet.)

HYNEK

How close to the trees was it? Did it have any trouble avoiding trees when it landed?

BETTY

It was all clear. Maybe little trees, but nothing big. It was a clearing in the woods with trees around it. Some clearing in front of it.

HYNEK

What were your thoughts as you drew closer to it?

BETTY

(After a brief pause.)

To get the "H" out of there if I could.

DR. SIMON

And why couldn't you?

BETTY

The man beside me—I kept saying "Barney, Barney, wake up . . .". And the man asked me if his name was Barney. I didn't answer because I didn't think it was any of his business. And when I saw this craft thing, I knew they were going to want us to go on it. I kept telling him I don't want to go—I won't go. They said they just wanted to do a simple test, and as soon as it was over, I could go back to the car.

DR. SIMON

What about when you were in the room with the leader or with the examiner? What kind of sounds did he make?

BETTY

He didn't make a mumbling sound, like the crew.

DR. SIMON

What kind of sounds did he make?

BETTY

It was more like words. Like sounds of words.

DR. SIMON

English words?

BETTY

No.

DR. SIMON

But you understood them?

BETTY

Yes.

DR. SIMON

How do you explain that?

BETTY

It was—all I could think of is when you are learning French . . .

DR. SIMON

Learning French?

BETTY

Yes.

DR. SIMON

Do you think it was French?

BETTY

No. No. But it was like learning French. When you first hear the French words, you think of them in English.

DR. SIMON

You heard these sounds in some language and you understood them as if they were in English. Is that it?

BETTY

I could understand everything the leader said, except there were some things the examiner said I couldn't understand.

(The session continued, with the narration that emerged almost exactly the same as that of the therapy. When Betty related how they began communicating with her, Professor Hynek began pressing down on this point:)

DR. HYNEK

How did they tell you what to do? Did they talk to you?

BETTY

The man I call the leader said, "Is his name Barney?"

DR. HYNEK

Did he actually say this in English? Clearly now, you can recall all these details. Did you hear him say this with your ears?

DR. SIMON

Clear and sharp now, Betty. You can recall this.

BETTY

I heard sounds.

DR. SIMON

You hear them now. Whatever they are, they are clear and sharp.

BETTY

He makes a sound, and I understand it in English.

DR. SIMON

Did you hear sounds coming out of their throats, their mouths?

306

BETTY

Yes.

DR. HYNEK

Tell me how they sounded to you.

BETTY

The crew made different sounds. Like a, like a humming sound. It went up and down, but it was a humming.

DR. SIMON

(He rises, crosses to Betty's chair.)

All right, Betty. When I touch your head, you'll be rested and relaxed. I don't want you to hear anything until I touch your head again.

(The communications aboard the craft had always been puzzling to understand. The Hills, especially Betty, were convinced that there had been communication, even though the way in which it was conducted was almost impossible to explain. The new session made some inroads into the puzzle, although the answer still remained vague. Barney had tried to explain it in the past by saying: "It was as if they placed their thoughts on ours," a suggestion of thought-transference. Dr. Simon now steered the questioning to explore this facet:)

DR. SIMON

(He touches her head, and she remains quiet.)

Barney, you can hear me now. You are comfortable and relaxed. You told me that you had gone into this vehicle. Is that right? They have taken you and put you on a table. And they talked to you. Is that right? Tell us how they talked. Answer Dr. Hynek on that . . .

DR. HYNEK

Did you see them, Barney, open their mouths? And if so, how wide did they open them?

BARNEY

(He is completely calm now.)

They were not talking to me. There were these eyes they burned into my head. They stayed in my head, and I knew whatever I was supposed to do, and they kept me calm. Whenever they wanted me to do something, this bright light was always in my head.

307

Is there any animal, Barney, that you can think of that made the sound that they were making?

BARNEY

No. It was no animal.

DR. HYNEK

Any human?

BARNEY

Is was no human.

DR. HYNEK

They were not human?

(*Barney begins to show signs of distress again, moving uncomfortably in his chair.*)

DR. SIMON

Easy, Barney!

BARNEY

They came down the road. They had spindly legs. They carried me out of the car. But the men inside did not have spindly legs. They moved. Their mouths moved. I could see them.

DR. HYNEK

And when their mouths moved, was there a sound coming from them?

BARNEY

Yes.

DR. HYNEK

Try to tell me what the sounds were. Do they represent anything you know?

BARNEY

No.

(*Then Barney suddenly makes an eerie humming sound that is partly a gargle as well as a hum.*)

Eerrgglhummmmmm . . .

DR. HYNEK

Did you understand what they were saying?

BARNEY

No I did not.

DR. SIMON

Did they talk to you?

BARNEY

No, they did not talk to me.

DR. HYNEK

They never spoke to you at all?

BARNEY

They just made these sounds.

DR. HYNEK

And could you understand what they were?

BARNEY

No.

DR. HYNEK

Did you think about them at all?

BARNEY

I thought: If only I could ball my fists up.

DR. SIMON

This is while you were on the table?

BARNEY

Yes.

DR. SIMON

I thought you were comfortable on the table.

BARNEY

I wasn't. I wasn't comfortable.

(*Now Barney begins closing and unclosing his hands again, squirming in his chair.*)

DR. SIMON

(*Quickly.*)

All right, Barney! You don't have to feel it. You can just talk about it.

309

BARNEY

(His voice is now quivering with emotion.)

I wanted to fight! I didn't know where Betty was!

(Perhaps the thought of this had made Barney jump out of his chair earlier in the session.)

And yet every time I would move or struggle, this bright light in my head would keep me calm . . .

DR. SIMON

(After consultation with Dr. Hynek.)

All right, Barney. I want to move ahead to the point after the abduction. You have just left the craft. You have been taken back to the car. You're both in the car now. Both of you are at the point where you saw the craft leave the ground. You don't know it yet, but it's about to leave. I want you both to tell exactly what happened.

(Dr. Simon touches Betty's head to bring her back into the session.)

BARNEY

(He is apparently addressing their dachshund who had been left in the car.)

Delsey!

BETTY

(Her voice in the trance is now measurably relieved.)

Delsey is scared to death!

BARNEY

Delsey! Delsey! Where's Delsey, Betty?

(He sounds confused.)

BETTY

(She is slightly laughing in relief.)

Barney, are you awake?

BARNEY

Yes, Betty.

BETTY

You have your eyes open now.

BARNEY

(He is apparently referring to Betty's acceptance that they are actually dealing with a UFO.)

Come on, Betty. Don't be ridiculous . . .

BETTY

Come on, get out of the car and watch it leave. Don't sit there.

BARNEY

Come on, Betty. Don't be ridiculous. Let's go.

BETTY

I want to see it leave, Barney.

BARNEY

(Suddenly his voice begins quivering in awe.)

There's an orange glow! Hey—look at that! Isn't that something?

(He talks as if he is watching the object begin to glow from a nearby location.)

BETTY

Delsey, Delsey—look at that!

(She is very excited.)

BARNEY

(Not at all convincing.)

It's the moon. I know. That's what it is. The moon!

BETTY

It's not the moon, Barney.

BARNEY

I'm not going to talk to you, Betty. I don't care. I'm going back to the car.

BETTY

Delsey's still excited.

BARNEY

(Sharply.)

Come on, Betty! Get in. You'd better, because I'm going to leave.

(He gets angrier.)

I'm not going to hang around here. Come get in the car, dammit. Geez, I'm tired of this foolishness. Get in the car, Betty!

BETTY

Okay. But look at Delsey. She's the only dog in the world who has seen something like this.

BARNEY

(The awe and wonder return to his voice.)

It looks like a satellite! Look at it go!

(He pauses, then resolutely:)

Oh, boy—I'll *never* tell anybody about this!

BETTY

I wonder where it's going . . .

DR. SIMON

(Driving hard for facts.)

Okay, now. Tell me now. What does it look like? How big is it? What is its color? What kind of movement does it show? Describe it in detail. Both of you. Just before it gets far from you. While it's still close.

BETTY

(Analytically.)

It has a swirling, orange glow.

BARNEY

It's getting brighter and brighter. And it's turning silvery in color. And it's moving very fast. And it's gone up in the sky.

DR. SIMON

(Firmly.)

Which direction? Straight up? Angle?

BARNEY

(Indicating with his hands. His eyes of course remain closed in a trance.)

It goes from this way—to this way. It never hit the trees. I'm away from the trees.

DR. HYNEK

Was it a clearing of some sort?

(Quizzically.)

There must be a clearing back there?

DR. SIMON

Is that right, Betty?

BETTY

There is a clearing.

BARNEY

Because I came out of the woods. When it went like that . . . it was gone.

DR. HYNEK

How big was it, Barney?

DR. SIMON

Before it left the ground, or just as it left the ground.

BARNEY

Sixty, eighty feet roughly.

DR. HYNEK

What do you know that is sixty or eighty feet long?

BARNEY

I compare it—I think when I saw it on the field—about as large as a plane with its wings outstretched.

DR. HYNEK

What kind of plane, Barney?

BARNEY

I thought of a B-47.

DR. HYNEK

What sort of sound did it make as it left?

BARNEY

No sound.

DR. HYNEK

No sound at all? Was there any swishing sound? How could something move in the air without making any sound?

BARNEY

(Solemnly.)

That's why I'm *never* going to tell nobody!

DR. HYNEK

Did it tip? Did it turn and rotate?

BARNEY

A huge ball—and then it tipped, and it was gone . . .

(At this point in the session, an unusual thing happened. In the room, Barney was sitting in an armchair on Betty's right. Yet in the flow of the regression, Barney was supposed to be in the driver's seat of the car. Regression in a trance state is so real to the subject that he actually believes he is back at the scene he is regressed to. In this case, it seemed to Barney that Betty was on the driver's side of the car,* when he should be there. He was hearing her voice coming from the wrong side, and it suddenly disturbed him greatly:)

BARNEY

Wait a minute. This is ridiculous. Betty's over here—when she should be there!

DR. SIMON

Easy, Barney.

BARNEY

Where are you?

DR. SIMON

Easy. Easy. Okay. I see.

BARNEY

I'm confused. Her voice is coming from here, but she belongs *there*. I'm driving the car.

DR. SIMON

Easy, easy. It's all right.

(But the vivid reality of the regression continued to disturb Barney with Betty still sitting in the "driver's seat")

Go on, Betty.

* i.e. Referring to the American car, with the driver's seat on the left.

314

Barney is still somewhat in a daze, after we see the object leave and get back in the car. And Barney is driving, and I say to him: "Do you believe in flying saucers?" And he says: "Don't be ridiculous!" And then we hear the beeping sounds again, and Delsey jumps up on the back seat and looks out the window.

DR. HYNEK

Was it at this time that you saw the craft cross between you and the moon?

BETTY

That was much earlier. But the moon is there.

DR. HYNEK

Was it above or below the moon, Betty?

BETTY

It was on the left hand side of the moon, about the middle of the moon, or a bit lower.

(At this point, Barney becomes more disturbed about the "driver's seat" problem.)

BARNEY

I'm driving this car . . .

DR. SIMON

Just a minute . . .

(Dr. Simon rises, and helps Barney and Betty change seats with each other, each of them still remaining in the trance state, eyes closed. Barney becomes considerably more comfortable after the change.)

Okay, Barney. Are you still confused?

(Barney nods his head. Dr. Simon instructs them to go back to the point where they first saw the object in the sky, before the abduction took place. This will be the first time that Barney and Betty have jointly re-lived the experience in regression together.)

BETTY

We're driving along . . . and Barney stops to look at it. I'm standing out there looking at it, and it goes across the moon . . .

DR. SIMON

You tell it to Barney. You're both in the car now.

BARNEY

(The puzzlement in his voice again.)

It turned, Betty.

BETTY

What do you mean, it turned?

BARNEY

Look out the window. You can see it's a plane. Geeez.

BETTY

Where are the binoculars?

BARNEY

(There is stress in his voice.)

Stop it, Delsey! Get down.

BETTY

(Chuckling.)

You see a plane coming towards us, and you're acting as if you're in Twilight Zone.

BARNEY

Just make the dog keep quiet. Delsey's agitated, and you're making me agitated. You're aggravating me.

BETTY

Okay, I'll just sit here and watch it through the binoculars and keep still. You keep still too, Delsey.

DR. SIMON

Now—we'll skip a little time now until it comes real close. It's coming real close, is it?

BETTY

I think. Barney, start the car. Barney, have you ever seen anything like this before?

BARNEY

(His resistance to the whole idea of UFO's is strong and determined.)

Come on Betty, I'm going to prove this damn thing. I'm going to prove it! I'm going to satisfy you, you hear?

BETTY

Look at it, Barney.

BARNEY

(More awe and wonder in his voice.)

I can see it!

(Again Barney begins to become disturbed in his chair. He leans forward tensely.)

DR. SIMON

That's all now, Barney. It's all gone now. Sit back in your chair.

BARNEY

(Shouting.)

Look at that!

DR. SIMON

Okay, Barney. You can do it from the chair.

BARNEY

(Absolutely awestruck.)

This is ridiculous!

DR. HYNEK

Describe it now.

BARNEY

(His voice trembling.)

Ohhhhhhh—it's *huge*! Ohhhh, my goodness.

DR. SIMON

What do you see through your binoculars?

BARNEY

I can see it! It's there!

DR. SIMON

Yes?

BARNEY

And . . . and . . . there's lights. I don't believe this!

(Breathless.)

I don't *believe* this.

Okay, okay. It's all right. Okay. Now tell us what you see.

(He is at the critical point of the encounter now, where his reaction has always been strong.)

Ohhhhhhhhhhh! A huge, huge, big thing! There are people and they are looking down.

(He begins to sob.)

God, help me get these binoculars down! God, help me get these binoculars down!

Calm, Barney. Calm. Tell us what you see.

I'm coming closer. I'm coming closer . . .

(He continues to sob.)

There's a man up there. He . . . he . . . he . . .

Describe the man's face. Describe it.

Oh, God!

Okay, okay. You see the eyes right now, but describe the craft. Describe it carefully. Tell me.

It's big.

How big?

It's biiiiggg . . .

Eighty feet?

Eighty feet. Big. Ohhhh—look at it! Two red lights . . .

DR. SIMON

Where are the lights? What's the shape? What's the shape, Barney?

BARNEY

Like a pancake.

(Stressing.)

I'm not going to say it! I don't believe it, flying saucers. I'm *not* going to say it. I don't ever want to say that word again.

DR. SIMON

You can say it to me.

BARNEY

God, that's what it looks like.

DR. HYNEK

How do you know what flying saucers look like?

BARNEY

(Calm again.)

I was looking in a magazine, I think it was the *Post* magazine . . .

DR. HYNEK

It looked like what you saw in the *Post* magazine, is that it?

BARNEY

Yes.

DR. SIMON

Yes, all right. Betty, what were you doing?

BETTY

I was in the car.

DR. SIMON

What was Delsey doing?

BETTY

I was sitting on the seat waiting for Barney, and I think Delsey was in the back seat. I'm waiting for Barney to come back, and I'm getting worried why he isn't coming back . . . and then he comes running to the car. He throws the binoculars in on the seat, and I don't know if he's laughing or crying, but he said: "Let's get the hell out of here, because they're going to capture us!"

Where was the craft at this time? Was it still in the air or had it landed?

BETTY

It was still in the air. And Barney kept saying: "Look out, look out, it's right over us." So I put the window down and I stuck my body out through, up to my shoulders.

DR. HYNEK

Did you see her do this, Barney?

BARNEY

Ohhhhhhhhh—I gotta get back—ohhhhhhh . . .

DR. SIMON

Okay, Barney, let's listen to Betty . . .

(Betty continues with the story of their experience as the first beeping sound is heard, to bring the session back to a full cycle.)

* * *

When Dr. Simon finally closed the session and took the Hills out of their trance state, I felt a strong sense of relief. Watching the vivid reactions on the part of Barney and Betty made it almost impossible not to believe in the validity of their encounter and abduction. Dr. Hynek agreed.

After the follow-up session with Dr. Hynek, I listened to and studied the tapes at length, trying to discover if they stood up under careful critical examination. The most important aspect of the case to me seemed to be Barney's total resistance to the whole idea of UFO's. He literally fought against acceptance of the phenomenon both consciously and under regressive hypnosis. But when he listened to his own voice on the tapes, he found himself in the position that he was forced to believe it, whether he wanted to or not.

The consistency of their recall also impressed me. The variances between Barney and Betty were so minor that they served only to buttress the validity of the experience. Their testimony was never pat or slick. Their response to hard-driving questions was immediate and non-contrived, and their emotional response in the re-living of the scenes was uncontestably convincing. When Barney apparently was re-experiencing the instrument used to examine his genitals, or when he was trying to ball up his fists to strike out at his purported abductors, the emotions revealed were so intense and the sense of reality so vivid, it was hard to conceive how they could be the passive recall of a dream or a fantasy.

With Barney's reactions so strong and overpowering, I could not see how the dream-transference theory could stand up. This theory would require the dreams to be transferred with such an impact that Barney would see, feel, re-experience, re-enact and sense every aspect of the dreams. Further, there were many details that Barney recalled that Betty did not—the details of his own physical examination, his view through the binoculars, the impact of the "eyes", the stumbling over the bulkhead, and of course the extreme reaction during his regression for *Look*.

There were other things that lent validity to the experience which were hard to ignore. One is that the amnesic veil fell at precisely the same time and place for both Barney and Betty. I have been unable to find any other cases of double amnesia in medical records prior to that of the Hills. Yet both began the period of unconsciousness at the sound of the beeping, and both had to break through that moment in the therapy to a period of hazy recall.

Other events that have taken place after this book appeared are of unusual interest. For instance, one of the points that Dr. Simon could not accept was Betty's recall of the needle that was inserted in her navel at the time of the examination aboard the craft. "There's no such medical procedure that would use direct needle through the abdomen to examine a condition of pregnancy," Dr. Simon told me. "This is the sort of thing that makes me doubt the story of the abduction. It simply has no basis in medical practice."

Yet shortly after the initial publication of *The Interrupted Journey*, it was announced in both medical journals and the lay press that a totally new method had been developed to examine the amniotic fluid—by the insertion of a needle through the abdomen. Beyond that, in 1971, it was announced that a procedure was being developed to obtain eggs from fertile women by using a needle through the navel. An article in *Look* titled *The Test Tube Baby Is Coming* described the process:

> "This involves a pencil-like viewing device that, once inserted through the umbilicus or navel, provides a panoramic view of the peritoneal cavity and its contents. Once the scope is fixed on the ovary, the doctor inserts a needle through a tiny incision in the lower abdomen. Then, looking through the scope, he guides the needle and uses it to aspirate the egg from its follicle. The procedure generally requires only one night in the hospital and minimizes scarring."

The question arises whether this function was the motive of the purported alien beings in Betty's case, and in the apparent removal of semen from Barney. This is of course speculation, but the medical confirmation of this sort of procedure several years after Betty recalled it under hypnosis creates an oddly prophetic ring.

A most important discovery after the fact was made by Professor Hynek in checking the Air Force records of UFO activity on the exact time and date of the Hills' encounter with the vehicle. Following up the Hill case, Dr. Hynek and his associate, Jacques Vallee, discovered an overlooked Air Force radar report that showed a radar contact with an unidentified flying object in the exact vicinity where the Hills had their experience. Previous attempts to find any such report had failed.

Since the Hill case, there have been many similar reports of UFO abduction, and some of them have had extensive investigation. In October, 1973, in a town by the name of Pascagoula, Mississippi, two shipyard employees who were fishing from a dock went into panic when an odd-looking airborne craft approached them a few feet above the water. It moved closer, emitting a strange blue haze. Both the men, Charles Hickson and Calvin Parker, were frozen with fear as three humanoid beings emerged from the craft, and seemed to float in the air toward them. The fishermen became numb, then began to feel themselves lifted and taken toward the craft.

Parker lost consciousness, but Hickson remembers vaguely feeling as if he floated toward the craft, airborne by the creatures. He recalled consciously being given some sort of a scanning examination by a machine, and described the humanoids as being pale, about five feet tall, with strange eyes—very similar to the Hills' experience, although they never had read the Hill story or knew about it.

Within forty-eight hours, Dr. Hynek arrived with an NBC-TV producer named Ralph Blum, and an intensive examination was begun. Dr. James Harder, a professor of engineering at Berkeley, also arrived from California. He was a consultant to the Aerial Phenomena Research Organization, known as APRO, and a cautious researcher in the UFO field.

What attracted this group was the assurance of the sheriff's department that the men were of good reputation, were genuinely upset by the experience, and were very reluctant to report it. Further, the men volunteered for lie detector tests, which they passed with flying colors. With the co-operation of a local psychiatrist, Dr. Harder hynpotized the men. At a press conference, Dr. Hynek said:

"There's simply no question in my mind that these men have had a very real, frightening experience, the physical nature of which I am not certain about—and I don't think we have any answers to that. These men are absolutely honest. They have had a fantastic experience, and I also believe it should be taken in context with experiences that others have had elsewhere in this country and in the world."

Hynek's experience with me in witnessing the hypnosis session of the Hills made some of the comparisons obvious, expecially when more information was gathered from the men, including the police investigation. Verbatim statements from Hickson show the close parallels in his encounter with the creatures:

—One of them made a little buzzin' noise, and two of them never made no noise . . .

—A little buzzin' sound—nnnnnnnnn, nnnnnnn . . .

—No force, they didn't hurt me. I didn't feel nothin' . . .

—Some kind of instrument, I don't know what it was . . .

—I couldn't move. Just my eyes could move . . .

—(Describing the mouth) Like a slit—and I never saw that opening move . . .

Parker had his recollections that matched some of Barney Hill's recall:

—My damn arms, my arms. I remember they just froze up, and I couldn't move . . .

—I paralyzed right then. I couldn't move . . .

—It's hard to believe . . . I know there's a God up there . . .

—All I know is how scared I was when I turned and saw them coming toward me.

Another case that took place on December 3, 1967, involved a Patrolman named Herbert Schirmer, of Ashland, Nebraska. Shortly before three in the morning, he was in his police cruiser on a road near Highway 63, when he saw what he thought was a truck broken down ahead of him. Within moments, the vehicle he thought was a truck took off abruptly in the air, with brilliant lights flashing around its perimeter. He entered the incident on the police blotter, but it was only later, when a writer named Eric Norman arranged for Schirmer to undergo regressive hypnosis, that the detailed story emerged.

With his memory sharpened, he recalled seeing the object settling on the ground, as it extended a sort of telescopic landing gear. Patrolman Schirmer's recall matches some of the Hill case incident in several parts. Like Barney Hill, he could not start his car to escape:

—I'm being prevented . . . something in my mind . . . I want to go home . . . they're getting out . . . they're coming toward the car . . . it can't be . . . I'm trying to draw my revolver . . . I am being prevented . . . the one in front of the car is holding up an object . . . he's pulling something out of a holster . . . my God, he's pointing it at me . . . paralyzed . . . passing out . . . can't remember anything . . . it's all black . . .

323

Other details also emerged that showed other similarities. The crewmen are about five feet tall. One pair of eyes burns into Schirmer's consciousness which he cannot escape. A ladder descended from the ship. The mouth is a slit which does not move. There are large, slanted Oriental eyes. And the purported spaceman seems to communicate both by speaking and through the mind. As Schirmer put it under hypnosis:

—Through my mind, somehow, he is telling me things . . . the one who is talking with me speaks with a voice, with a sort of broken English . . .

Schirmer voluntarily took a polygraph test that showed no evidence that he was lying.

In a book titled *The Andreasson Affair*, UFO investigator Raymond Fowler recounts the story of Betty Andreasson, involved in a highly strange UFO abduction case in a small town in Massachusetts. Fowler spent a year investigating the case, utilizing the help of several UFO experts and a skilled hypnotist from the New England Institute of Hypnosis. On January 25, 1967, Mrs. Andreasson found her home plunged into darkness, as a pulsating glow showed up in her backyard outside her window. She and several members of her family were stunned and unable to move when several humanoid creatures entered her kitchen, took her out to the craft, and, like the Hills, subjected her to a detailed physical examination.

Again, the investigation revealed many marked similarities to the Hill case. Mrs. Andreasson's sketches of the creatures were almost identical to those of Betty Hill. Under hypnosis, details emerged that showed remarkable parallels.

First, Betty Andreasson's daughter explains why she took no action:

—Sideways, he didn't have a mouth . . . when he turned, he did. It was like a wrinkle in clay, not a line but like a line . . . I can't see any nose . . . the only thing I can see really good is the big eyes . . . I can't do anything—can't move . . . I'm not afraid of him because there's a feeling he's not going to hurt me . . .

In her trance, Mrs. Andreasson describes a ship very similar to the one the Hills described, including legs that seemed to adjust to the ground, and a circular craft that contained an examination room and complicated instruments. Betty Andreasson's commentary describes various things she encountered:

—Large, wrap-around catlike eyes . . . holes for noses and ears . . . shiny dark blue form fitting uniforms . . . he called me Betty. It seemed like an oral sound, but I think it was a transformation of sound . . . but it seemed oral . . .

324

Describing her physical examination under hypnosis, Betty Andreasson gets into further detail:

—There a long block they have me on . . . lights coming from the walls . . . wires, needle wires . . . they inserted a long silver thing through my belly button, my navel . . . they said there were some parts missing, because I had a hysterectomy, I guess . . . they're saying something about some kind of test . . .

There are many other "close encounters of the third kind", some of them heavily documented. Common among them are these similar details that suggest a pattern that is more than coincidence. Consistently, there are the descriptions of floating or gliding on the part of both the reported humanoids and the subject, the constant inability of the subjects to strike out or fight back, the temporary amnesia, the ability to communicate by thought transference and inarticulate sounds, the sense of authority on the part of the captors whose commands, however, are most often tempered with gentleness. As bizarre and exotic as these cases are, there is a level of sincerity, rationality, and believability in the testimony under regressive hypnosis that can't simply be brushed aside.

No other case, however, has had the advantage of being examined over a long period of months by a medical scientist of Dr. Simon's stature. His stern objectivity and dispassionate point of view have added greatly to the quality of investigation of the Hills' case. In the face of this, there was no question of the implanting of ideas in the minds of the Hills. If anything, the doctor's objective questioning challenged the whole idea of the abduction, especially in the follow-up session. Yet the testimony stood up.

An independent follow-up of Betty Hill's star map over a period of years has caused somewhat of a ripple of excitement among astronomers, as reflected by an article in the December, 1974 *Astronomy* magazine, a publication highly regarded by both professional and amateur. Marjorie Fish, a health physics technician at Oak Ridge National Laboratory and a competent amateur astronomer, was both intrigued and puzzled by the star map Betty Hill had drawn under post-hypnotic suggestion. When she first read the story and saw the map in *Look*, she had no interest or belief in UFO's. It was only when she came across Jacque Vallee's book *The Anatomy of a Phenomenon* that she began to take serious interest.

What intrigued her was that there was no visible configuration of stars in the sky that could conform to Betty Hill's sketch. She speculated that the formation would logically not be from the point of view of the earth, but from a point familiar to the home base of the UFO craft that had confronted the Hills. With the help of Dr. Walter Mitchell, an astronomer from Ohio State University, she began constructing a series of models, using only those stars considered likely to be able to support planetary systems.

She finally was able to find the star pattern that duplicated Betty Hill's map, confirmed by a computerized program set up by Dr. David Saunders, a member of the Condon Committee who had found the UFO evidence to be overwhelmingly persuasive. Marjorie Fish's findings from her patient reconstruction of a stellar model indicated that the focal point of Betty's map was the star Zeta Reticuli. Most interesting was the fact that when Betty drew her map in 1964, she represented this star as a double star, while astronomers then knew it only as a single star. Nine years later, the astronomer Van de Camp ultimately discovered that Zeta Reticuli actually was a double star, confirming the accuracy of Betty Hill's map. The *Astronomy* article went on to say: "If some of the star names on the Marjorie Fish map sound familiar, they should. Ten of the sixteen stars are from the compact group that we selected earlier based on the most logical direction to pursue to conduct interstellar exploration from earth." The *Astronomy* article also adds: "Both Zeta Reticuli 1 and Zeta Reticuli 2 are prime candidates for the search for life beyond earth. According to our current theories of planet formation, they both should have a retinue of planets something like our solar system."

The star map findings were later confirmed by Dr. Frank B. Salisbury, Director of the Plant Science Department of the University of Utah. His observation is: "The final map has sixteen stars that form a flattened rather than a spherical cluster. The viewing position is immediately suggested by the two close stars and the triangle of stars (correct data for which only appeared in the 1969 catalog). The final breakthrough came in September of 1972, when Miss Fish assumed that the star Zeta Tucanae was directly behind Zeta Reticuli. This further refined the viewing position. Thus when one views the model from the proper position, only fifteen of the sixteen stars are visible—matching the number on Betty's map."

Not being an astronomer, I have no way of evaluating the star map portion of the story. I would have to leave this to expert opinion, which seems to be divided. I am very wary of over-acceptance of the UFO evidence, but am equally wary of those who dismiss it without thorough examination. Intelligent appraisal of the evidence is faced with two problems. On one side is the non-discriminating enthusiast who is naive and gullible, and buys everything that comes down the pike. This creates so much static and high noise-level that it discourages intelligent study of the phenomenon.

On the other side is the closed-minded skeptic who refuses even to examine the data, or if he does, he seizes on irrelevant data to dismiss the entire subject. Some scientists, in an attempt to discredit *all* UFO's simply because *some* reports are unfounded, unfortunately resort to the most unscientific means of doing so.

For instance the famous 1969 Condon Study, commissioned by the United States Air Force, was marred from the start by its project director, Robert J. Low, who wrote in a memo outlining the approach of the project: "The *trick* (italics added) would be, I think, to describe the project so that, to the public, it would appear a totally objective study but, to the scientific community, would present the image of a group of non-believers trying their best to be objective but having almost zero expectation of finding a saucer."

This "trick" cost United States taxpayers over half a million dollars, and resulted in a report that set back careful examination of the subject for many years. Instead of zeroing in on the hundreds of carefully documented cases, the project dissipated its energies exploring obviously weak cases, which should have been dismissed as unworthy of study to begin with.

Jacques Vallee tells the story about a French colleague who explained his sudden interest in UFO subject by noting that the Condon Report spent so much time in trying to explain something away, that there must be something to it. The stance adopted by Condon himself and Walter Sullivan of the *New York Times*, who wrote the introduction, seems to be contradicted by many of the cases described in the report. As Vallee notes, if the report were read backwards, saving Condon's and Sullivan's con- clusions for the end, a strikingly positive picture would emerge. But the report is so loaded with irrevelant material, only the most dogged reader could get through it.

Another aspect of the UFO phenomenon is the effect it has on those who have undergone the "close encounters of the third kind". The first problem they run into is the strong probability of ridicule. This in turn causes the subjects to keep quiet about their encounters. The Hills, for instance, waited several years before they made their case known, and only then because of the press leak that made it public.

The entire subject of UFO's cries out for more intelligent scientific and governmental attention, but this does not seem to be forthcoming. The Condon report has carried more weight that it ever deserves, dis- couraging other governments and scientists from exploring the area. A 1979 proposal for an intensive UN inquiry into the subject has resulted in a half-hearted resolution for a world-wide study on the part of the UN Outer Space Committee, but it seems to be wallowing in the lack of funding.

Another 1979 resolution was proposed in Mississippi as House Resolution No. 14, calling for a complete U.S. Senate investigation of UFO sightings, but it was defeated by failure to meet a legislative deadline of February, 1979.

In January, 1979, the British House of Lords debated the UFO issue, under the prompting of Lord Clancarty, who pointed out that the number of sightings and landings throughout the world were increasing at an alarming rate, and the need for a government study was great. He was supported by the Earl of Kimberley, Lord Davies of Leek, and Lord Kings Norton, who called the UFO's "a very serious matter," and pointed out a recent flap of sightings in New Zealand and Italy, that included very startling film sequences. "It is no good just laughing it off," he added. "The true origins of the phenomena are a matter of great importance and some urgency."

The New Zealand sightings remain one of the more baffling UFO cases, especially because of the careful technical follow up on the motion picture film conducted by optical physicist Dr. Bruce Maccabee on behalf of Hynek's Center for UFO Studies.

The first of this series in New Zealand involved the disappearance of pilot Fred Valentch, who radioed that his plane was being approached by an enormous unidentified object. His radio suddenly blacked out, and he and his plane disappeared forever. Within two months after that, on December 21, 1979, an Argosy air freighter took off from Blenheim at 12:35 A.M. for a routine flight to Christchurch. Cruising at 220 knots, Captain John Randle noticed a brilliant white light "too powerful to be a vehicle's headlamps", which lit up the landscape below it. A flight service officer at Blenheim control spotted the same thing from the ground, while radar control at Wellington discovered five unidentified targets moving up and down the coast.

After eliminating the possibility of weather balloons and military aircraft, Wellington radar continued to monitor the strong blips, receiving one signal that moved like an aircraft at 120 knots, only to stop and hover for half an hour some forty miles southeast of Wellington. Meanwhile, Christchurch radar confirmed that they were following the same targets.

At 3:30 A.M., another Argosy freighter took off from Blenheim under the command of fifty-five-year-old Vern Powell, a veteran of 18,000 hours flight time. They were asked to investigate the radar targets, especially one that appeared to be about twenty miles to port. Within moments, the second Argosy flight spotted a bright white light with a reddish tinge that changed color intermittently. At 10,000 feet the plane was level with the object, while Wellington radar noted that the target hovered without motion until the plane caught up with it. The object appeared on radar as large and solid as the Argosy, and began a path that followed the plane some twenty miles to the east of it. Powell watched it do this for ten or twelve minutes, until it disappeared when he changed course to starboard. As he did, the object also disappeared from the Wellington radar screen.

But as Captain Powell's plane approached Christchurch, his own weather radar picked up an object crossing its flight path. At the same time, a brilliant object swept by his plane visually, blazing like a strobe light and covering about twelve miles in five seconds, an incredible speed. An observer on the ground also reported a similar object.

But the events were not over. Captain Randle in the other Argosy was now flying north toward Auckland, when he spotted the five objects again, "four times the strength of landing lights," flashing white and amber lights, and leaving a reflection on the water.

It was because of these sightings that Melbourne's TV station sent out a film crew on duplicate Argosy flights ten days later. Not only were there repetitions of many of the radar-visual sightings observed before, but the film footage shot by the crew recorded much of the activity under difficult conditions of filming. Physicist Maccabee's painstaking analysis, after ruling out atmospheric conditions and secret military maneuvers, indicates that the objects remain unidentified, and a landmark case among UFO observations.

But cases like this, including radar-visual-airborne-ground control observations by seasoned and competent observers, are many. They cannot be brushed off. Yet official resistance to a crash program and study of the world-wide, continuing sightings remains strong. Probably one of the chief reasons for this is the fear of the unknown, and the threat to conventional laws of physics. UFO critics continue to seize on the most unscientific reasons to avoid examining palpable evidence. A careful study of the massive evidence requires a great deal of time and concentration, and officials who make the ultimate decisions are most often unable and unwilling to do this.

A few years ago, I was directing and producing a documentary film for ABC Television about the future of space travel in the NASA space program. I interviewed at length Chris Kraft, a top NASA official, on the subject of possible contact with other extra-terrestrial civilizations. He stated without equivocation: "There is no question in my mind that in the future, we will visit other civilizations, and they will visit us."

The question still remains, in the light of *The Interrupted Journey*: Have we already been visited? As Walter Sullivan stated in his introduction to the Condon Report: "If, as many people suspect, our planet is being visited clandestinely by spacecraft, manned or controlled by intelligent creatures from another world, it is the most momentous development in human history."

Only further, deeper, unprejudiced investigation into the thousands of UFO sightings that are constantly being reported, without let up, will let us know.

APPENDIX

APPENDIX

The following is the recall of Betty's dreams, which she wrote down as notes to herself after the incident had taken place. It will be noted that they are substantially the same as the recall she describes as having actually happened during the amnesic period. It is not uncommon for dreams resulting from an experience of shock to be literal; i.e., a complete re-enactment, so to speak, of an event that actually took place. On the other hand, such a dream neither proves nor disproves such an event.

Betty Hill's detailed notes are printed here for those readers who would like to compare in detail the content of her dreams with her recall of the amnesic period as it came out under hypnosis.

The similarities are marked.

* * *

(Dreams that occurred following the sighting of the UFO in the White Mountains on Sept. 19–20, 1961.)

Two events happened of which we are consciously aware; these are also incorporated in my dreams. First, we sighted a huge object, glowing with a bright orange light, which appeared to be sitting on the ground. In front of this, we could distinguish the silhouette of evergreen trees. Our reaction was to say, "No, not again," and then we consoled ourselves with the self-assurance it was the setting moon. At this point in the highway, we made a sharp turn to the left. Second, at the termination of this, I asked Barney if he believed in flying saucers now? He replied, "Don't be ridiculous. Of course not." I will attempt to tell my dreams in chronological order, although they were not dreamed in this way. In fact the first dream told was the last one dreamed. My emotional feelings during this part was of terror, greater than I had ever believed possible. [Betty Hill recalls almost bolting out of bed during this dream.]

333

We were driving home from the sighting, when we saw the bright orange glowing shape; we saw a very sharp left-hand turn in the road and found that the road curved back to the right. At this moment, I saw eight to eleven men standing in the middle of the road. Barney slowed down to wait for them to move, but the motor died. As he was trying to start the motor, the men surrounded the car. We sat there motionless and speechless, and I was terrified. At the same time, they opened the car doors on each side, reached in and took us by the arm.

(This is the first dream I had.) I am struggling to wake up; I am at the bottom of a deep well, and I must get out. Everything is black; I am fighting to become conscious, slowly and gradually I start to become conscious, I struggle to open my eyes for a moment, and then they close again; I keep fighting, I am dazed and have a far-away feeling. Then I win the battle and my eyes are open. I am amazed! I am walking through a path in the woods, tall trees are on both sides, but next to me on both sides is a man; two men in front; two men in back; then Barney with a man on each side of him; other men in back of him. I become frightened again, and I turn to Barney and say his name, but he is "sleep-walking," he does not hear me and does not appear to be conscious of what is happening. The man on my left speaks to me and asks if his name is Barney; I refuse to answer. Then he attempts to reassure me: that there is nothing to fear—Barney is all right; no harm will come to us. All they want to do is make some tests; when these are completed in a very brief time, they will take us back to the car and we will go safely on our way home. We have nothing to fear.

During this time I become conscious of several things [She is referring to her dream, as all through this account]. First, only one man speaks, in English, with a foreign accent, but very understandably. The others say nothing. I note their physical appearance. Most of the men are my height, although I cannot remember the height of the heels on my shoes. None is as tall as Barney, so I would judge them to be 5′ to 5′4″. Their chests are larger than ours; their noses were larger (longer) than the average size although I have seen people with noses like theirs—like Jimmy Durante's.

Their complexions were of a gray tone; like a gray paint with a black base; their lips were of a bluish tint. Hair and eyes were very dark, possibly black.

The men were all dressed alike, presumably in uniform, of a light navy blue color with a gray shade in it. They wore trousers and short jackets, that gave the appearance of zippered sports jackets, but I am not aware of zippers or buttons for closing. Shoes were a low, slip-on style, resembling a boot. I cannot remember any jewelry, or insignia. They were all wearing military caps, similar to Air Force, but not so broad on the top.

They were very human in their appearance, not frightening. They seemed to be very relaxed, friendly in a professional way (business-like). There was no haste, no waste of time.

After reassuring me that there was no cause for fear, the "leader" ignored me, and we continued to walk. I would turn back to Barney, and he still was not aware of what was happening. Incidentally, he remained ın this state until we were returned to the car at the end.

We reached a small clearing in the woods. In front of us was a disc, almost as wide as my house is long. It was darkened, but appeared to be metallic. No lights or windows were seen, and I had the impression that we were approaching from the back of it. We stepped up a step or two to go onto a ramp, leading to a door. At this point I became frightened again and refused to walk. The leader spoke, firmly but gently, reassuring me that I had no reason to be afraid, but the more delay I caused by my uncooperativeness, the longer I would be away from the car. I shrugged my shoulders and agreed that we might as well get it over with; I seemed to have no choice in this situation.

We entered the disc. I found a corridor, curving to the contours of the ship. We started to enter the first room, leading from the corridor, but then I found that Barney was being taken further down the hall. I objected to this, and questioned why we both could not be examined in the same room. The leader showed some exasperation with this question and my objections, and explained, as though I were a small child, that the exam would take twice as long this way, as they only had equipment to test one person at a time in a room, and he thought that I wanted to be on my way as quickly as possible. So I agreed.

About four or five men entered the room with us, but when another man came in, they left. This man was the examiner and also spoke English. He was very pleasant, reassuring. He asked questions; some I had difficulty understanding, as his English was not as good as the first man's. My answers puzzled him at times. He asked my age, also Barney's. He shook his head as though he doubted me. He asked me what I ate; when I told him, he asked questions, what did vegetables look like? My favorite one? Squash—what did it look like; how do we eat it? I told about peeling it, cooking it, mashing it, putting salt and pepper, butter on it. He was puzzled. I tried to explain the color of it—and looked for some yellow coloring in the room, but could not find any. I tried to tell about meat, milk, but he did not understand the meaning of the words I was using.

Then the examiner said that he wished to do some tests, to find out the basic differences between him and us; that I would not be harmed in any way and would not experience any pain. Also he would explain what he was doing as he went along. Just a few simple tests. The leader returned and remained in the room the rest of the time I was there. He was an observer during the testing. First, I sat on a stool, the examiner in front of me, with a bright light shining on me. My hair was closely examined, and he removed a few strands and then cut a larger piece on the back left-hand side. I was not able to see what he used for cutting purposes. Then he looked in my mouth, down my throat, in my ears, removing some ear wax or something. They examined my hands and fingernails, taking a piece of my nail. They removed my shoes and looked at my feet. They showed much interest in my skin and pulled out some type of apparatus which they held close to my arm on the top and inside. He seemed to be adjusting this, and I wonder if he was getting a magnified view or taking a picture. He took a slender long instrument, similar to a letter opener, and scraped along my arm. As he took these samples, he would hand them to the leader, who carefully placed these on a clear material like glass or plastic, cover with another piece and wrap them in a piece of cloth. Very similar to a glass slide.

Next he pulled a machine over, and asked me to lie down on an examining table. This machine resembled the wires of an EEG [an electroencephalograph, which records electrical brainwaves], but no tracing machine was seen. On the end of each wire was a needle. He explained that he wanted to check my nervous system. He reassured me that there would be no pain. Very gently he touched the ends of the needles to different parts of my body. He started with my head, temples, face, neck, behind my ears, back of my neck, all my spine, under my arms, around my hips, and paid particular attention to my legs and feet. Sometimes only one needle would be held against me, then two, then several. A few times he would touch a spot on my body, and I would jump, or my arm or leg would jerk; a slight twitch. Both men were highly interested in this test; and I feel that a recorder was being used, although I did not see one. Also during this exam, my dress was removed, as it was hindering the testing.

They said the next test was a pregnancy test. The examiner picked up a very long needle, about four to six inches long. I asked what he planned to do, and he said that it was a very simple test, with no pain, but would be very helpful to them. I asked what kind of pregnancy test he planned with the needle. He did not reply, but started to insert the needle in my navel with a sudden thrust. Suddenly I was filled with great pain, twisting and moaning. Both men looked very startled, and the leader bent over me and waved his hand in front of my eyes. Immediately the pain was completely gone, and I relaxed. At that moment I became very grateful and appreciative to the leader; lost all fear of him; and felt as though he was a friend. I kept repeating my thank-you's to him for stopping the pain, and he said that they had not known that I would suffer pain from this test; if they had known, they would not have done this. I could feel his concern about this, and I began to trust him.

They decided to end the testing. The examiner left the room, the leader gathered up all the test samples and put them together in a drawer, and I put on my dress and shoes. Upon questioning where the examiner had gone, he told me that he was needed to complete the testing on Barney, that his was taking longer than mine, but soon we would be going back to the car.

I spent the time waiting, by talking with the leader and walking around the small room. There was an absence of color in the room, and it was of a metal construction—like stainless steel or aluminum. Cabinets and one door were on the curved side; the remaining two walls were intersected like a triangle. There was a bright overhead light of bluish shade. Together in one corner was the equipment used in the testing. After the leader had put away all the things, we stood on the right-hand side of the door and talked. I mentioned that this had been quite an experience and I had never had anything like this happen before. He smiled and agreed and said that of course in the beginning I had been badly frightened. They regretted this fright and had wanted to do all they could to alleviate it. I admitted that I had completely recovered and was now enjoying this opportunity to talk with him; and there were so many questions I wanted to ask. He volunteered to answer all that he could.

At this point, some of the men came hurriedly into the room. Their excitement was apparent, and they were talking with the leader, but I could not understand what they were saying. They were not using words or tones with which I was acquainted. The leader left the room with them, and I became frightened that something had gone wrong with Barney's testing. The leader was gone only a short period of time; he opened my mouth and was touching my teeth, trying to move them. When he stopped, very puzzled, he said they were confused. Barney's teeth were removable, mine were not. This was an amazing discovery! The examiner returned and checked my teeth. I was laughing most heartily about this, and went on to explain that Barney had dentures, the reasons for this, while I did not need these yet, but I would as I became older; that all people lose their teeth with old age. All were very amazed, and all the men were going back and forth to Barney and then me, to look at our teeth, and to see the difference. They were unbelieving, shaking their heads.

After they left, the leader asked what was old age. I said that a life span was believed to be a hundred years, but people died at age sixty-five to seventy from degeneration and disease usually; some died in accidents and illnesses at all ages. I attempted to explain aging—the skin wrinkles, the graying hair, etc. He asked what was a hundred years, and I could not tell him, only a way to measure time.

Then I broached the subject again of this whole experience being so unbelievable to me; that no one would ever believe me; that they would think I had lost my mind; I suggested that what was needed was absolute proof that this had happened; maybe he could give me something to take back with me. He agreed and asked what I would like. I looked around the room and found a large book. I asked if I could take this with me, and he agreed. I was so happy and thanked him. I opened the book and found symbols written in long, narrow columns. He asked jokingly if I thought I could read it, and I said that this was impossible, I had never seen anything like it. But I was not taking this for reading purposes, but this was my absolute proof of this experience and that I would always remember him as long as I lived.

Then I asked where he was from, and he asked if I knew anything about the universe. I said no, but I would like to learn. He went over to the wall and pulled down a map, strange to me. Now I would believe this to be a sky map. It was a map of the heavens, with numerous sized stars and planets, some large, some only pinpoints. Between many of these, lines were drawn, some broken lines, some light solid lines, some heavy black lines. They were not straight, but curved. Some went from one planet to another, to another, in a series of lines. Others had no lines, and he said the lines were expeditions. He asked me where the earth was on this map, and I admitted that I had no idea. He became slightly sarcastic and said that if I did not know where the earth was, it was impossible to show me where he was from; he snapped the map back into place. I said that I did not intend to anger him but had told him that I knew nothing of such things. But there were many people here who did have knowledge of these things, and I knew that they would love to talk with him and would understand him. Then I suggested the possibility of arranging a meeting between him and these people, that this would be a momentous meeting; a quiet meeting with scientists or top people of the world. While I was saying these things, I was wondering if I could do this, but felt that it could be worked out some way. He asked why, and I said that most people did not believe that he existed; he would have a chance to meet us and to study us openly. He smiled and said nothing. I was in the middle of trying to sell him this idea, when several men appeared with Barney, who was still in a daze. I spoke to him, and he did not answer. I asked when he would be fully awake, and the leader said as soon as we were back in the car.

We started to walk out the door, when one of the men said something, not understood by me. They all stopped and were talking excitedly. The leader went back and talked to them. A disagreement had occurred, and the leader seemed to be in the minority. He came up to me and took the book. I protested, saying that this was my only proof; he said that he knew this, and this was the reason why he was taking it. He said that he could see no harm in my having the book, but that it had been decided that no one should know of this experience, and that even I would not remember this. I became very angry and said that somehow, somewhere, I would remember—that there was nothing he could do to make me forget this. He laughed and agreed that I might possibly do just that—to remember, but that he would do his best to prevent me from this, as this had been the final decision. He added that I might remember but no one would ever believe me; that Barney would have no recollection of any of this experience; in case Barney might ever recall, which he seriously doubted, he would think of things contrary to the way I knew them to be. This would lead to confusion, doubt, disagreement. So if I should remember, it would be feasible to forget. It could be very upsetting.

We left the ship and walked through the woods. This time it seemed like a very short time. I spent the time saying that I would always remember and asking that they return; please, please return. The leader said that it was not his decision to make; he did not know if he would come back. I said that I was very happy about meeting him, and honored, and thanked him for being kind. All the men accompanied us.

We came to the car, and the leader suggested that we wait and see them leave. We agreed. Barney seemed to wake up as we approached the car, and he showed no emotion, as if this were an everyday occurrence. We stood on the right-hand side of the car, Barney was leaning against the front fender, and I was by the door. As we were waiting, I thought of Delsey. I opened the car door and Delsey was under the front seat. She was trembling badly, and I patted her for a moment. She came out, and I picked her up, and held her, again leaning against the car door.

Suddenly the ship became a bright glowing object, and it appeared to roll like a ball turning over about three or four times and then sailing into the sky. In a moment it was gone, as though they had turned out the lights. I turned to Barney, and I was exuberant. I said that it was the most marvelous, most unbelievable experience of my whole life. I patted Delsy and said, "There they go. And we are none the worse for the wear."

We got in the car and Barney started driving. He said nothing during this whole experience, so I turned to him and asked, "Do you believe in flying saucers now?" He replied, "Don't be ridiculous." Then we heard the beeping on the car again, and I thought, good luck, good-by, and I am going to forget about you. If you want me to forget, I will, and I will not talk."